6405

Women and Language
in Transition

Women and Language in Transition

edited
by

Joyce Penfield

STATE UNIVERSITY OF NEW YORK PRESS

6405

Published by
State University of New York Press, Albany

© 1987   State University of New York

For information, address State University of New York
Press, State University Plaza, Albany, N.Y., 12246

Library of Congress Cataloging-in-Publication Data

Women and language in transition.

  Includes index.
  1. Women—United States—Language.   2. Sexism in
language.   3. Feminism—United States.   4. Language
planning—United States.   5. Sociolinguistics—United
States.   6. English language—Sex differences.
I. Penfield, Joyce.
P120.W66W64 1987   401'.9'0973   86-23113
ISBN 0-88706-485-X
ISBN 0-88706-486-8 (pbk.)

10   9   8   7   6   5   4   3   2   1

To my sisters around the world.

Contents

Part III. Women of Color

Acknowledgments

I owe the motivation for this anthology to my sisters in West Africa whose unrewarded patience with patriarchy and inequality made me challenge my own assumptions and perspectives about white women and women of color in the United States and led me to ardent feminism. This collection of essays reflects a promise I made to myself to contribute toward identifying and changing gender inequity throughout the world.

Many colleagues have helped me explore the role of language in gender inequity and I am thankful to them. This anthology began as a result of a Faculty Development Grant from the University of Texas at El Paso for a lecture series on "Gender Differences in Speech and Writing: Implications for Teaching." Through their presentations, the following speakers contributed to the inception of this book: Isabel Crouch, Betty Lou Dubois, Carole Edelsky, Nancy Henley, Alleen Pace Nilsen, and Vera John Steiner.

The Introduction and the chapters were improved thanks to the comments of several scholars with expertise in sociolinguistics: Susan Gal, Paul Garvin, Nancy Henley, Cheris Kramarae, Jacob Ornstein-Galicia, and Ana Celia Zentella. My thanks go also to Michele Martin at SUNY Press for her editorial assistance and to Pratima Shastri for proofreading the manuscript. I am especially indebted to my close companion and friend, Benjamin Rigberg, for his editorial acuity and his help in forcing me to clarify the ideas presented in the Introduction. And, of course, the book would not exist without the support and patience of the authors of the chapters.

I am grateful to Rutgers University for the one-semester leave which gave me a continuous block of time to complete the editing of these chapters.

Introduction

Women's Liberation: The Socio-Historical Context

The rise of Women's Liberation in the past two decades reflects women's struggle to counter the extensive gender inequity which they face from birth. Much progress has been made in this short time. The book market is now flooded with historical accounts of the contributions of individual women and creative literature caters to a feminist audience.[1] Intellectually there has been a clear transformation leading to more positive images of women. A great deal of attention has focused upon self-definition and identity construction through contemporary historical and literary works.

At the institutional level, women have made less progress in reforming the social conditions and legal boundaries of inequity in which they find themselves. Some legal gains have been achieved, most notably, Affirmative Action enforcement. But for the most part women have had to recognize, albeit reluctantly, that social changes leading to gender equity have been constrained by a male-constructed and male-dominated framework held fast by centuries of tradition. How to change that framework which defines, controls, and deprecates women has thus become a central concern of Women's Liberation. To use a simple metaphor, this view of Women's Liberation suggests that women are not so much interested in how to play the game or how to improve their skill as players but rather how to change the rules of the game and to become equal, active participants in forming future rules.

Language plays a critical role in this struggle for gender equity and therefore deserves careful examination. Language is the most obvious and universal aspect of humanity. It is "the source from which intellectual, spiritual, and individual existence springs."[2] Yet it is both personal and social. Liberating language, making both the internal structure and external function of language gender equal, touches the most ingrained and unconscious aspects of our personal and social identities.[3] Language is the system through which we are all socialized. It is a framework that inherently and traditionally comes loaded with gender inequity. The fact that it is unconsciously integrated in our daily behavior makes it resistant to planned change.

This anthology focuses on the role of language in the feminist experience and, more especially, on the struggle of women to achieve gender equity *in* and *through* language. One hopes that the examination and analysis of language change will lead to a greater understanding of women's liberation and the struggle for equality. Language is intricately bound to the various institutions of our lives; therefore, women's struggle to transform institutionalized gender inequity can best profit from a multidisciplinary approach.

Part I of this anthology, Liberating Language, focuses on historical attempts to liberate English, with special attention to the means and strategies used, primarily by white women. This section reflects some of the changes in language and the political approach to achieving them which accompanied the Women's Liberation movement of the 1970s. Part II, Identity Creation, deals with the close relationship between identity construction and the alteration of that portion of language which serves to name women and their experiences. Part III, Women of Color, is concerned with the unique situation of women of color.

Women of color find themselves in a much more complicated social context than do white women. They are caught between two social systems in which they participate simultaneously: the mixed-gender majority society—with its strong pressures for acculturation—and the male-dominated structure of their own communities. Today's scholarship has yet to approximate an understanding of the complexities with which women of color must deal. An analysis of the role of language in the experiences of women of color can offer deep insights into some of these complexities. The most obvious of these experiences is bilingualism, which places women of color on the "cutting edge of change." Here women of color play two contradictory roles, that of enforcer of tradition and that of language innovator. The problems posed for women of color and the obstacles they must confront make their feminist experiences unique.

Conceptual Frame of Reference

Women's liberation has been concerned with the creation of new and equal frameworks. Historically, women have been concerned with freeing themselves from exploitation and male domination. To this extent, their struggle parallels the experiences of various ethnic or cultural groups in the world who have fought for independence and self-determination.[4] This anthology is concerned with attempts to alter language in line with the feminist experience.

Language, here, is conceptualized in its broadest sense as "the strongest and most significant bond which unites the various cultural expressions of a people."[5] Language is social behavior, but it is also the bridge between the personal and social aspects of women's lives. Consequently, it is not surprising that one finds gender inequity conveyed in and through language in a society marked by gender inequity. In the past decade several excellent scholarly works have focused on various aspects of this language inequity in English.[6] There are at least four different notions of language in which gender inequity has been examined: (1) the internal makeup of English as in vocabulary, pronominal reference, and so forth; (2) patterns of language use, as in mixed-sex discourse versus female-female discourse; (3) verbal labels and other images used to refer to women and their experiences; and (4) character images of women portrayed in creative literature. A broad conception of language necessarily entails an understanding of the social and historical context in which attempts have been made by individuals, political groups, creative artists, and institutions to make language gender equal. The author assumes that the liberation of language is directly linked to the liberation of white women and women of color, and consequently must be placed in this context. For this reason, the point of departure here is the development of the feminist movement.

In the past two decades feminists have struggled for the right of self-determination and self-definition in a male-dominated society. As I have noted, to some extent their struggle is similar to one of the strongest intellectual forces in history—the evolution of modern nationalism.[7] In Europe, language consciousness played a prominent role in the achievement of equality and independence through nationalism. Part of this evolution in the nineteenth century meant breaking away from the intellectual and social shackles of superimposed languages as national languages began to develop.[8] I am arguing here that there are some attributes inherent in the struggle for language self-determination present in the initial stages of nationalism which can lead to an historical understanding of the role of language in the feminist experience.

In its initial stages, nationalism has been conceived of by scholars as an ethnic and cultural process involving a group of people who speak the same language (or closely related dialects), occupy the same territory, share a common history, believe they constitute a distinct society, and have a particular manner of initiating their youth into the ways of the group.[9] These four fundamental attributes interact to develop a unique group consciousness which the German writer Herder referred to as *Volksgeist*.[10] By this he meant a common core of values and beliefs that set a group apart from all others. It is argued here that at least three of these characteristics have been fundamental to the birth of the feminist community. Because of the ideological growth in the 1970s, the feminist community now views itself as an identifiable group with a common core of values and beliefs—a fellowship of sisters who share the same past and the same future[11]

With the emergence of Women's Liberation as a philosophy an explosion of scholarship took place which created a plethora of works by women about women. Scholarly and popular journals, such as *Signs: Journal of Women in Culture and Society*, were born. Feminist newsletters served as a path to networking and consciousness-raising, as did numerous regional conferences, workshops, and sessions or committees within professional associations.[12] A considerable number of historical analyses and accounts of the contribution of individual women and groups of women have appeared. Linguistic interest in language and women focused on sex-linked differences in language, leading to the publication of several scholarly books and at least one newsletter.[13] Within professional organizations such as the Modern Language Association (MLA), the Linguistic Society of America (LSA), and the National Council of Teachers of English (NCTE), caucuses and sessions were formed to lobby actively for women's concerns.[14] The integration of these activities helped women to see themselves as constituting a distinct community and sharing a common history. Women in the 1970s were entering the process of developing their own form of nationalism, a "feminist nationalism," that is a distinct form of cultural and ethnic nationalism rather than political or state nationalism. Feminist frameworks, values, and experiences were identified and legitimized. Along with the feminist declaration of self-determination and self-definition came the struggle for participation and power in those circles from which women had been excluded for so long. Consciousness-raising brought increasing awareness that the English language and discourse were subconscious and subtle agents of gender exclusion in which both sexes participated. Feminist research documented ways in which both male and female children acquired sexist veiws through language at a very young age.

Thus, early attention was focused on sexist patterns of socialization; in particular, how to reverse negative sex-role stereotyping in children. This interest led to attempts to liberate school curricula and all printed matter used by children. Feminists thus began to develop ways to initiate their youth into sex inclusive thinking, speaking, and acting.

As more and more research highlighted the extent of sexism in society, feminist activism addressed the question of when and how this behavior could and should be changed. Unlike many of the nationalist developments in modern Europe, it was a foregone conclusion that the solution to sexism did not lie in seeking a territorial separation or in developing a separate distinct language contrasting with that of the oppressors. With the exception of lesbian communities, territorial or linguistic separation from a male-dominated society was an impossibility. Women are integrated in every facet of mixed-gender society and are therefore faced with a task much different from simply withdrawing and forming a separate entity. They must work to build a new inclusive system which incorporates the feminist experience. This has been nowhere more apparent than in the alteration of the English language.

Historically, language has played a crucial role in raising group consciousness. The struggle to make English more gender equal, which increased in the 1970s, brought a high degree of language consciousness which no doubt has in turn contributed to *Volksgeist* or group consciousness. It can be argued equally that changing English to make it conform with these newly formed aspects of group consciousness served to instill prestige and pride in women. To this extent, alterations in English by feminists symbolically parallel the formation of national languages in nineteenth-century Europe.[15]

Alterations were first focused on changing linguistic aspects of English, such as the pronouns and vocabulary; later, other strategies for empowerment in mixed-sex discourse were also studied (see Henley, Part I, in this volume). As feminist scholars became aware of their inability to talk about themselves and their own unique experiences in English, they began to explore linguistic strategies for creating, reviving, or extending the meaning of current language forms to conform to the feminist experience.

The rise of feminist *Volksgeist* contributed in turn to the construction of new identities among women on both a personal and collective/social level. Women began to take an active part in defining themselves both individually and collectively. One could say that they had discovered symbolic value in the adage "You are who you say you are." However, they usually encountered social and legal resistance from the inherently sexist system in attempting to define themselves linguistically. The chapter "Surname Changing: The Struggle for Identity" (Part II) illustrates this difficulty in the simple matter of naming one's self. On the other hand, Van Den Bergh (Part II) suggests how collective renaming may serve to precipitate social changes.

It is worth noting that modern nationalism was first propagated by a small group of intellectuals and then spread among the masses. Feminist scholars constitute the intellectuals who inaugurate and carry forward feminist ideology through scholarly research, women's history, and creative literature. It is important to remember the role of the individual creative artist in the propagation of nationalism—or, in our case, feminist nationalsim. Henley (Part I) mentions how creative literary artists might introduce "new language" to help create new images of women.

Whereas feminist nationalism has no doubt been the work of feminist intellectuals—scholars and artists—it is the school, the church, and the press which have been responsible for spreading feminist ideology and philosphy among the masses. All three have served as important auxiliaries for the propagation of liberated language. During the 1970s, feminists reconstructed the English language to make English gender equal. Attention was also given to transforming negative sex-role stereotyping in children's books by making them inclusive. Withers (Part I) argues that teachers and religious educators are in fact agents of change who can instill gender equity in children through more inclusive curricula and patterns of interaction. Her annotated bibliography is rich in available resources for making the curricula more gender inclusive in words, images, and actions.

Some have noted how the English pronoun system has been affected by the initial stage in planned language. In many countries of the world such changes are planned and implemented by an officially designated group or organization.[16] However, the United States has no such centralized language planning body. There is no official or governmental policy-making body or group to suggest, institute, or enforce changes in language. Without central control and enforcement, it is not uncommon to witness several language alternatives emerging simultaneously for the same referent, resulting in a type of ambiguity of correctness for any given situation. Dubois and Crouch (Part I) rather humorously refer to this natural phenomenon as "linguistic disruption."

But for the most part, language planning in the United States is informally conducted by the press and broadcast media. They make decisions about the current nature and status of language norms in English and disseminate them. Since the press is sensitive to public opinion, policies are often formulated and carried out more often in line with public sentiment and political climate than with any set of rules. With the equal rights orientation and feminism of the 1970s came the introduction and enforcement of sex-fair stylistic guidelines in scholarly publications. Drawing on her experience as policy formulator and editor, Nilsen (Part I) recounts the development and implementation of sex-fair guidelines in the publications of a large professional association, suggesting some of the difficulties in implementing gender-equal or sex-fair language in writing.

Women of Color

Although white women and women of color do share a certain sisterhood, it is clear that the powerful social factors of race and ethnicity lead to somewhat different feminist experiences for the two groups. The prevalence of ethnic discrimination and racism have served to isolate women of color and to encourage group consciousness based on race, language, or ethnicity rather than on gender or nationality. It may be argued that languages *other than* Standard English have been a common defining characteristic among women of color. Any notion of nationalism or *Volksgeist* among women and men of color is no doubt tied not to nationality, region, or gender but to language and/or ethnicity. Both of these play a crucial role in the feminist experience of women of color who must function in two worlds which are culturally and linguistically different.

Men and women of color often find themselves caught between these two worlds. The power group or majority society in the United States, backed by a tradition of suspicion of bilingualism, seeks to impose total adoption of the English language. This pressure for acculturation has its roots in the ideology of American nationalism, which emphasizes the positive aspects of assimilation and the negative effects of remaining culturally or linguistically different.[17] An integral element of this ideology is the American dream, which promises economic and social mobility for all those willing to abandon their cultural and linguistic heritage and assimilate completely to Anglo-Saxon culture and the English language.

Two questions must be raised here. What role do women of color play in resisting or encouraging the process of acculturation and how are they affected by either of these processes?

Loyalty to the native language and ethnic/racial identity within minority communities has worked to resist the pressures of acculturation. The maintenance of the native language is one obvious way in which resistance occurs. Women have been noted to play a key role in this resistance as enforcers of tradition and guardians of culture (see Medicine, Part III in this book). This tends to reinforce the view expressed by such linguists as Robin Lakoff that women are extremely conservative when it comes to language.[18] Yet, research on patterns of language used in minority communities suggests equally that women are on the cutting edge of change. They play the role of innovator and cultural broker between their own community and the majority culture. Usually, these dual roles that women play are most apparent in their pattern of bilingualism. Zentella (Part III) suggests one way in which younger Puerto Rican women act both as enforcers of tradition and as innovators.

Women of color do not exist in total isolation. Various aspects of their lives—such as child rearing, language, and their relationships with their men—are influenced by changes brought about by contact with society-at-large. Thus, a deep understanding of the socio-historical context in which minority communities find themselves is a critical factor for interpreting the feminist experience of women of color. Robins and Adenika rely heavily on this socio-historical context in their chapter in this book (Part III). They illustrate in detail how the struggle for power and equality in the Black community in the 1950s, 1960s, and 1970s redefined the interests and concerns of Black women.

Just as white middle-class women have struggled for the right of self-determination and equality, minority women have also been involved in the effort to define themselves. The socio-political events of the 1960s remind us of the many successful attempts of what might be considered "liberal" nationalism in which oppressed nationalities sought to free themselves from alien domination by reviving national traditions and history, arousing popular enthusiasm for traditional figures, and giving greater prestige and loyalty to their own ways of speech. In the same sense, advances in the feminist movement have transformed the social image of women. In turn, these new patterns have given rise to changes in the social order itself, as Van Den Bergh argues in this book. In this transformation of the feminist experience, language—the visible sign of change—has also been the critical index of that change.

In conclusion, the question may be raised: Has there been progress in the women's movement in the past two decades? To ask the question is to answer it. When one compares the self-consciousness of women of two decades ago with that of today's women, one notes that the intervening years have produced vast changes in the way women identify themselves. This is reflected in the inclusive language which has become part of our society. It is also reflected in the achievements of women in the business and corporate world, in the professions, and in many other vocational areas. It is reflected in the *near* acceptance of women's right to choose the number of children they will have, in the sharing of household chores (especially the care of children), and in divorce settlements in which husbands remain partners in the care of children. Though much remains to be done, much has been achieved. The fact that the national environment of the 1980s is now threatening these achievements does not diminish the magnitude of the advances. In this context, the language changes which have preceded and accompanied the alteration in the status of women provide the *raison d'être* of this book.

Notes

1. Many presses now have a Women's Studies series, including Pergamon Press, State University of New York Press, The University of Tennessee Press, Indiana University Press, and Transaction Press. There are also several presses that publish books only on, about, and by women, such as the Feminist Press.

2. Boehm (1933:236) also refers to language as the key to the most essential traits of a people.

3. The "internal structure" refers to the structural make-up of a language system, such as sentence patterns, pronunciation, and word patterns of English. The "external function" refers to the meaning and social signficiance of a given internal structure and explains why the same words or pronunciation or sentence pattern may have a different meaning depending on the dynamics of the linguistic and social context. Both linguistic concepts are taken from Garvin (1972).

4. According to Hayes (1933), cultural and political nationalism became part of nineteenth century liberalism and thus created popular support for the struggle of "oppressed nationalities" to free themselves from alien domination. National traditions and national languages were then revived.

5. See Boehm (1933: 236).

6. One of the first scholarly collections in the field focused on power and language: *Language and Sex: Difference and Dominance*, edited by Barrie Thorne and Nancy Henley (1975). This work documented numerous research studies in its annotated bibliography. More recently, the bibliography has been extended, along with current articles by leaders in the field, in *Language, Gender and Society* (Thorne, Kramarae, and Henley, 1983).

To date there have been over a dozen books published on language and gender. Some have resulted from conference, such as *Communication, Language, and Sex* (Berryman and Eman, 1980) and *The Sociology of the Languages of American Women* (Dubois and Crouch, 1976). Others have offered critical insights and frameworks for analysis; these include *Women and Men Speaking: Frameworks for Analysis* (Kramarae, 1981) and *Words and Women: New Language in New Times* (Miller and Swift, 1975). At least one edited collection has dealt with language from a literary standpoint—*Women and Language in Literature and Society* (McConnell-Ginet, Borker, and Furman, 1980). A few others have offered suggestions for dealing with linguistic sexism in the school setting; for example, *Changing Words in a Changing World* (Nilsen, 1978) and *Sex Role Stereotyping in the Schools* (Weiner, 1980).

7. For a more complete discussion on the development of nationalism, see Hayes (1926 and 1931).

8. Garvin (1972) has defined a national language, using nonlinguistic criteria, as a language which "serves the entire territory of a nation rather than just some regional or ethnic subdivision" and which functions as a national symbol.

9. These four criteria were proposed by Hayes (1926) in *Essays on Nationalism*.

10. *Volksgeist* refers to the tracing of the history and culture of a people to one common root (Boehm 1933: 233).

11. It is in the initial stages of national development, when cultural nationalism is evolving, that the comparison seems most relevant. It is not so apparent in the maturer stages, when political nationalism is too often followed by the oppression of minorities. Nor is the characteristic of a separate territory of significance to a feminist community.

12. Advances have been made within professional organizations. Sessions on Language and Sex were organized by Kramarae and Schulz for the ninth and tenth World Congress on Sociology, bringing many researchers together. In addition, national organizations—e.g., MLA (Modern Language Association) and LSA (Linguistic Society of America)—organized an active Women's Caucus to lobby for women's interests and especially to further research in gender, language, and literature. The MLA has been especially active in women's concerns; they established a Commission on the Status of Women in the Profession. Some regional organizations also formed special sessions at their annual conferences, for example, NEMLA (Northeast Modern Language Association), which holds a session on Linguistics and Women's Studies.

13. *Women and Language News*, edited by Kramarae and Treichler, appears

three times per academic year with updates on continuing research. This newsletter originally began when the field of language and gender was first developing, and it served as a form of networking. *Signs: Journal of Women in Culture and Society* offers a forum for scholarly papers on several topics, especially language, communication, and gender.

14. The Committee on the Role and Image of Women in the National Council of Teachers of English (NCTE) was active in obtaining a resolution at the 1974 NCTE convention directing the Council to create style guidelines ensuring the use of nonsexist language in NCTE publications. (For the 1985 version of the NCTE Nonsexist Style Guidelines, see Nilsen, Part I, in this book).

15. See Hayes (1926; 1933) for a more thorough discussion.

16. Language planning is a discipline applied throughout the world often with the purpose of instituting linguistic equality and the legitimization of dialects and languages through conscious, planned, deliberate change initiated by social institutions, agencies, commercial institutions, or cultural promotion societies.

17. See Conklin and Lourie (1983) for discussion.

18. Some research has noted the conservative nature of women's use of language in speech communities around the world. Nichols (1983), in her study of Black residents of a rural coastal area and a river island in South Carolina, closely links social context with language use by women. She found that women exhibited both innovative and conservative behavior, depending on the occupational and education experiences to which they had access.

References

Berryman, Cynthia and Virginia Eman, eds. 1980. *Communication, Language and Sex: Proceedings of the First Annual Conference*. Rowley, Mass.: Newbury House.

Boehm, Max H. 1933: "Nationalism" *Encyclopaedia of the Social Sciences* 11: 231-40.

Conklin, Nancy & Margaret Lourie. 1983. *A Host of Tongues: Language Communities in the United States*. New York: The Free Press.

Dubois, Betty Lou and Isabel Crouch, eds. 1976. *The Sociology of the Languages of the American Women*. Papers in Southwest English, IV, San Antonio, Texas: Trinity University.

Garvin, Paul. 1972. "Linguistics as a Resource in Language Planning." Paper presented at the Symposium on Sociolinguistics and Language Planning, Mexico City.

Hayes, Carlton. 1926. *Essays on Nationalism*. New York: Macmillan Company.
_____. 1933. "Nationalism." *Encyclopaedia of the Social Sciences* 11:240-248.

_____. 1958. *The Historical Evolution of Modern Nationalism*. New York: Russell & Russell.

Kohn, Hans. 1968. "Nationalism." *International Encyclopaedia of the Social Sciences* 11: 63-70.

Kramarae, Cheris. 1981. *Women and Men Speaking: Frameworks for Analysis*. Rowley, Mass.: Newbury House.

Lakoff, Robin. 1975. *Language and Woman's Place*. New York: Harper & Rowe Publishers.

McConnell-Ginet, Sally; Ruth Borker; and Nelly Furman, eds. 1980. *Women and Language in Literature and Society*. New York: Praeger Publishers.

Miller, Casey and Kate Swift. 1975. *Words and Women: New Language in New Times*. New York: Doubleday & Co.

Nichols, Pat. 1983. "Linguistic Options and Choices for Black Women in the Rural South," in *Language, Gender, and Society*. by Barrie Thorne, Cheris Kramarae, and Nancy Henley. Rowley, Mass.: Newbury House.

Nilsen, Alleen Pace. 1980. *Changing Words in a Changing World*. Newton, Mass.: Educational Development Center.

Thorne, Barrie and Nancy Henley, eds. 1975. *Language and Sex: Difference and Dominance*. Rowley, Mass.: Newbury House.

Thorne, Barrie, Cheris Kramarae; and Nancy Henley, eds. 1983. *Language, Gender, and Society*. Rowley, Mass.: Newbury House.

Weiner, Elizabeth Hirzler, ed. 1980. *Sex Role Stereotyping in the Schools*. Washington, D.C.: National Education Assocation.

White, William, Jr., ed. 1972. *North American Reference Encyclopedia of Women's Liberation*. Philadelphia, Pa.: North American Publishing Company.

Part I

Liberating Language

This New Species That Seeks a New Language: On Sexism in Language and Language Change

Nancy M. Henley

In this chapter the author provides a comprehensive overview of sexism in the English language. She reviews types of gender inequity and social factors that resist change, she discusses and refutes conventional arguments for resisting change, and she concludes with suggestions for language planning, in particular, the role of the creative artist in creating new language forms.

This article is grounded in both a theory of language change and in practical language alteration, with suggestions for individual and group-initiated ways of liberating language.

The title of this paper is taken from Monique Wittig's lyrical novel of a female society, *Les Guérrillères,* which records many sayings of "the women"—"They say, take your time, consider this new species that seeks a new language" (1973:131). That is what I seek to do here—consider this "new species," consider why it wants a new language, why it has a right to demand a new language, what stands in the way to the new language, and what is being done and can be done to achieve it.

Sexism in Language

Sexism in language takes many forms, though these may be reduced to three types: language ignores, it defines, and it deprecates women. As a result, women and girls are hurt both psychologically and materially by it. In addition, such usages as the "generic" masculine do not serve their intended linguistic function and are often ambiguous. Martyna (1980), Miller and Swift (1976), and others summarize these arguments well.

Defining

Language and usage reflect and help maintain women's secondary status by defining them and their "place." Whereas men are often referred to in

3

occupational terms, women are more often referred to in relational terms, for example as *wife* or *mother*, or by titles which denote the presence or absence of an authorized relation to a male (*Miss, Mrs.*). Neutral occupational terms take on feminine modifiers—*lady judge, woman doctor*—which remind us that prestige occupations are male-identified. When naming the sexes, males commonly come first, as in *men and women, males and females, his and hers, he or she, Adam and Eve, Samson and Delilah*, and so on ad nauseam. This male-precedent usage, by the way, follows rules explicitly stated centuries ago, as Bodine has noted (1975:134), for example, by Wilson in 1560: ". . . the worthier is preferred and set before. As a man is sette before a woman."

And finally, the male power to define through naming is seen in the tradition of a woman's losing her own name upon marriage, having thrust upon her the man's name, and giving birth to children that will have the man's name (Stannard, 1977). The terms *lady* and *girl* are euphemisms for *woman* which define her by denying woman's sexuality, maturity, and capability (Lakoff, 1973, 1975; Lerner, 1976).

Deprecating

The deprecation of women in the English language is seen in the connotations and meanings of words applied to female and male things. Different adjectives are often applied to the actions or productions of the different sexes: women's work may be referred to as *pretty* or *nice*, men's work as *masterful* or *brilliant* (Nilsen, 1977b). While words such as *master, prince, lord*, and *father* have all maintained their stately meanings, the similar words *mistress, madam*, and *dame* have acquired debased meanings (Lakoff, 1973, 1975).

A woman's sex is commonly treated as if it is the most salient characteristic of her being, but this is not the case for males. This situation is the basis of much of the defining of women, and it underlies much of the deprecation. Sexual insult is overwhelmingly applied to women: Stanley (1976), in researching terms for sexual promiscuity, found 220 terms for a sexually promiscuous woman but only 22 terms for a sexually promiscuous man. Furthermore, trivialization accompanies many terms applied to females. While male-based terms suggest concerns of importance, like *fraternalism* and *mastermind*, female-based terms tend to refer to unimportant and/or small things, such as *ladyfingers, ladybird, maidenhair fern* (Nilsen, 1977b). The feminine endings *-ess* and *-ette* are added to many words which are not in actuality male-limited, resulting in trivialized terms such as *poetess, authoress, majorette*, and *usherette*.

Ignoring

The paramount example of the way in which language ignores females is the "generic masculine," or "pseudo-generic," as Stanley (1978) has termed it; that is, the use of the masculine to refer to human beings in general. It is common in such terms as *chairman, spokesman, the man in the street, the working man, the Black man, men of good will, the two-man boat*. Especially prevalent is the "generic" *he* and its forms. Grammarians have typically prescribed that *he* must follow reference to sex-indefinite or mixed-sex antecedents, as in "Each of the children wrote his name on the board." Linguists have claimed that this usage, one of many examples of "marking" in the language (Greenberg, 1966), includes women and is not biased but innocuous. Evidence I will describe later, however, demonstrates that *he* and other masculine terms do not function generically and in fact do bias interpretation.

Women and girls are also ignored in the language simply by not being the topics of discourse. An extensive study of children's schoolbooks, for example, found that of 940 uses of *he*, 97% referred to male human beings, male animals, or male-linked occupations; only 3% referred to sex-unspecified persons. Male pronouns outnumbered female ones by about four to one, and the mention of men over women was about seven to one (Graham, 1975). So, compared to specific male reference, actual generic usage is rare. Nevertheless, generic masculine usage is so frequent that MacKay (1980a) has estimated that highly educated Americans are exposed to generic *he* a million times in a lifetime.

Resistance to Changing Sexist Language

There is much general belief that language changes slowly, that language change can't be forced, and especially that the pronoun system is quite unlikely to be changed by feminist efforts, which are seen as naive at best. Lakoff (1973, 1975) argues that since linguistic change follows social change, putting pressure on the pronoun system is wasted energy. Nilsen (1973:9) similarly urges that feminists concentrate their efforts on "educating children and the general public to the way language is rather than by trying to change the language."

Most telling have been the emotionality and vehemence of the opposition to suggestions of change, which have generally been stronger than the original feminist suggestions. Periodically, some underinformed and overincensed male columnist displays what he considers wit with diatribes using his projected version of the threatened "newspeak." Feminists for language change have been accused of "a willful exercise in intellectual dishonesty," of "contemplating social follies and injustices," of "a misguided attempt to change herstory," of committing "social crime," and of "pronoun envy" (Nilsen, 1977a, and Martyna, 1980, give good accounts of these responses). Both common sense and Sigmund Freud tell us that such vehemence attaches itself to nontrivial, core conceptions. We must conclude that the artificially induced sex polarization that props up male supremacy is fundamentally encoded in our masculist language and will be defended vehemently by those who will fight to retain male privilege.

Arguments against changing the language may take any of the following forms:[2]

Argument 1. Linguistic sexism is largely imaginary; specifically, there is a distinction between the use of the masculine as generic and the use of the masculine to reference gender.

The argument distinguishing two forms of masculine denotation involves the linguistic principle of marking, mentioned previously: many pairs of terms have an "unmarked" member which may be used to characterize both terms, and a "marked" one which cannot and is seen as specific and limited. Some linguists argue that the unmarked masculine in our language is solely a linguistic feature, not a social phenomenon, and that it is naive to question it. However, as one linguist has written, "The question deserves a better answer than: 'What a coincidence that the masculine is unmarked in the language of a people convinced that men are superior to women'" (cited in Miller & Swift, 1976: 69).

A large number of research studies now demonstrate that *he* does not function generically, that is does not reference both female and male, but rather most readily produces images and ideas of males (DeStefano, Kuhner, & Pepinsky, 1978; Eberhart, 1976; Hamilton, 1985; Hamilton & Henley, 1986; Harrison, 1975; Harrison & Passero, 1975; Hyde, 1984; Kidd, 1971; MacKay, 1980b; MacKay & Fulkerson, 1979; Martyna, 1978; Moulton, Robinson, & Elias, 1978; Schneider & Hacker, 1973; Shimanoff, 1977; Silveira, 1980; Wilkinson, 1978).

These studies have involved subjects of various ages, from five years to adult, and have used various methods. The basic structure of the research is similar, however: Subjects are given written or spoken phrases, sentences, paragraphs, or stories, with a generic noun or pronoun—neutral, masculine, or feminine. They are asked to respond by drawing a picture, bringing in a picture, or selecting a picture from a given set, which represents the person or persons referred to; or by describing or naming the person or writing a story about the person; or by choosing a yes/no or multiple-choice response in answer to whether a sex-specific word (female/male) or picture applies; or by answering questions about imagery experienced when exposed to the stimulus material. The criterion measures have been the sex of persons shown in the pictures, named or described in writing, or seen in imagery, or the sex chosen as applying; reaction time for the response has also been examined. In these studies, a number of which consist of several studies themselves, it has been universally found that "generic" masculine is interpreted to indicate predominantly males—in other words, it does not function generically to indicate to hearers both females and males.

Interestingly, various studies have found sex differences in the production or comprehension of the masculine generic. Females are less likely to use it, and are more likely to interpret it generically, that is, as applying to both females and males, when they encounter it (DeStefano, et al., 1978; Hamilton, 1985; Hamilton & Henley, 1982; Harrison, 1975; Hyde, 1984; MacKay & Fulkerson, 1979; Martyna, 1978; Wilson, 1978). Although in two studies no sex differences were found (Eberhart, 1976; MacKay, 1980b), in none have males been found to use the masculine more inclusively.

Memory (Crawford & English, 1984) and comprehension (Hamilton & Henley, 1982) have been found to be affected detrimentally by the masculine generic form. Studies have also found such usage to affect attitudes toward women, girls' self-esteem (Henley, Gruber & Lerner, 1985), and beliefs in females' ability to perform a job (Hyde, 1984).

In addition, there are findings that gender marking other than in the generic influences people's behavior. Preschool boys' achievement and perseverance were increased by hearing a story of male accomplishment, and girls' achievement was increased by hearing a story of female accomplishment (McArthur & Eisen, 1976); women had higher levels of aspiration for tasks labeled as feminine than for ones masculine-labeled, and performed better at them (Jackaway, 1975); high school students responded preferentially to jobs cued to their own sex (Bem & Bem, 1973). Consistent with these findings, Kutner and Brogan (1976) have constructed a model of sex discrimination in education in which biased curricular and text materials are components in the education system which function as an independent variable contributing to sex inequalities in educational achievement.[3]

Feelings and evaluations are also affected by gender marking. Students in a New York high school and at Yale University, asked to give their opinions about some courses described, rated them less enjoyable and less intellectually stimulating when they were to be taught by a *Miss* or *Mrs.* than when they were to be taught by *Ms., Mr.,* or an untitled instructor (Heilman, 1975). In another study, evaluations of paragraphs ascribed to professional women were lower when the woman had a sex designator of "lady" or "-ess" than when she had one of "woman" or "female" (Glenn, 1976). In yet another study, ratings of a character in a story, an applicant for a high-level management position, characterized her as tougher, a better leader, smarter, more rational, dignified, and otherwise qualified when she was referred to as *woman* than when she was referred to as *girl*; and the salary that subjects thought the *woman* should get was $6000 higher than that assigned to the *girl* (Brannon, 1978; however, Hamilton, et al., 1983, with revised material, did not find these differences). Finally, women exposed to the feminine generic have reported feelings of pride, importance, superiority, freedom, and power (Adamsky, 1981).

Of course, whether or not the harm done by sexist language has been "proved" conclusively does not negate the extensive documentation of women's own perceptions nor the evidence of harm in parallel situations, such as race or class discrimination. We can only guess that the argument that changing sexist language is a trivial matter is put forward because the offended group is women. Sexism is still *de rigeur* in our culture, despite a surface and token egalitarianism in some environments, such as the academic world.

Argument 2. Linguistic sexism is superficial and trivial compared with the "real" problems of today; it is overblown by a lunatic fringe brewing a tempest in a teapot.

Despite arguments that change is unnecessary, the detrimental effects of sexist language outlined above and the desire to protect our daughters and ourselves from it point to the necessity of understanding and changing such language. It is a hard course for scholars to have to choose between concern for physical survival and concern for psychological survival, which is the underlying meaning of this objection (when it is not simply a hypocritical evasion). But more and more we are coming to learn how much the major problems affecting our lives are interwoven with and supported by what has been regarded as trivial. Many are now coming to see, for example, the devastation of "little (psychological) rapes" as a problem of parallel concern to, and augmenting, the devastation of physical rape. Studying sexism in language is not a diversion from study of important problems, but it does need integration with studies of other areas of inequality so that the larger picture may be pieced together.

Argument 3. Language may be sexist—i.e., exclude and deprecate females—but changing it is unnecessary. We can educate ourselves to what is happening and make efforts to think of both sexes for all examples given.

Of course, there is no reason why we need choose between, on the one hand, educating ourselves and others to the sexism in our present speech, and, on the other hand, inventing better ways to say what we really want to express—the equality of human beings.

Argument 4. Language change might be desirable, but the changes proposed are inelegant and awkward; or the effort would be too great and most people would not join in it.

Efforts at change are not a new invention, and neither is their characterization as inelegant. Jespersen wrote in 1922 of "the cumbrous use of *he or she*" in Fielding; for example "the reader's heart (if he or she have any)," "each one made his or her comment" (1922, 1964:347). Here Jespersen remarks in a footnote, "This ungainly repetition is frequent in the Latin of Roman law. . . ." But, regarding these terms *cumbrous* and *ungainly*, often applied today, Barber (1966:8), writing on linguistic change, points out that contemporary change is generally characterized as "vulgar, or careless, or ungrammatical, or uneducated," while change that took place in previous ages is considered quite respectable.

Argument 5. Attempting linguistic change is impossible because language is too deeply ingrained, slow to change, shaped by other forces than social movements.

On the contrary, we may consider the change in the late 1960s from the prevalence of *Negro* to that of *Black* (see Van Den Bergh, Part II, in this book). It occurred practically universally, within written media, within the space of about a year; it was accepted for speaking, albeit at times grudgingly, by most Americans in urban centers; and it occurred as a result of the spoken preference of Black leaders of the Civil Rights movement. Lakoff (1973, 1975) uses this as an example of her thesis that linguistic change follows social change; the time, she says, was ripe for such a proposal, but it is not yet ripe for change in linguistic sexism.

However, we have seen broad change due to the women's movement in recent years, in coinages such as *sexism/sexist* and *chairperson,* extensions like *male chauvinism* and *sisterhood* or *orgasm* used as a verb, and wider use of such existing terms as *Ms.,* as well as innovative usage like *gynergy* and *gynocide.* *Androgyny* has taken extended meaning thanks to the work of psychologist Sandra Bem, and it now has most frequent reference to psychological rather than physical androgyny.

But do pronouns change? In contemplating the possibilities for changing the generic use of the masculine pronoun, one depressing conclusion that has been forwarded is that, like male supremacy, the generic masculine is practically universal. Lakoff (1975: 43–44) states the following:

In English, as indeed in the great majority of the world's languages, when reference is made individually to members of a sexually mixed group, the normal solution is to resolve the indecision as to pronoun choice in favor of the masculine: the masculine, then, is 'unmarked' or 'neutral,' and therefore will be found referring to men and women both. . . .

There is strength in numbers, and if anything can make the masculine "generic" sound "normal" and rational, and wanting to do away with it abnormal and irrational, it is knowing that "the great majority of the world's languages" take this "normal solution." But just how common is this form?

Jespersen, in *Language: Its Nature, Development and Origin* (1922, 1964:347), wrote as follows:

Most English pronouns make no distinction of sex: *I, you, we, they, who, each, somebody,* etc. Yet, when we hear that Finnic and Magyar, indeed the vast majority of languages outside the Aryan and Semitic world, have no separate forms for *he* and *she*, our first thought is one of astonishment; we fail to see how it is possible to do without this distinction.

How common can the male pronoun as generic be if the "vast majority of languages outside the Aryan and Semitic world" don't even have a male pronoun?

We are aware that our own language has indeed changed in many ways, including its pronoun system, and the trend has been toward simplification—i.e., loss of distinctions. We no longer have singular and plural second person, but one form, *you,* for all. (And third person singular is the *only* term in which gender is distinguished in our pronouns.) These changes in the past *were* often slow; but it is impossible to estimate the speed with which language may change today, since we see that social change is speeded up, and there has been a revolution in communications. Bodine (1975:141), as a matter of fact, has stated that "looking at the wider context of language change in general, it can be seen that pronominal systems are particularly susceptible to alteration in response to social change." She cites the persistence of singular *they* and *he or she* as evidence that there is a countermovement against sex-indefinite *he* which is unlikely to disappear. Because it now has more supporters and "more explicit social and ideological buttresses," she writes that it is reasonable to predict that the countermovement will affect English pronominal usage.

Bodine is one of a number of linguists who have called for close watch over the rapidly changing pronoun usage today. She even fears that the language is changing so fast that study will lag behind (Bodine, 1976). Similarly, Dubois and Crouch (1976), writing about attempts to change sexist language, state that "In the 1970s, . . . one can observe an ongoing, not to say precipitate, language disruption deliberately forced by social pressure." Examples of the effect of this "language disruption" are detailed by them in this book.

Argument 6. To make people give up certain usages is a form of censorship and infringes on freedom of speech.

Of course, no one can *make* people change their language in all contexts. But we accept that there are some limits on freedom of speech, for example that one ought not shout "Fire!" falsely in a crowded hall, or use derogatory racial and ethnic epithets. Sexist language, of course, is similar to these derogatory epithets which many people on their own reject, and which most publications will not print; but sexist language is not so widely rejected or banned. One may also argue that it is *women* who have been censored *out of* language and that the switch to nonsexist forms is an attempt to remove that censorship rather than impose any. Furthermore, censorship really applies to the suppression of ideas, imposed by a ruling elite on those less powerful; the present attempt at change is the opposite case, an attempt by the suppressed to free themselves and to reassert an idea.

Nevertheless, the changes sought *are* prescriptive grammar, and I advocate barring people from using "generic" masculines in certian contexts, particularly publications. If this is censorship, so is the refusal to allow *ain't, we is,* and *nigger,* and so are the requirements to type articles double-spaced, to capitalize proper names, and to use only three forms of subheadings.

Alternatives in Change

We may first consider language change not only as change in "the" language as a whole but as changes in individuals' speaking habits, which may occur before the changes are accepted by the larger speech community or by its most influential members. Sturtevant (1917) labels a language innovation in an individual speaker *primary change;* the spread of the innovation to others, *secondary change.*

At the individual or primary change level, many of us have adopted alternatives to the masculine generic by referring to human beings as *people, humans, individuals, persons,* and so forth, rather than *man, men,* or *mankind.* Publishing houses and professional organizations have printed guidelines in recent years to suggest ways to avoid sexism in language. (See Nilsen, "Guidelines Against Sexist Language: A Case History," in this book, for a brief history of the development and application of these guidelines; Miller & Swift, 1980, and Persing, 1978, are excellent guidebooks now available.)

Blaubergs (1978) has pointed out three approaches to changing sexism in English: (1) "indirect," through social change; (2) direct—"change via circumvention," that is, change to sex-neutral forms; and (3) direct—"change via emphasis on feminine terms." The first approach (through social change) is that of Lakoff (1973, 1975) and other linguists who suggest that once social equality is reached, we can assume the language will no longer reflect an inequality. Of course, this method is slow and chancy; it allows the continuation of damage in the interim, and is really no guarantee of language change anyway, since we have many remnants of earlier ideology remaining in the language. Moreover, to favor indirect change is to ignore the relation between linguistic change and social factors. (For more detailed discussion of the relationship between these two, see Van Den Bergh in this book.)

Of the two means of direct change, many people assume that the only feminist position is to favor sex-neutral terms; indeed, this proposal has occasioned the most discussion in print and in speech from feminists and others. However, one should recognize that there is also a strong feminist argument for emphasis on sex-specific terms. Stanley (1977a) and Shepelak (1977) are two who have taken exception to the push for a sex-unspecified pronoun, pointing out that other "neutral" terms tend to raise male images, not female ones. Stanley suggests we mark gender explicitly, for example use both *Chairwoman* and *Chairman.* A different approach to restoring the female to language is taken by Shepelak (1977:22), who proposes an equal-probability usage of both feminine and masculine cues, as in the following example:

The social scientist views the child . . . as an individual who has come to know of and about himself in relation to others in his environment. And indeed, it may be the case that the child is an active participant in her gender role development since she may purposefully be selecting and imitating the behavior of her chosen models.

What options do we have for direct change which emphasizes sex-neutral terms? There is a rich assortment of alternatives here. Various writers (e.g., Blaubergs, 1978; Miller & Swift, 1976, 1980; Nilsen, this book; Stanley,

1977a; Withers, this book) have summarized them. Miller and Swift (1976) list sixteen tips for avoiding sexist language, and Blaubergs lists eleven, such as plurals, indefinites, parallel female/male constructions, and so on. The Guidelines for Nonsexist Use of Language (Cofer, Daniels, Dunham, and Heimer, 1977) prepared for the *Publication Manual* of the American Psychological Association take up thirty examples of common usages which may be changed, and other such guidelines do similarly.

Changes in the pronoun system, to produce a neutral word for the sex-unspecified third person, have been proposed in abundance, though none has been widely adopted. Miller and Swift (1976, Chapter 8) and Baron (1981) give good accounts of the various proposals. Henley and Dragun (1983), in a questionnaire study, found surprisingly that 61% of their respondents answered Yes or Maybe when asked whether there is a need for a sex-neutral pronoun in English, compared with 29% who responded No and 9% who responded Not Sure (1% did not respond). The wish for a sex-neutral third person pronoun must go as far back as the use of the singular *they*, which itself dates back at least four hundred years. Bodine (1975:131–132) points out that "prior to the nineteenth century 'they' was widely used in written, therefore presumably also in spoken, English." It persisted until the eighteenth century, along with *he or she,* when grammars took up an attack on the singular *they,* culminating in an 1850 Act of Parliament which legally replaced *he or she* with *he* to "shorten the language used in Acts of Parliament." This became the prescriptive grammar in texts from the nineteenth century to the present, and is justified by an emphasis on agreement in number, ignoring the parallel problem of agreement in gender.

The linguist Otto Jespersen (1922:347) also wrote of the desire for a sex-neutral pronoun.

> . . . it is at times an inconvenience to have to specify the sex of the persons spoken about. Coleridge (*Anima Poetae* 190) regretted the lack of a pronoun to refer to the word *person,* as it necessitated some stiff and strange construction. . . . Anyone who has written much in Ido [an artificial language] will have often felt how convenient it is to have the common-sex pronouns *lu* (he or she), *singlu, ultru,* etc.

Though the proposed alternative pronoun systems have not caught on, they are being tried out in pockets of the population, in written and spoken language. Miller and Swift (1976) report the adoption of *co* and *cos* by the Twin Oaks Community in 1972, and in other communities since then, as well as by the publication *Communities.* They also report the attempt to adopt *tey, ter, tem* by the student newspaper of the University of Tennessee in 1973—an attempt that was aborted within a few months in the face of ridicule and backlash. *Co* and *cos* were also used in a book on therapy (Glenn & Kunnes, 1973), and *tey,* in a major psychological paper on measuring attitudes toward women (Spence & Helmreich, 1972).

In *The Cook and the Carpenter,* a novel, June Arnold (1973) adopted the pronouns *na* and *nan* (and *naself*), explaining tongue-in-cheek:

> Since the differences between men and women are so obvious to all, so impossible to confuse whether we are speaking of learned behavior or inherent characteristics, ordinary conversation or furious passion, work or intimate relationships, the author understands that it is no longer necessary to distinguish between men and women in this novel. I have therefore used one pronoun for both, trusting the reader to know which is which.

Other writers and speakers have eliminated obvious sexism from their language by simpler means, without new pronoun systems. Several psychologists and pediatricians (e.g., Carl Rogers, 1977, Benjamin Spock, 1977) alternated the use of the masculine and feminine generic in their books. However, Blaubergs (1978) pointed to a failure in such an attempt—alternation can be used stereotypically and die out early in the course of a book.

Dorothy Tennov (1975), in *Psychotherapy: The Hazardous Cure,* used female pronouns to refer to patients and clients in psychotherapy because her focus was on female psychotherapy patients, but she used male terms for therapists "Because psychotherapy is largely based on patriarchal assumptions and because most therapists are male" (pp. xii–xiii). Tennov was dissatisfied with this usage, however, and did not recommend it to others. Still other writers have used alternative constructions such as plural, passive, omission of the pronoun, and other forms.

The option for personal change in usage is presumably open to all who wish to change. However, milieu pressures such as inaccessibility of the knowledge of options, disapproval by living or work companions or by superiors, and lack of general social support, as well as initial socialization and resistance to extra effort, all limit the availability of the option for change (see Bate, 1978). In all cases of individual change, as in structural change, the larger system is involved—one does not change alone.

New Words and Their Effects: Science Fiction as Laboratory

An interesting laboratory for the study of change in the generic reference is the genre of science fiction, which deals with beings of different sexual structure from ours or in utopian societies. David Lindsay, in *Voyage to Arcturus*

(1920, 1946), describes the odyssey of an earth man who meets many strange people (all human forms) on another planet. In one encounter

he experienced another surprise, for this person, although clearly a human being, was neither man nor woman, nor anything between the two, but was unmistakably of a third positive sex, which was remarkable to behold and difficult to understand. In order to translate into words the sexual impression produced in Maskull's mind by the stranger's physical aspect, it is necessary to coin a new pronoun, for none in earthly use would be applicable. Instead of "he," "she," or "it," therefore, "ae" will be used.

The pronouns *ae* and *aer* are used for the brief period of the book that this androgyne remains.

Ursula LeGuin has a world of androgynous characters in her *Left Hand of Darkness* (1969). She has been criticized for her use of the masculine pronoun for these beings who are usually neuter but at times become either of the sexes (anyone may become either sex at different times, depending on what sex a love partner is becoming). LeGuin (cited in Sargent, 1975, p. xxxv) later explained her choice of pronoun.

I know that the use of the masculine pronoun influences the readers' imagination, perhaps decisively. . . . Alexei Panshin and others have demanded an invented neuter pronoun. I did consider this carefully, and I decided against it. The experiment was tried by Lindsay in *A Voyage to Arcturus,* and it is to my ears a failure, an exasperating preciosity; three hundred pages of it would be intolerable.

(The author further defends her choice by pointing out that the narrator of the novel is a male earthling, who would refer to the ambisexuals by a male generic term.)

In a later essay, LeGuin (1976: 137–138) analyzes her own book and admits that

the central failure in this area comes up in the frequent criticism I receive, that the Gethenians seem like *men,* instead of menwomen.

This arises in part from the choice of pronoun. I call Gethenians "he" because I utterly refuse to mangle English by inventing a pronoun for "he/she." . . . But I don't consider this really very important. The pronouns wouldn't matter at all if I had been cleverer at *showing* the "female" component of the Gethenian characters in action.

Marge Piercy (1976), in *Woman on the Edge of Time,* writes of future earth people who maintain distinctive sex, though coupling may take place between two of any sex; in their society, the sexes have been equalized, and with them the language. The author invents a new pronoun, *person,* and its objective and possessive form *per,* for the third person (sex is *never* specified pronominally), as in "Person does not switch jobs but is permanent head of this house of children. It is per calling."

The examples from science fiction, far from being simply a curiosity, have implications for our own concerns about language usage. For one thing, these stories assume that when a community does not have gender as a primary social criterion for allocation of its goods and status, it does not need, nor wish, to specify sex in its pronouns. And they do not depict sexuality as suffering when sex is not distinguished linguistically. In fact, as in many utopian views, a much freer sexuality is generally portrayed—as we might expect when one sex does not dominate and the other does not have to barter its sexuality for survival. These possible futures develop our intuition that sexist language is closely bound to sexist society; but further, the stories imply that if women are moving toward economic, political, psychological, and social equality with men, a changed language is necessary and perhaps inevitable. We see in the alternatives being tried out in various places the gropings toward a language that will express the ideology and later, the reality, of equality.

What is the response to these coined pronouns? Readers of books using alternative pronouns have frequently remarked on (1) the initial consciousness-raising jolt at being made aware of one's own expectations and biases coded in the language, and (2) the ease with which they adapted to the coinage by the time they were well into the book. In fact, contrary to LeGuin's expectations, after reading *Woman on the Edge of Time* (Piercy, 1976), I found myself going around thinking in the new pronoun *person,* and others have recounted similar experiences. Perhaps adaptation is easier than we thought; certainly there are many who have changed their speaking habits to eliminate the generic masculine and accomplished it so that they were at ease with the new speech within a few months.

To date, very little controlled research has been done on response to novel pronoun systems or to other such changes. Adamsky (1981) investigated the effect of an instructor's use of the feminine as the generic singular on student language use and attitudes. Students in her experimental group were given a brief statement at the beginning of the semester describing what the instructor's usage would be, but no suggestion was given to copy it. However, their written work showed that their use of the generic feminine significantly increased (compared with that of a control group), their use of the generic masculine decreased, and their use of these two pronouns was more specifically attached to referents of the appropriate sex. The response of most women to the feminine generic usage was positive and self-enhancing (though one claimed she "felt unfairly included" by the pronoun). Interestingly, of those who used the feminine generic, none of the males indicated in a questionnaire that they felt it was difficult, while 52% of the females felt it was. The majority of both sexes, not surprisingly, believed that an inclusive pronoun is needed.

How Change Might Come About

Language change is always taking place, though in some periods and in some groups change is faster than in others, creating extra tension between the necessary conservative and innovative forces of language.

Change may occur not only in *usage* but in *acceptance* of forms which are already in existence but not recognized as "standard." Both of these types of change may occur at different levels of formality of the written and spoken language. The situation of the singular *they*, so common in informal and spoken usage, may be one of progress toward acceptance in writing and in more formal circumstances. Its persistence over the centuries suggests two things: (1) that this is the weak point of the pronoun system, or of sexist language as a whole, and the point therefore at which it will break; (2) that the speech community does feel the strain of referring to females with the masculine, and that *they* is a major way to avoid that strain. Jespersen (1922, 1965:348) points out that:

The substitution of the plural for the singular is not wholly illogical; for *everybody* singular is much the same thing as "all men," [sic] plural and *nobody* is the negation of "all men" [sic] . . .

While language purists and linguistic sexists decry the awkwardness of proposed changes to nonsexist language, such change could well represent in fact a retreat *from* strain, that is to *less* awkward and dissatisfying language. Furthermore, the proposed reform of the pronoun system would be in keeping with the trend to simplification which the system has undergone over the years.

Bate (1978) has studied nonsexist use in transition through study of printed materials, observation of faculty meetings, and interviews with members of a university faculty. Her results suggest some of the factors that will influence *how* change will take place. She found, for example, that sounds of proposed forms constitute a constraint on change—not knowing how to pronounce something (e.g., *s/he*) or finding it awkward (e.g., *his or hers*), will make it unlikely that speakers will make the transition.

Bate found that change occurs gradually in an individual and begins with

terms most dissonant to the individual or most often mentioned by a respected other. To adopt an alternative form, one must first have heard of it, so
information is a key factor. But the presence of that "significant other" is
important too; men, especially, described the influence of one or more females as important to their changing. The audience was also important to
men; they were most likely to change their speech when females were active
members of the audience. Audience was also an important factor in the
change away from the term *Negro* to *Black* and *Afro-American* (Rafky, 1970)
in the 1960s. Blacks were also more likely to use the new racial terms, as we
see women more likely to be active in the transition from sexist language
today.

Various influences located within the individual or in the environment may
encourage language change. Participants in a questionnaire study (Henley
and Dragun, 1983) most often cited "Own conclusions from reading, social
justice considerations, etc." (cited by 43%) as an impetus to change their
sexist language; other frequently named influences were "Speech of those
around me (was nonsexist)" (24%) and "Female friend's influence" (21%).
More formal influences, such as "Influence of articles and books on sexist
language" (16%), "Requirements of others (e.g., editor)" (15%), and "Influence of authority" (13%), were less frequently cited.

Studies of language change find other social and personal factors active:
Labov (1972) has studied phonologic change that takes place over time
synchronically, that is, in a single time, by studying the factor of age. Older
speakers tend to cling to the old form, and younger, to adopt the new.
Similarly, in the racial terminology study, the adoption of new racial terms
was most prevalent in younger rather than older Blacks. Change was related,
among academics, to their political attitudes, personal history, academic field,
and social class.

Some of Labov's (1972: 179–180) discoveries about change suggest patterns by which change in sexist language may develop. Labov noted that the
change spread to the extent that the values of the original subgroup with the
change were adopted by other groups in the speech community.

If the group in which the change originated was not the highest-status group in the
speech community, members of the highest-status group eventually stigmatized the
changed form through their control of various institutions of the communication
network. . . .

Under extreme stigmatization, a form may become the overt topic of social comment,
and may eventually disappear. It is thus a *stereotype*, which may become increasingly
divorced from the forms which are actually used in speech.

But if the change originated in the highest status group of the community, it became a prestige model for all members of the speech community.

Applying his observations to change in sexist language, we would expect such change to occur first among those most affected by it—women; particularly young, educated, socially conscious, perhaps employed and mobile women, whose active presence will constitute pressure on speakers to use nonsexist forms. These women will in turn exert influence through example and argument on others to change. To the extent that nonsexist values are adopted in the speech community, nonsexist forms may be adopted by other groups within it. The first ones to use changed forms, however, being of lower prestige (as women), may be stigmatized, and their speech may become the overt topic of social comment and stereotyped, a phenomenon we have already seen taking place. However, if the change is put forward in sectors of higher prestige, it has more chance of being adopted.[4]

The Next Stage

The next stage of transition to nonsexist language, in addition to continuing adoption of the forms on an individual level, should be one of active pressure on the larger speech community. While many personal options exist for excising the prescriptive masculine pronoun, we will have to face the need for an altogether new pronoun. Singular *they* is an excellent alternative for many situations, but Donald MacKay (1980a) has illustrated problems of ambiguity and inadequacy of singular *they* when one examines the whole range of uses to which prescriptive *he* is applied. I consider *they* and other strategies such as use of the plural, use of the passive, and repetition of the nominal as transitional forms.

Kramer, Throne, and Henley (1978:651) point out the following:

In times of changing social custom, it is common for several forms of behavior to be optional for a given situation and for the "correctness" of a form to be ambiguous (as in current mixed-sex door opening). The existence of a variety of alternatives to the pronoun system, as well as to other forms of sexism in language, and ambiguity over the correctness of certain forms, all point to the climate of change in our langauge at this time.

Nichols (1978:1,4) writes, "The time is now ripe for language planning by a new generation of academic grammarians," and that

Recent work in the area of language planning suggests that certain changes can be directed if we understand both the linguistic structures involved and the institutional influence which may be brought to bear on their use.

Nichols states further that "we as language scholars have a particular responsibility to plan for efficient and graceful change" in this area of animate pronouns. Nichols does not advocate the introduction of a new pronoun, however, but rather greater usage of forms already available—*they, he or she,* and repeat of the nominal.

There is a field and a developing literature of language planning which has predominantly been applied to other countries (e.g., Rubin, 1977; Rubin & Jernudd, 1971; Rubin & Shuy, 1973). But how would one go about such language planning for this linguistic problem in our current state of development in the United States? First, one would demonstrate an inadequacy and a need. The inadequacy of the prescriptive masculine forms for referencing both female and male in our language has been more than sufficiently demonstrated. The need is, first, to abandon masculine pseudogeneric, and that is being done by many people, agencies, and institutions, and being encouraged by professional organizations and publishers.

However, this need leads to another need. Adequate alternatives to the pseudogeneric don't exist, or the existing ones will not be universally adopted. It seems that a new form will be necessary. A testing program by which we might assess the relative merits of proposed alternatives has been outlined by MacKay (1980a:364); this program includes the following factors:

. . . simplicity, lexical availability, connotation, conceptual availability, comprehensibility, imageability, memorability, producibility, learnability, topic, sentence complexity, linguistic side effects, case, function, ambiguity, context, written vs. spoken speech and formal vs. informal registers. . . . political and sociological factors. . . .

The adequacy with which alternatives meet these criteria should be compared with the adequacy with which the current prescription—the masculine pronoun—meets them, rather than with some ideal.

Once the inadequacy and need are demonstrated, the criteria developed, the testing program completed, and an alternative form found, the thrust of the language planning program becomes one of implementation. Since in the United States we do not have a central agency charged with preserving or regulating the language, nor any particular body with direct control over it[5], association and example will be better teachers of new forms than overt prescription. Our task will then be to search out and identify the agents of change and arbiters of language in our national speech community. The expertise in this area will come from sociological knowledge of innovation spread and sociopsychological knowledge of persuasion and resistance to change, from communications studies of influences on speech, and identification of influential speakers and speech sources.

It might be found, for example, that major speech influences are the television and news media, English teachers, and publishers and editors (including governmental sources of publications). With our modern communication instancy, we might say that if *CBS News,* the *New York Times,* and *Time* magazine began to use a new pronoun this week, it would be fairly nationally spread by next week.

Grass-roots spreading of information will also contribute to change. There might be speakers, in cities large and small all over the country, speaking to women's groups, parents' groups, book clubs, and so on. Such a campaign might be coordinated within already existing organizations and networks, such as the National Organization for Women or women's political caucuses.

The popular media would undoubtedly play a part; articles in popular magazines, for example, could help. There is an advantage here because popular media have already given attention to the topic of sexism in language; this may be considered a disadvantage, though, because the attention that has been given the topic has been often misinformed and sexist in the extreme. It may also be a disadvantage if the novelty of such attention is played out by the time a scientifically arrived at, well-planned language change is introduced. My own opinion is that it will be a help that new proposals will build on a base already created in popular media, particularly if serious attention is given to stimulating informed media coverage.

Research must be carried out at a variety of interdisciplinary levels so that careful planning may be effected. The following questions need to be addressed:

1. What will the proposed change(s) be? Are there limiting contexts?
2. What are the stages of language change and the influences on it?
3. What sectors of the population are to be reached and by what means?
4. What arguments must be met and how should they effectively be met?
5. What agencies, persons, and media of influence are to be used?
6. What is the timetable for each proposed change?

The kind of change that is being suggested in this paper is on a large scale, similar in some ways to the change from *Negro* to *Black,* or to the adoption by many print media a few years ago of the Pinyin system of Chinese transliteration, or to the attempted conversion to the metric system.[6] In retrospect, only a few years ago such a grand plan would not have seemed feasible; but today the climate is different. Encouraging signs of change away from sexist language happen more frequently. For example, there are now the sex-neutral occupational titles devised by our government, a *Thesaurus for Nonsexist Indexing and Cataloging* for librarians (Marshall, 1977), and many sets of guidelines to nonsexist writing. Even in that staid bastion of scholarly writing, *The New York Review of Books*, an article has been seen to use the singular *they*.

At this time, a variety of forms exists, indicating that we are in a time of transition. Bodine (1976), Dubois and Crouch (1979 and this book), and Nichols (1978) have pointed out that the pronoun system *is* susceptible to change and that social factors may influence that change. The time is now right. Social events are influencing the use of language, and pronoun usage as part of language use. We have a marvelous opportunity for intelligent study and application of social science knowledge, coordinated with existing factors.

Research at the intersection of gender and language is truly an interdisciplinary enterprise. It is an opportunity like no other we have had before to pool our knowledge and skills; it represents excitement for the milions of women cut out of the language and for ourselves and our daughters who are seizing back the language by rejecting that which has excluded us. A grand enterprise awaits us, one that both demands of us our best and will give back to us information on language, social processes, and language planning that has not been available before. In the words of Monique Wittig (1973:131):

They say, take your time, consider this new species that seeks a new language. A great wind is sweeping the earth. The sun is about to rise. The birds no longer sing. The lilac and violet colours brighten in the sky. They say, where will you begin?

Notes

1. Based on papers delivered at the meeting of the Association for Women in Psychology, Pittsburgh, 1978, and the Conference on Language and Gender, Santa Cruz, California, 1979. I wish to thank Joyce Penfield for her extensive help with revision and to acknowledge the influence of Barrie Thorne, Cheris Kramarae, and Wendy Martyna on the paper.

2. See also Blaubergs (1980) for another analysis of arguments against changing sexist language.

3. In the studies cited here, the effect of language is not separated from other operating cultural influences (e.g., content) which might bias response.

4. The adoption of nonsexist language by women and men in higher educa-

tion, and by institutions themselves, may have preserved the possibilities of change before we were aware of what danger they were in.

5. Indeed, it is safe to say that Americans would react vehemently and negatively to any attempt to control their speech and writing, which probably accounts for some of the reaction to feminist criticism of phallocentric language.

6. In fact, it may be most like the latter in scope, an attempt which met with little success and great resistance, although it had comprehensive planning. It is therefore a dismal comparison. However, while there are some elements in common with metric conversion, there are important differences; first, governmental pressure should be avoided in the case of language; and second, the metric system does not have the history of popular need and resistance to the prescribed form, the current social force and awareness of injustice, or the existence of an already-occurring transitional stage such as we have with pronouns now.

References

Adamsky, Catheryn. 1981. "Changes in Pronominal Usage in a Classroom Situation." *Psychology of Women Quarterly* 5:773-779.

Arnold, J. 1973. *The Cook and the Carpenter*. Plainfield, Vt.: Daughters, Inc.

Barber, C. 1966. *Linguistic Change in Present-day English*. University, Alabama: University of Alabama Press.

Baron, Dennis E. 1981. "The Epicene Pronoun: The Word that Failed." *American Speech* 56:83-97.

Bate, Barbara. 1978. "Nonsexist Language Use in Transition." *Journal of Communication* 28:139-149.

Bem, Sandra L., and Daryl J. Bem. 1973. "Does Sex-biased Job Advertising 'Aid and Abet' Sex Discrimination?" *Journal of Applied Social Psychology* 3:6-18.

Blaubergs, Maija S. 1980. "An Analysis of Classic Arguments Against Changing Sexist Language." *Women's Studies International Quarterly* 3:135-147.

_____. 1978. "Changing the Sexist Language: The Theory Behind the Practice." *Psychology of Women Quarterly* 2:244-261.

Bodine, Ann. 1975. "Androcentrism in Prescriptive Grammar: Singular 'They', Sex-Indefinite 'he,' and 'he or she.'" *Language in Society* 4:129-146.

_____. 1976. "Workshop B. Investigating the Generic Masculine." In *Papers in Southwest English IV: Proceedings of the Conference on the Sociology of the Languages of American Women*, edited by B.L. Dubois and I. Crouch. San Antonio, Texas: Trinity University.

Brannon, Robert. "The Consequences of Sexist Language." Paper presented at the American Psychological Association, Toronto, August 1978.

Cofer, Charles N., Robert S. Daniels, Frances Y. Dunham and Walter Heimer. 1977. "Guidelines for Nonsexist Language in APA Journals." *American Psychologist* 32: 486-494.

Crawford, M. and L. English. 1984. "Generic Versus Specific Inclusion of Women in Language: Effects on Recall." *Journal of Psycholinguistic Research* 13:373-381.

DeStefano, J., M.W. Kuhner, and H.B. Pepinsky. "An Investigation of Referents of Selected Sex-Indefinite Terms in English." Paper presented at Ninth World Congress of Sciology, Uppsala, Sweden, 1978.

Dubois, Betty Lou and Isabel M. Crouch. 1979. "Man and Its Compounds in Recent Prefeminist American English Prose." *Papers in Linguistics* 12:1, 261-269.

Eberhart, Ozella Mae Yowell. "Elementary Students' Understanding of Certain Masculine and Neutral Generic Nouns." Doctoral dissertation, Kansas State University, 1976.

Glenn, W.G. March (1977). "Feminine Designators: A Quantitative Study." *Women and Language News*, p. 2 (Abstract).

Glenn, M. and R. Kunnes. *Repression or Revolution? Therapy in the U.S. Today.* New York: Harper, 1973.

Graham, A. "The Making of a NonSexist Dictionary." In *Language and Sex: Difference and Dominance*, edited by B. Thorne and N. Henley. Rowley, Mass.: Newbury House, 1975.

Greenberg, Joseph H. *Language Universals*. The Hague: Mouton, 1966.

Hamilton, M.C. 1985. "Linguistic Relativity and Sex Bias in Language: Effects of the Masculine 'generic' on the Imagery of the Writer and the Perceptual Discrimination of the Reader." *Dissertation Abstracts International*, 46: 1381B (University Microfilms No. 8513117).

―――――― and Nancy M. Henley. 1986. "Sex Bias in Language: Effects on the Reader/Hearer's Cognitions." Paper submitted for publication.

―――――, W. Wong-McCarthy, N.M. Henley, L. Devillers, E. Kelly,and R. Armentrout. August 1983. "The Consequences of Sexist Language Revisited." Paper presented at the meeting of the American Psychological Association, Anaheim, California.

Harrison, Linda. 1975. "Cro-Magnon Woman—In Eclipse." *Science Teacher*, 42:4, 9-11.

―――――― and R.N. Passero. 1975. "Sexism in the Language of Elementary School Textbooks." *Science and Children*, 12:4, 22-25.

Heilman, M. 1975. "Miss, Mrs., Ms., or None of the Above." *American Psychologist* 30:516-518.

Henley, Nancy M., and D. Dragun. August 1983. "A Survey of Attitudes Toward Changing Sex-biased Language." Paper presented at the meeting of the American Psychoiogical Association, Anaheim, CA.

_____, B. Gruber, and L. Lerner. March 1985. "Studies on the Detrimental Effects of 'generic' Masculine Usage." Paper presented at the meeting of the Eastern Psychological Association, Boston.

Hyde, J.S. 1984. "Children's Understanding of Sexist Language." *Developmental Psychology* 20:697-706.

Jackaway, R. 1974. "Sex Differences in Achievement Motivation, Behavior, and Attributions about Success and Failure." Doctoral dissertation, State University of New York at Albany.

Jespersen, Otto. 1964. *Language: Its Nature, Development and Origin.* New York: Norton. (Originally published 1922).

Kidd, V. 1971. "A Study of the Images Produced Through the Use of the Male Pronoun as the Generic." *Moments in Contemporary Rhetoric and Communication* 1:25-30.

Kramer, C., B. Thorne, and N. Henley. 1978. "Review Essay: Perspectives on Language and Communication." *Signs* 3:638-651.

Kutner, N.G., and D. Brogan. 1976. "Sources of Sex Discrimination in Educational Systems: A Conceptual Model." *Psychology of Women Quarterly* 1:50-69.

Labov, William. 1972. "On the Mechanism of Linguistic Change." Chapter 7 of *Sociolinguistic Patterns.* Philadelphia: University of Pennsylvania Press.

Lakoff, Robin. 1973. "Language and Woman's Place." *Language in Society* 2:45-79.

_____. 1975. *Language and Woman's Place.* New York: Harper & Row.

LeGuin, U.K. 1969. *Left Hand of Darkness.* New York: Ace.

_____. 1976. "Is Gender Necessary?" In *Aurora: Beyond Equality,* edited by S.J. Anderson and V.N. McIntyre. Greenwich, Conn.: Fawcett.

Lerner, H.E. 1976. "Girls, Ladies, or Women? The Unconscious Dynamics of Language Choice." *Comprehensive Psychiatry* 17:295-299.

Lindsay, D. 1946. *Voyage to Arcturus.* London: V. Gollancz. (Originally published 1920.)

MacKay, Donald G. 1980a "On the Goals, Principles, and Procedures for Prescriptive Grammar." *Language in Society* 9: 349-367.

_____. 1980b. "Prescriptive Grammar and the Pronoun Problem." *American Psychologist* 35:444-449.

_____, and D.C. Fulkerson. 1979. "On the Comprehension and

Production of Pronouns. *Journal of Verbal Learning and Verbal Behavior* 18:661-673.

Marshall, J.K. 1977. *On Equal Terms: A Thesaurus for Nonsexist Indexing and Cataloging.* New York: Neal-Schuman.

Martyna, Wendy. 1978. "Using and Understanding the Generic Masculine: A Social-Psychological Approach to Language and the Sexes." Doctoral dissertation, Stanford University.

──────────. 1980. "Beyond the He/Man Approach: The Case for Linguistic Change." *Signs* 5:482-493.

McArthur, L.A., and S.V. Eisen. 1976. "Achievements of Male and Female Storybook Characters of Determinants of Achievement Behavior by Boys and Girls." *Journal of Personality and Social Psychology* 33:463-473.

Miller, Casey, and Kate Swift. 1976. *Words and Women.* New York: Doubleday.

──────────. 1980. *Handbook of Nonsexist Writing: For Writers, Editors, and Speakers.* New York: Lippincott.

Moulton, Janice, G.M. Robinson, and C. Elias. 1978. "Sex Bias in Language Use: 'Neutral' Pronouns that Aren't." *American Psychologist* 33:1032-1036.

Nichols, Pat. 1978. "Planning for Language Change." Paper presented at the meetings of the Modern Language Association, New York.

Nilsen, Alleen Pace. December 1973. "The Correlation Between Gender and Other Semantic Features in American English." Paper presented at meeting of the Linguistic Society of America, San Diego.

──────────. 1977a. "Linguistic Sexism as a Social Issue." In *Sexism and Language,* by A.P. Nilsen, H. Bosmajian, H.L. Gershuny, and J.P. Stanley. Urbana, Ill.: National Council of Teachers of English.

──────────. 1977b. "Sexism as Shown Through the English Vocabulary." In *Sexism and Language,* by A.P. Nilsen, H. Bosmajian, H.L. Gershuny, and J.P. Stanley. Urbana, Ill.: National Council of Teachers of English.

Persing, B.S. 1978. *The Nonsexist Communicator.* East Elmhurst, N.Y.: Communication Dynamics Press.

Piercy, M. 1976. *Woman on the Edge of Time.* New York: Knopf.

Rafky, D.M. 1970. "The Semantics of Negritude." *American Speech* 45: 30-44.

Rogers, Carl. 1977. *Carl Rogers on Personal Power.* New York: Delacorte.

Rubin, Joan. 1977. *Language Planning in the United States.* The Hague: Mouton.

──────────, and B.A. Jernudd, eds. 1971. *Can Language be Planned? Sociolinguistic Theory and Practice for Developing Nations.* Honolulu: University Press of Hawaii.

_____, and R.W. Shuy, eds. 1973. *Language Planning: Current Issues and Research*. Washington: Georgetown University Press.

Sargent, P. 1975. "Women in Science Fiction." In *Women of Wonder*, edited by P. Sargent. New York: Vintage.

Schneider. J., and S. Hacker. 1973. "Sex Role Imagery and the Use of the Generic 'Man' in Introductory Texts." *American Sociologist* 8:12-18.

Shepelak, Norma J. 1977. "Does 'He' Mean 'She' Too? The Case of the Generic Anomaly." Paper presented at meetings of the Association for Women in Psychology, St. Louis.

Shimanoff, Susan B. 1977. "Man-Human: Empirical Support for the Whorfian Hypothesis." *Bulletin: Women's Studies in Communication* 1:2, 21-27.

Silveira, Jeanette. 1980. "Generic Masculine Words and Thinking." *Women's Studies International Quarterly* 3:165-178.

Spence, J.T. and R.L. Helmreich. 1972. "Who Likes Competent Women: Competence, Sex Role Congruence of Interests and Subjects' Attitudes Toward Women as Determinants of Interpersonal Attraction." *Journal of Applied Social Psychology* 2:197-213.

Spock, Benjamin McL. 1977. *Baby and Child Care*. New York: Pocket Books.

Stanley, Julia P. 1977a. "Gender-marking in American English: Usage and Reference." In *Sexism and Language*, by A.P. Nilsen, H. Bosmajian, H.L. Gershuny, and J.P. Stanley. Urbana, Ill: National Council of Teachers of English.

_____. 1971b. "Paradigmatic Woman: The Prostitute." In *Papers in Language Variation*, edited by D.L. Shores & C.P. Hines. University, Ala.: University of Alabama Press.

_____. 1978. "Sexist Grammar." *College English* 39:800-811.

Stannard, Una. 1977. *Mrs. Man*. San Francisco: Germain Books.

Sturtevant, Einar H. 1917. *Linguistic Change: An Introduction to the Historical Study of Language*. Chicago: University of Chicago Press.

Tennov. D. 1975. *Psychotherapy: The Hazardous Cure*. New York: Abelard-Schuman.

Wilkinson, Louise Cherry. 1978. "Teachers' Inclusion of Males and Females in Generic Nouns." *Research in the Teaching of English* 12:155-161.

Wittig, Monique. 1973. *Les Guérrillères*. New York: Avon.

Linguistic Disruption: He/She, S/He, He or She, He-She[1]

Betty Lou Dubois and *Isabel Crouch*

One popular way proposed to liberate language is to neutralize it. Basically this means to create forms which are unmarked for gender. For many languages of the world this simple solution presents some challenging linguistic problems. English is a major example. Dubois and Crouch searched through several years of writing to provide numerous examples of attempts to make English gender neutral.

This chapter originally was not meant as an intellectual discussion or theoretical treatise; rather it was written and presented as a theatrical piece to humorously highlight some of the difficulties in creating greater gender equity by neutralizing the English pronoun system. The editor has altered it to conform to the stylistic approach of this book.

One of the striking aspects of current feminism is its concern for language, both *of* women and *about* women. The great "he/she" battle has involved language *about* women. This article takes a lighthearted look at how various writers and speakers have been affected by attempts to make the pronoun system of English less sexist.

All languages are constantly in flux, but usually linguistic changes occur so slowly that they often go unnoticed by the users themselves.[2] At the initial stage of language change, it is not uncommon to find what appears to be inconsistency or what we shall refer to here as "linguistic disruption."[3] The use of alternations or multiple options sometimes causes confusion in the message content. In other cases, it simply calls attention to some aspect of language which is in the process of change. This essay notes various categories of linguistic disruption related to the "he/she" battle, drawing on a data base taken from everyday texts in print and speech collected by the authors over a six-year span. One underlying point of the discussion is that there may be no easy solution to the elimination of linguistic sexism in the English pronoun system. And more importantly, at the first phase of language change, it is not uncommon to witness the use of many different alternatives, which gives the idea that language is being used inconsistently.

The Pronoun Problem

Poets and other creative writers used the double alternative *he or she* or *him or her* long before pronouns became an issue. Walt Whitman is one such example.

> Vocalism, measure, concentration, determination and the divine power to speak words.
> Surely whoever speaks to me in the right voice, *him or her* I shall follow as the water follows the moon, silently, with fluid steps, anywhere around the globe!

Virginia Woolf in the 1930s is another example (Nicolson and Trantmann, 1979).

> What I thought about the article—and I read it again, after your letter—was that the *man or woman* was so much engaged in imitating, first me, then someone else—for it went on differently—that *he or she* had never got away from the looking glass at all, and therefore had quite forgotten to say anything about Jane Austin.

But by far the majority of writers before the 1970s did not worry about the use of pronouns. There was little use of *he or she, she,* generic special antecedents, or plural pronouns in order to avoid gender; nor were people concerned about the use of *man* as generic. Today, we find a myriad of possibilities in the "pronoun problem," sometimes in the same paragraph or even the same sentence. One of the most common solutions is *he or she* or *his or her.*

> We must fight the tradition that forces the actor to accept poverty as a precondition of *his or her* profession (Farr, 1975).

Less commonly used is *she or he* and *her or him.*

> Read to children and let them participate from time to time by telling what they think the author would add if *she or he* was present with them (Allen, 1976).

Along with the alternation solution often comes inconsistency, as the author either tires of using both or forgets, as reflected by Vladimir Nabokov when writing about the Moscow Art Theater.

> The enthusiastic spirit of this high service animated every single member of the troupe; and if any other consideration became to *him or her* of greater importance than

the search for artistic perfection, then *he or she* had no place in this theatrical community. Carried away by the profound artistic enthusiasm of its founders, living like one big
family, the actors worked away at every one of the productions as if this were to be the
one and only production in their lives. There was religious awe in their approach;
there was moving self-sacrifice. And there also was amazing teamwork. For no actor
was supposed to care more for *his* personal performance of success than for the general
performance of the troupe, for the general success of the performance.

Does this mean that although the members of the troupe are both male and
female, actors apparently are only male?

Inconsistency in the use of pronouns is equally reflected in titles where
three females of the same age and marital status may be referred to quite
differently:

Miss Minerva Jimenez has been added to the credit unions staff as a teller to replace
Rosemary Gonzales who will be taking care of the RSW Accounts. Also *Ms. Darlene
Whitcomb* joined the staff in early December as a teller (Dona Ana County Teachers
Federal Credit Union Newsletter, 1976).

One would assume that there would be little difficulty in pronoun choice for a
Women's Caucus, but the Speech Communication Association Women's
Caucus makes it clear that they accept several different options.

S/he shall be ex-officio member of all standing committees.
S/he shall serve as representative of this association to other related organizations.
S/he primary responsibility shall be arrangement of programs. . . .
It shall be *her/his* duty as treasurer to keep oficial count of all funds of the association.
In addition, *she/he* shall mail and tabulate election ballots.

Typical of the "pronoun solution" is the alternation of pronouns throughout a text from one paragraph to another or one chapter to another. For
example, in *Developing Second-Language Skills: Theory to Practice* (Chastain,
1976) we find the following:

At the age of three, then, the child appears capable of true speech. However, *he* still
makes many pronounciation errors.
. . . it should be obvious that the two processes are greatly different due to chronological time in the life of the individual and *her* situation . . .
If the teacher spent more time concentrating on what the student is saying rather than
how *he* is saying it, the process would be more rapid.
Speech in a grammatical sense usually occurs around the time the child is one-and-one-

half-years old. By the time *she* is three-and-one-half, *she* already has the elementary syntactical patterns of the language.

For example, a child will not repeat, "Daddy is going to work," until *he* has reached a certain level of linguistic and cognitive maturing.

The child until a certain age will not join the two words into a single phrase, even though *she* may babble much longer sentences.

Occasionally, pronoun choice is very revealing of the author's bias about the nature of the referent. For example, a supermanager may be assumed to be a male (*Family Weekly*, 1976).

One clearly identifiable characteristic of the supermanager is that *he* talks as little as possible, especially in public. This is partly because words waste time, and most *men of true action* are deeply, instinctively conscious of the way in which time, which is also money, runs through the fingers.

However, males don't always fare that well. In other consistent cases, they are burglars, introverts, or liars, according to the New Mexico State University Police Department.

What to do before the burglar comes:

Not if *he* comes, but when *he* comes. Because, say the statistics, *he's* coming. Down your street. And looking for easy targets. *He's* looking for easy targets because *he's* not a professional as a rule. *He's* an amateur. And so *he* must find easy target.

And in an article on extroverts and introverts (*Family Weekly*, 1978):

Psychological surveys conducted at the University of London show that extroverts are more frequently and more actively involved in romantic situations with members of the oppositve sex. It's not that the introvert doesn't like women, but *he's* more cautious in involvements in which affairs of the heart are concerned.

In the above example, it is obvious that "he" is not "generic," since the introvert is specifically defined by reference to the opposite sex, women.

Not unexpectedly, women often get an even more negative association, as illustrated by a question answered on Monty Hall's television show, "Let's Make a Deal" (*Family Weekly*, 1976).

What do you do with all the animals you don't give away on the show?

The owner brings them to the show and takes them back afterward. If anyone wins one via a "zonc," *she* can keep it.

Since many writers are conscious of the "pronoun problem," they often put their heart in the right place but eventually "overcorrect," making singular pronouns into plural ones, as illustrated in a student's term paper.

It is the purpose of this learning experience to use a linguistic approach to bring awareness to my students of *his/her* own language usage.

And in a student newspaper (New Mexico State University Round-Up):

Begay was able to show the Native American students the many possibilities open to *him or her* . . .

At some point, hypercorrection becomes downright ridiculous, especially for educators (NEA-New Mexico Advocate).

Congresswoman Mink, currently serving her sixth term, called on women educators to write letters in support of child care centers and the right for *women* to control *her* own body.

It was observed that at the New Mexico Women of Achievement award program that alternative pronouns are sometimes used in a totally inappropriate context.

We have looked at the credentials in *her or his* field.

It is too often the case in writing that the confusion over which pronoun to select results in the destruction of the intended meaning (Sanchez, 1979).

But, it is right for our kids and we are providing taxpayers more for *his or her* money.

In other cases, the rule seems to be: When in doubt, alternate from one to another. This is exemplified by an article in the *Albuquerque Journal* entitled "Injuries to Head Need Prompt Aid" (Andelman, 1976).

Following a head injury, have the patient lie down and remain completely quiet no matter how *she* feels. Have *him* do this even though he acts all right and insists that you leave *her* alone. Keep the patient flat on *his* back (or face down if *he's* vomiting) if *her* face is gray, blue or pale.

We have found that many writers in fact practice what could be called "gender tokenism," in which they throw in one *he* and an occasional *she* or whatever; women are thereby included in this excerpt from an article in *Family Weekly*, "Keeping the Life of the Party Alive" (1977).

What do you do when the party's over and an intoxicated guest who shouldn't drive insists that *he* will? . . . the last thing you should do is let *him or her* drive . . . the old remedy of pumping your guest full of coffee will only make *him* a wide-awake drunk.

Occasionally, the use of parenthesis serves the same purpose (Nolan, 1976).

Here, Doctor Nolen discusses the personal and emotional after-effects which many *male (and female)* heart-attack victims face.

And which pronoun is appropriate in those cases where sex has been changed through surgery or other alterations? Thomas Szasz created his own solution when he wrote about Richard Raskind who, after marrying and fathering a child, had a sex-change operation and became Renee Richards (*The New Republic*, 1976). His solution was the hypen.

I submit, then the Raskind-Richards is a fake,—that is, male-woman. *He-she* is no more a woman than a bogus Renoir is a Renoir. *He-she* may look like a woman, act like a woman, claim to be a woman, but *he-she* is, in fact, a man who pretends to be a woman.

Generic Nouns

If attempts to make progress for women by changing pronouns have been unsuccessful, what about the attempts to eliminate generic nouns, for example, "man" to mean "human race"? Perhaps, we would suggest, these "generic nouns" never were so generic anyway, because even now a woman is a *chairperson* but a *man* is still a *man*—a *chairman* (*Chronicle of Higher Education*, 1977).

Margarette P. Eby, *Chairperson* of Humanities at U. of Mich. at Dearborn, to Dean of the College of Humanities and Fine Arts and Professor of Music at U. of Northern Iowa.
David W. Hamilton, Assoc. Professor of Anatomy at Harvard, to *Chairman* of Anatomy at U. of Minnesota.
Eileen T. Handelman, *Chairperson* of Science at Sinon's Rock Early College, to Dean of Academic Affairs.
Elaine B. Harvey, Acting *Chairperson* of Graduate Pediatrics at Indiana U. to Dean of the School of Nursing at Fort Hays Kansas State U.
Philip E. Hicks, Professor of Industrial Engineering at New Mexico State U., to *Chairman* of Industrial Engineering at North Carolina A & T State U.

Sometimes, however, a woman gets slightly closer to being a *chairman*.

Dear *Chair (wo)man* Betty Lou Dubois:

Substituting nowadays for "generic" *man*—almost obsolete—is *person*. But who knows exactly what *person* refers to at different points of linguistic disruption? It is now used as a verb (*TESOL/ALSIG Newsletter*, 1977):

The information booth will be *personed* by volunteers from the ALSIG membership.

and as a compound (Today Show, 1977):

Marian McPortland and an *all-person* jazz group.

But even the liberated women of Berkeley agree that there is a limit to neutralizing language, and certain words are just not acceptable. In fact, certain combinations appear quite ridiculous, and the following example from the Los Angeles Times so well points out:

At Thursday night's city council meeting, a routine purchase matter was presented for passage. It called for bids on sewer cleaning equipment, chemicals and new *personhole* covers.
When the item was read, Councilwoman Shirley Dean asked to speak. The cover on a sewer she said, "is not an acceptable desexed word." The councilmen agreed to call them *manholes*.

Conclusion

Numerous examples from everyday English found in speech, meeting reports, textbooks, creative literature, newspapers, announcements, and advertising circulars quickly depict the changes which the great "he/she" battle have brought about. In many cases, the result has been a sort of linguistic disruption, rather humorously ending in the confusion of the message content. Our view is that at this stage the battle has not yet resulted in effecting change in language or in referential associations. The examples cited above, while often humorous, are not meant to make light of the battle for equality. They are simply presented to illustrate the state of linguistic disruption which is a natural by-product of change and one in which we currently find ourselves.

Where is the victory in the great "he/she" battle? This we leave to others. We have only tried to point out briefly here that perhaps as John Kenneth Galbraith (Smith, 1981) has suggested: "It is almost as important to know what is not serious as to know what is."

Notes

1. The underlining of pronouns, generic nouns, and the use of quotes in this essay are used to point out a more conscious awareness of the disruption on the part of the authors.

2. The field of linguistics has developed a variety of analytical tools for studying the process of language change. Diachronic linguistics scientifically sketches out the processes of linguistic change.

3. The notion of "linguistic disruption" was first mentioned and discussed in Dubois and Crouch (1979).

References

Allen, R. (1976). *Language Experiences in Communication*. Boston: Houghton-Mifflin.

Andelman, S. L. (M.D.) February 19, (1976). "Injuries to Head Need Prompt Aid," *Albuquerque Journal*, Section D, p. 1.

Chastain, Kenneth. 1976. *Developing Second Lanugage Skills: Theory to Practice*. 2nd ed. Chicago: Rand McNally College Publishing Company.

Chronicle of Higher Education. July 5 (1977), p. 15.

Constitution of the Western Speech Communication Association, Women's Caucus.

Dona Ana County Teachers Federal Credit Union Newsletter, March 1, (1976).

Dubois, Betty Lou, and Isabel M. Crouch. 1979. "*Man* and Its Compounds in Recent Prefeminist American English Prose." *Papers in Linguistics* 12:1-2, 261-269.

Family Weekly. October 10 (1976), p. 34. (From the *Common Millionaire* by Robert Heller, Delacorte Press.)

—————————. February 15 (1976), p. 26.

Farr, Louise. 1975. "Kathleen Nolan: From Sit Com Star to SAG Prexy," *Ms. Magazine* 5: 9-15.

Frost. Robert. 1945. "A Masque of Reason." In *Complete Poems*. New York: Holt, Reinhart, & Winston, Inc.

Galsworthy, John. 1922. *The Forsyte Saga*. New York: Charles Scribner's Sons.

Guess Who's Coming to Dinner. Brochure of the New Mexico State University Police Department.

"Keeping the Life of the Party Alive," *Family Weekly*, Oct. 9 (1977), p. 34.

"Manhole covers to Stay: Libbers say Enuf's Enuf." *Los Angeles Times*, April 17 (1976).

"More than Shyness Separates Extroverts from Introverts." *Family Weekly*, February 26 (1978), p. 24.

Nabokov, Vladimir. 1981. "I: Maxim Gorki (1868-1936)." *New York Review of Books*, 7:14, 49-52

NEA-New Mexico Adovcate. April (1976)

Nicolson, Nigel, and Joanne Trantmann, eds. 1979. *The Letters of Virginia Woolf*. New York: Harcourt Brace Jovanovich.

Nolan, William A. (M.D.) Aug. 29, (1976). "My Life After Heart Attack," *Family Weekly*, p. 4.

Round-up (New Mexico State University student newspaper). February 11, (1976).

Sanchez, Susan. April 15 (1979). "Special Ed Funding May Change." *Las Cruces Sun News*.

Smith, Jack. December 27 (1981). "Humorists: They're Funny That Way." *Los Angeles Times*.

Szasz, Thomas. 1975. "Male Women, Female Men." *The New Republic*, 15:8-9.

TESOL/ALSIG Newsletter. March (1977).

Whitman, Walt. 1942. "Vocalism." *Collected Poems of Walt Whitman*, edited by E. Holloway. Garden City: Blue Ribbon Books.

Guidelines Against Sexist Language: A Case History

Alleen Pace Nilsen

In the chapter which follows, Nilsen examines the role of style guidelines and editorial boards in eliminating sexist language in scholarly and professional publications. The author draws on her experience as a committee member formulating nonsexist guidelines for the National Council of Teachers of English (NCTE) —a powerful organization of eighty thousand members. In her experience as editor of the *English Journal*, she describes some of the problems encountered in implementing sexfair language in educational publications.

The "Guidelines for Nonsexist Use of Language in NCTE Publications," published by the National Council of Teachers of English, can be considered a representative example of many such guidelines developed and adopted during the 1970s by educational publishers such as Macmillan; McGraw-Hill; Scott, Foresman; and Holt, Rinehart and Winston. They also resemble the guidelines against sexist language adopted by other professional organizations, including the American Psychological Association. However, the NCTE guidelines are of special interest for the following three reasons:

1. the large number of people involved (NCTE has over eighty thousand members);
2. the members' expertise and special interest in matters related to language; and
3. the potential for effecting widespread change, since NCTE members are English teachers in either elementary schools, high schools, or colleges.

Although the guidelines were ostensibly prepared to help authors and editors of council publications (semiannual or bimonthly journals and several books each year) to avoid using sexist language, the underlying assumption was that as English teachers became aware and learned to use "sex-fair" language, they would naturally pass their attitudes and knowledge on to their students, as shown by the concluding sentences of the guidelines:

Whether the members work as teachers, authors, or editors, they not only help shape students' language patterns but are also viewed by the public as custodians of what is "correct" in the language. The very newness of these changes in our language offers English teachers a unique opportunity. Under their guidance, eliminating sexism can bring a new vitality to the English language.

In general, English teachers have the justly deserved reputation of being conservative when it comes to matters of usage. So it is to be expected that they would not be among the first to jump on the bandwagon for changing the English language. McGraw-Hill and Scott, Foresman published their guidelines against sexist language in 1972. The NCTE Guidelines did not come out until four years later. During those four years, articles—mostly critical or sarcastically humorous[1]—began appearing regularly in popular magazines and newspapers. The profession faced a quandary. Grammar and usage had suddenly become of interest to the popular culture. In a startling change from the days when the confession of being an English teacher served as a STOP sign to light, social conversation, English teachers began to be sought out at cocktail parties to either settle disputes or add fuel to the fire as people argued about the feminist movement and its relation to language. Pressure came from two sides. One philosophy was that if there is any group who is going to get together and agree on a concerted plan of action, it should be the English teachers. But from the other side came the opinion that if there is any group who ought to know better than to try to impose patterns of usage on people, it should be the English teachers.

By the mid-1970s, the issue could no longer be ignored. The Committee on the Role and Image of Women in the Council and the Profession (the name was later shortened to the Women's Committee) which had been established in 1971, pushed for action from the Council as a whole. At the 1974 annual convention, this committee brought a resolution to the floor (which was passed) calling for the preparation of guidelines for nonsexist language in NCTE publications. Some sixty participants in a two-day preconvention workshop on the subject of sexism and language contributed ideas to a preliminary version of "Guidelines for Combating Sexism in Language." I was on this original committee and remember being relegated to the bathroom with my portable typewriter because I was still working when everyone else wanted to go to sleep.

Looking back on what we came up with, I am surprised at how timid we were. We presented our observations in the form of questions, the kind of language that Robin Lakoff would later describe as being typical of out-of-power women.[2] These questions were printed and distributed to the members as "A Preliminary Version" of "Guidelines for Combatting Sexism in Language."

Do you expect or promote a different kind of written and oral expression from boys than from girls?

Do you refer to teachers as *she* while principals, professors, and department heads are *he*? Are doctors and lawyers automatically *he*, while nurses and secretaries are always *she*?

Do you personify bad practices in English teaching as always female (i.e., *Miss Fidditch* or *Mrs. Grundy*)?

In literary criticism do you use the word *masculine* as a positive term, as in "masculine (or perfect, strong) rhyme," and *feminine* as a negative term, as in "feminine (or incomplete, weak) rhyme"?

Do you support the men of letters stereotype by going along with publishers who hide the fact that their author is a woman by using either masculine sounding pen names or initials?

Do you give the impression that female writers are somehow apart from the mainstream by singling them out with the titles *poetess* and *authoress*?

Do you mentally exclude women from the business world and teach your students to do the same by heading letters to unknown people with either *Gentleman*: or *Dear Sirs*:—even though chances are good that the letters will be opened and read by women?

Where practical, do you promote the use of unambiguous terms such as *people* rather than man?

Do you understand and teach your students about the imperfect correlation in modern English between grammatical gender and the sex of the referent? Children need to be taught this peculiarity of the language both formally and informally. For example, in your school do you make sure that illustrations are equally representative of males and females when generic terms such as *man*, or one of its alternatives, are used in books and films or on bulletin boards?

If you can answer no to the first seven questions and yes to the last two, you are helping combat sexism in language.

The mildness of these questions may have influenced the Board of Directors, a governing body made up of three hundred leaders in NCTE, which in 1975 adopted a formal policy statement reading in part: "The National Council of Teachers of English should encourage the use of nonsexist language, particularly through its publications and periodicals." This policy statement was taken to mean the approval of guidelines; however, the guidelines themselves were not voted on. The reason given was that according to the NCTE constitution, if they had been voted on by the Board of Directors, then any subsequent change would also have to be voted on by this large, unwieldy body which meets only at the annual conventions.

I was not involved in the behind-the-scenes governance decisions, but I suspect that someone was happy to find this reason for not putting the actual guidelines up for voting. It is always easier to get large numbers of people to agree in principle to a worthy-sounding goal than to get them to agree to make specific—what many consider nit-picking and others consider blasphemous—changes in their own behavior. The policy was adopted in November, and in March the guidelines were published in each of the council journals. A note of explanation from Robert F. Hogan, the NCTE Executive Secretary, credited their writing to the Women's Committee, the editors of council journals, and professional staff members at NCTE headquarters. It was actually the latter group which was responsible for the content and the wording, although they acknowledged heavy reliance on previously published guidelines.

Apparently many members found the guidelines to be more extensive and specific than they had expected. Controversy raged. In the December 1976 issue of *English Journal*, Lance Alter, a high school teacher from Russiaville, Indiana, argued that

at best the guidelines . . . are mischievous and unnecessary. At worst, they introduce ideology and partisian activism into the language arts. The authors of the Guidelines are creating problems which only exist in the minds of certain ideologues. They emphasize social policy rather than standards of quality in language and literature. . . .

Although the guidelines have been just as vigorously defended and have brought significant editorial changes to the NCTE publications, criticism similar to Alter's continues. See, for example, Robert L. Spaeth's "The Nonsexist Assault on Language or A Memorandum to the National Council of Teachers of English" in *Change* July/August, 1981. Spaeth is Dean of the College of Arts and Sciences of St. John's University in Collegeville, Minnesota, and was offended when someone put a copy of the guidelines in his mailbox with a suggestion that he urge the contents on faculty members. He bemoaned the power of some radical fringe that was able

to convince as large and responsible an organization as the National Council of Teachers of English to advocate changes in English usage that would do considerable violence to the language.

Both the spirit and the substance of the NCTE guidelines are objectionable. Altogether the guidelines treat the language like an innocent puppy waiting to be neutered for the convenience of his human masters. . . .

Ordinary speakers and writers of English automatically turn to English teachers for professional assistance in understanding and protecting the language. One naturally wonders how the unnamed English teachers who wrote these guidelines could have such an advanced social conscience and yet fail to defend the very language they profess to love.

Within NCTE, the controversy took a legalistic turn. Leading the opposition to the guidelines was former NCTE president, Harold Allen, a respected linguist and professor emeritus from the University of Minnesota. Professor Allen had a friend who submitted an article to an NCTE publication. The editor, in keeping with the guidelines' suggestion against the use of masculine pronouns to refer to people of both sexes changed pronoun usage throughout the article. The author refused to have the article published in its altered form. Professor Allen brought the matter up at the 1978 annual meeting, making an impassioned plea against the kind of "censorship" which his friend had suffered.

The eventual result was that at the 1979 meeting a compromise amendment was passed.

Council Publications

Manuscripts which are judged by the Council editor to contain sexist language but are otherwise acceptable for publication should be handled either of these ways: a) returned to the author with a copy of these "Guidelines" and a letter of explanation, encouraging the author to rewrite the article so that the language is nonsexist; or b) returned to the author with specific suggestions from the editor for eliminating sexist language, citing these "Guidelines".

If the author refuses to make these changes, the manuscript shall be published, but shall include a note that the sexist language appears at the author's express stipulation.

In the four years since these two paragraphs were added to the guidelines, what some people would judge to be sexist language has undoubtedly appeared in NCTE publications. But as far as I know, it has not been acknowledged with editorial footnotes. I would judge that in most cases when it has appeared, it was the result of an editorial lapse rather than of someone's desire to make a statement. The main publications of the Council are its monthly journals. Approximately fourteen thousand college teachers receive *College English*, forty-five thousand high school teachers and English educators at the college level receive *English Journal*, while twenty thousand elementary teach-

ers and educators at the college level receive *Language Arts*. Specialized journals include *Research in the Teaching of English, English Education*, and *College
Composition and Communication*. The Council also publishes several original
books, three convention programs, a catalogue, and miscellaneous
newsletters and brochures each year.

I am now in my third year as co-editor (with Ken Donelson) of the *English
Journal* and so can describe how the guidelines influence the editing of this
particular Council journal; but since all the other editors operate at their own
college campuses with a fair degree of independence, there is no guarantee
that their attitudes and procedures are the same as ours.

When Professor Donelson and I applied for the job of EJ co-editors, we
promised to make the journal a model of *inconspicuous sex-fair language*. We
used the term *sex-fair* rather than *nonsexist* because we thought it more accu-
rately described our goal of using language forms and patterns to give equivalent or fair treatment to both sexes. Contrary to the opinion of those critics
who complain that feminists are out to "neuter" the language, we did not
intend to remove all references to sex or gender, but only to make them
accurate.

We had both practical (or political) and philosophical reasons for using
inconspicuous as a modifier. From the practical standpoint, *English Journal*
does not have a captive audience. Unlike the case with some trade unions or
with highly technical, specialized fields where practitioners must keep up with
the latest research, there is little pressure on teachers to pay their annual dues
of thirty dollars, for which their main benefit is receiving the Journal. Since
the whole issue of sexism and language guidelines is so controversial, we do
not want to highlight language problems that will make readers on either side
of the issue feel uncomfortable and, therefore, less likely to subscribe to the
Journal.

From the philosophical standpoint, the purpose of most guidelines on
sexism and language is to downplay the matter of sex—to make it so that
people will be able to fill roles in society based on something other than what
sex they happen to be. But when readers are met with dual pronouns such as
he/she or *himself/herself*, with artificially created pronouns such as *tey* or *him-
mer*, or even with standard but unexpected pronouns, then the focus of the
sentence—regardless of the subject—is pointed toward the matter of sex.
Some writers choose to do this as a consciousness-raising technique, but the
practical necessity of having our journal appeal to as many readers as possible
precludes this as an option for us.

English Journal falls somewhere between a popular or trade magazine and a
scholarly journal. Because we feel that we must woo our readers with sharp,
crisp prose, we wield heavy editorial pencils. We edit first for wordiness and
lack of clarity, and then for the kind of puffed-up jargon some educators use

when trying to impress colleagues. Then we look for grammatical errors and sexist language. On both our style sheet and the consent-to-publish form which contributors sign, a warning is given that the editors reserve the right to edit all manuscripts. Authors do not see their edited manuscripts, nor do they read proofs.

What we have done to accommodate the 1979 amendment saying that authors may use sexist language if they prefer, is to make the following note on our style sheet under the heading "Sex-fair Language":

EJ will follow the "NCTE Guidelines for Nonsexist Use of Language." Any author objecting to these guidelines should make that clear at the time the article is submitted.

For any authors who so inform us—none have, as of yet—we will treat the manuscript as suggested in the 1979 amendment, corresponding back and forth until some sort of agreement is reached. But in the absence of such a note, we edit for sexist language in the same manner that we edit for everything else. It is physically impossible for us to correspond concerning each editorial change we make. The idealized picture of careful scholarship and consultation that the committee who drew up the amendment envisioned bears little resemblance to the hectic pace of life in the EJ editorial office. NCTE provides us with a twenty-hour-per-week secretary, most of whose time is taken up handling the clerical details relating to the fifteen hundred manuscripts we receive each year and typing the edited version of the two hundred we have space to print. Arizona State University releases both Professor Donelson and myself from teaching one class per semester, the equivalent of ten hours of work per week. Of course, editing a monthly journal the size of EJ (it varies between 96 and 128 pages per issue) takes more time than this, and so we place a premium on efficiency.

As a specific illustration of how our editing is influenced by the guidelines, I have gone back to the original manuscripts that we edited for the November 1982 *English Journal* and have compared them to the galleys to see just where we made changes related to sexism. Taking all examples from a single issue will probably result in a fairly objective description, whereas if I allow myself to cite examples from our whole two-and-a-half years of editing, I might present only those extreme examples of sexism which stick in my mind months or even years after we struggled with them. I chose the November issue simply because we are currently reading page proofs on it. However, the editing was completed two months ago, so it was not influenced by the knowledge that this issue would later be used as part of a case history.

Editorial changes were made on all twenty-four articles, but on only ten of them were changes made related to sexism. We also edited fifteen shorter pieces (three hundred-word statements) for the Our Readers Write section, resembling a Letters-to-the-Editor page. On four out of these fifteen, changes were made because of sexist language. On another six articles, we considered making changes, but did not. Statistically then, we changed slightly over one-third of the articles we used, and we worked with the matter of sexist language on one-half of them.

Among those that we worked with but did not change was one in which the author used what might be considered stereotyped sample sentences. While we do not hesitate to delete material from articles, we are cautious about stepping into an author's shoes and writing new material. Therefore, since the sentences were not blatantly sexist, we left them as they were. In another article, an author used a boy as her sample student. All the way through she used masculine pronouns. Since it was unclear whether she taught girls as well as boys and was actually referring to both, we left it as she wrote it and hoped that we would soon have an article using a girl as the sample student. A third article that some people would interpret as promoting sexism was about a class writing an old-fashioned love ballad. It relied on dozens of traditional stereotypes about male/female relationships, but without those there would have been no ballad and hence no article.

A difficult boundary for us to decide on is that between sexist language and sexist content. We are authorized to change the former but not the latter; of course, when articles are submitted we are free to reject them for whatever academically honest reason we see fit, including sexism. But when we first evaluate manuscripts, there are so many things we look for that it is easy not to notice occasional paragraphs that express sexist attitudes. This means that when it comes time to edit, we are sometimes faced with a dilemma. Part of the problem is that not everyone—including *English Journal's* two editors—agrees on what is sexist. Guidelines help, but they can't possibly foresee every problem, and so we are left to decide on a case-by-case basis. The three examples below show the continuum of our responses.

At one end, we do nothing because it is clear that the statement is an honest reflection of the author's beliefs—not simply an oversight caused by the vagaries of the English language. For example, we were concerned that in an article about a first year teacher's experience with twenty-seven remedial English students (twenty-five of them boys), she used only masculine pronouns; but then came a paragraph explaining her reasoning.

My first few days with "the boys," as I secretly called them, were horrifying and a direct threat to my physical and emotional welfare. . . . I failed to describe either of the two girls in the class largely because they both tried very hard to be recognized as anything *but* girls. I spent many free periods telling L. R. that she was pretty and had a feminine voice when she wasn't hurling obscenities down the hall. This September L. R.

appeared at my classroom on the first day of school. Her blonde, curly hair was styled into a bouncy Afro. Her nails were polished and she had curtailed her profanity. We talked more calmly than ever before. Finally I said, "Laura, you've changed—what happened to you?" The grin on her face betrayed her attempts to be smug. She seemed to be relishing my recognition of her transformation. . . ."

I may personally disapprove of this teacher's attitude and the differences that she expected from her male and female students, but the magazine is to represent a variety of viewpoints, not just the editor's. We therefore left this paragraph and her use of masculine pronouns untouched.

At an interim level, we can soften or tone down a statement in order not to help to solidify the tendency teachers have to jump ahead of their students and preselect "books for boys" and "books for girls."

ORIGINAL VERSION	EDITED VERSION
Of course many of the girls in an average classroom probably won't be too interested in a western, but there are all sorts of books that might be equally attractive.	Perhaps girls in an average classroom might not be interested in a western, but there are all sorts of books that might be equally attractive.

The most extreme thing we can do is to delete the offending paragraph; that is, if the piece will hold together without it. This is what we did in an article on creative teaching where the paragraph below was put in as a kind of side note explaining that there will always be poor teaching going on. The sexist part of the statement is the personification of the bad English teacher as *Miss Fidditch*.

Of course, this isn't exactly the way things happened, history being, inevitably, one person's attempt to figure out what was going on. Those who embraced Moffett style student-centeredness were never more than a feisty minority, perhaps, and —right in the room next to mine—Miss Fidditch was holding forth on the difference between direct and indirect objects, just as she had done in 1955 and will continue to do in 1985. There'll always be a Miss Fidditch teaching English in my school, and in yours too.

A year before, we had been faced with a similar problem when an article had a whole page about Miss Fidditch. The discussion was crucial to its main point concerning English teachers' public image. We solved the problem then by changing *Miss Fidditch* to *Old Fidditch*, but we hardly felt proud of ourselves for substituting ageism for sexism. The stereotype of the ineffective and overly fussy woman English teacher runs deep within our profession. Before we were editors, one clever author managed to get around the guidelines and still communicate the stereotype by referring to "a kind of elitist, 'Vassar-trained,' carefully speaking person."

Most of the writers whose articles we edit fall into one of the following three categories:

1. Writers who are aware and skilled but uncommitted (or hostile) to the idea of sex-fair language.
2. Writers who are simply unaware of the issue.
3. Writers who are aware of the issue and apparently committed to the idea of sex-fair language but lack writing skills needed to handle the matter smoothly.

The smallest group, but the hardest to deal with, are those skilled writers in category 1. They play games with editors and pride themselves on creating sexist metaphors and symbols. They are like the headline writer for a New York tabloid who set out to prove that the matter of sexist attitudes could not be solved by anything so simple as naming hurricanes after men as well as women. In the summer of 1979, this person was responsible for the headline "David Rapes Virgin Islands." Another response by this kind of person is to use an overabundance of dual pronouns, as many as five or six pairs in a single paragraph, as if to say, "I'll use dual pronouns if you say so, but just look how dumb they sound!"

On the surface, an article from this kind of person may appear very much like one from a writer in the largest group, those who are simply unaware of the issue. More than half of our problem authors fall into this category. They begin the letters that accompany their manuscripts "Dear Sir:"; and whenever they refer to an unknown person, they use a masculine pronoun—as in the following example.

ORIGINAL VERSION	EDITED VERSION
The Mexican American child is encouraged to be responsible and independent, aggressive and assertive as long as he is achieving for the family or his community and/or protecting it. The Mexican-American child is encouraged to always view himself as an integral part of the family or community.	Mexican-American children are encouraged to be responsible and independent, aggressive and assertive as long as they achieve for the family or their community. Mexican-American children are encouraged to always view themselves as integral parts of the family or community.

We do not automatically change masculine pronouns to inclusive pronouns. First, we try to make sure that the author really was referring to both females and males. For example, we left all the masculine pronouns in an article written by a teacher at a boys' school, but we changed them in the two following examples. The first was from an author named *Lois* writing about her vision of an ideal English department. The second was from the academic supervisor of a large public school district writing about teachers making sacrifices.

ORIGINAL VERSION	EDITED VERSION
Perhaps it will be that we regard each other as individuals. Everyone will plan his own lessons, select his own text, teach his own course.	Perhaps we will regard each other as individuals, each planning our own lessons, selecting our own texts, and teaching our own courses.
Sacrifice, however, is made more willingly when those asked to make it are asked by one who has demonstrated it himself. If the person in the leadership position has exemplified sacrifice with the departmental welfare in mind, then when that leader asks for the same from his colleagues, it will be easier for them to believe the sincerity of the request and accept the rationale.	Sacrifice, however, is made more willingly when the person in the leadership position has exemplified sacrifice with the departmental welfare in mind. When that leader asks for the same from colleagues, it will be easier for them to believe the sincerity of the request and accept the rationale behind it.

It was especially interesting that the writer of this last piece (it was a three hundred-word-long letter to the editor) used masculine pronouns in the three paragraphs describing the leader's role, but in the final paragraph describing the teacher's part, he switched to dual pronouns.

ORIGINAL VERSION	EDITED VERSION
When one member eschews personal gain to help his/her colleagues, he/she fosters a spirit of cooperation and respect foreign to an autocratic organization.	When one member eschews personal gain to help colleagues, a spirit of cooperation and respect foreign to an autocratic organization is fostered.

Another problem that these writers have is the unwitting use of terms that are offensive to more aware readers, as in this article about a class studying *Hamlet*.

ORIGINAL VERSION	**EDITED VERSION**
Most of us agreed that a Women's Libber would sneer at Ophelia, yet many girls in class admitted thoughts of suicide on breaking up with their boyfriends.	Most of us agreed that a feminist might sneer at Ophelia, yet many girls in class admitted thoughts of suicide on breaking up with their boyfriends.

Editors less middle-of-the-road than we are might have deleted this sentence entirely or changed *girls* to *women*, since many feminists are uncomfortable with the term *girls*. If the females we wrote about had been college rather than high school age, then we would have been inclined to take this suggestion seriously; but as it is, we used whichever term the original author chose as most appropriate. Another reason that this sentence might offend people is the statement that girls in class admitted thoughts of suicide on breaking up with their boyfriends. Did the teacher think to ask boys about their feelings when breaking up? Or if the teacher did, would the boys have been as free to admit their distress as were the girls?

This is another example of the difficulty in distinguishing between sexist language and sexist content. I think this is sexist content and really not our business to edit out; but I will confess that had this article been one paragraph too long to fit on the page when we were doing layout, this is the paragraph I would have been tempted to delete.

We make almost as many changes in the writings of people who are aware of the issue but are unskilled in techniques for handling it as we do in articles by those who are oblivious to the whole matter. The newly aware writers try too hard and fill their articles with dual pronouns, many of which are unnecessary, as shown in the examples below:

ORIGINAL VERSION	**EDITED VERSION**
Every student recalled writing in his/her English class.	Every student recalled writing in English class.
Not one student called himself/herself a poor writer.	No students called themselves poor writers.
In checking for any relationship between the student as a writer and his/her parents' education . . .	In checking for relationships between the students' writing ability and their parents' education . . .

Another problem that this category of writer has is that of inconsistency. Like the public school academic supervisor cited above, these writers switch back and forth between dual pronouns. The switching seldom appears to be random. There is usually some telltale evidence that reveals the author's thought process, as in the above example where the teachers were *he/she* but the leader was *he*; or in the book description below, which reveals people's tendency to think of their family roots as predominantly male.

ORIGINAL VERSION	EDITED VERSION
An epic novel which traces the Sandoval family from the first Sandoval who came into the United States to make a better life for himself to the grandchildren who end up in the barrio of East Los Angeles.	An epic novel traces the Sandoval family from the first member who enters the United States to make a better life to the grandchildren who end up in the barrio of East Los Angeles.

Sometimes dual pronouns are necessary to get the thought across, and so we try to reserve their use for those cases—as in this question suggested for teachers to ask students studying "Hamlet":

Suppose this new parent, like Claudius, had your father or mother killed just to take his or her place? Then what?

The teacher was trying to connect Hamlet's family situation with that of any student in the class who belonged to a reconstituted family. He wanted to emphasize that it could be either parent—not just the father, as in Hamlet—who was replaced, and so his use of the dual pronoun was crucial to communicate the thought.

A minor problem that we had in this issue was deciding how to write a biographical note at the end of an article. We originally wrote "Adrian B. Sanford is a retired teacher from Carlmont High School, Belmont, California. She is currently a free-lance writer." But then it occurred to us that Sanford might be a man, so we changed the note to read ". . . is a retired teacher and a free-lance writer."

Another problem representative of what happens whenever we deal with historical pieces was our Too Good to Miss feature, which is an extended review of a book we want to bring to teachers' attention. The book this month happened to be Rollo Brown's *How the French Boy Learns to Write*, originally published in 1915, when indeed the students that people were concerned about were boys. We never change direct quotes, although occasionally we have paraphrased historical quotes that have stood out in contrast to the pronoun pattern used in the rest of an article. Throughout this particular book review, we were pleased that the author talked mostly about *pupils* and *students* rather than *boys*, but whether or not she did this consciously we have no way of knowing.

We have no comparison data, but I'm under the impression that more of our writers are aware of the issue and are more skilled in dealing with it than they were two-and-a-half years ago when we started receiving manuscripts. However, it is hard to know the extent to which authors have struggled to use sex-fair language, because the more successful they are the less it shows.

We get frequent references to department *chairpersons*. We prefer a less obvious term, such as *deparment head* or *department chair*, but we hesitate to assign people titles they may not feel comfortable with. This problem came up once in the November issue, and we solved it through deletion.

ORIGINAL VERSION	**EDITED VERSION**
Our first gathering is in the fall. After receiving a humorous invitation from our department chairperson, new teachers are not quite sure what to expect.	Our first gathering is in the fall. After receiving a humorous invitation, new teachers are not quite sure what to expect.

One of the ways we know that our authors are becoming more aware is that they sometimes do their own editing on the manuscript. Perhaps when they turn to the masthead in the Journal to get the address and final directions for submitting articles, they notice the statement that NCTE has adopted guidelines for nonsexist use of language and so go back and re-read their manuscripts with this in mind. Or perhaps a friend proofreads and edits for them. On one of the manuscripts for the November issue, the typed copy read, ". . . that in this teaching there was often a contradiction between what the teacher supposed it was doing and what it was *actually* doing." In red ink, both uses of *it was* were crossed out and replaced with *he/she was*. Then these too were crossed out and replaced with *they were*. It's hard to know whether the revision was originally inspired by the problem of sexism or simply by the unclearness of the reference, but it's obvious that whoever did the revising considered the matter of accurate gender reference.

The one article that was the best example of increased skill on the part of our writers was "Food for Thought—and Writing." In it, Marc Glasser suggested creative ways to get students to write about eating; for example, by developing the thesis that smorgasbords reveal eaters' personalities. In writing about *The Mincer*, *the Monster*, and *the Masher*, he carefully avoided using pronouns. And when it came to describing a very picky eater, the kind who storms out of a restaurant, he labeled the paragraph *Persnickety Pete or Pam* and took turns ascribing obnoxious actions to each one. The one place that he relaxed his scrupulous fairness was in a paragraph about the condemned prisoner's last meal, where he suggested that students "describe through comparison and contrast, the way parts of the convict's last meal force him to recall happier moments from his past and the contrast created in his mood by his present surroundings."

We left the manuscript as it was, but smiled to ourselves about how unlikely it was that anyone would notice and think it sexist. After all, the guidelines state only that "When we constantly personify *the judge, the critic, the executive, the author,* etc., as male by using the pronoun *he,* we are subtly conditioning ourselves against the idea of a female judge, critic, executive, or author." They do not mention *convict, hoodlum, gangster,* or *felon.*

In conclusion, these are some of the things I've learned from working with the NCTE Guidelines:

1. Guidelines dealing with sexism in language are different from other parts of a publication's style manual, because the reactions of both readers and writers are influenced by emotional and political overtones quite apart from standard considerations of grammar, usage, and style.

2. For editorial purposes, it is extremely hard to decide what is sexist content and what is sexist language, and in a "sponsored" publication such as *English Journal* just how much obligation or authority the editor has in dealing with each.

3. The creators of guidelines are not so wise as to foresee every possible problem. Therefore editors bear a heavy responsibility both in recognizing and in dealing with facets of sexism.

4. So much is left to the discretion of the editor that the mere adoption of guidelines will not guarantee that a publication is written in sex-fair language. An editor who does not feel a genuine commitment to linguistic sex-fairness is not likely to add the considerable task of editing for sexism to the already long list of responsibilities traditionally held by editors.

5. Using sex-fair language requires skill as well as commitment. Since the writers for *English Journal* are English teachers, one would assume that their writing skills are higher than average; yet when trying to be nonsexist, many of them create extremely awkward sentences in which the readers' attention is drawn to matters of grammar rather than to the

thought being communicated. There is need for research and development of training materials to teach committed people how to be successful in using sex-fair langauge.

Notes

1. See for example, "Sispeak: A Msguided Attempt to Change Herstory," by Stefan Kanfer. TIME Magazine, October 23, 1972.

2. See Lakoff's discussion of why women make statements in the form of questions in *Language and Woman's Place* (Harper & Row, 1975), pages 14-19.

References

Guidelines for Nonsexist Use of Language in National Council of Teachers of English (NCTE) Publications (Revised 1985).

Kanfer, Stefan. October 23, 1972. "Sispeak: A Msguided Attempt to Change Herstory," *Time Magazine*.

Lakoff, Robin. 1975. *Language and Woman's Place*. New York: Harper & Row.

Appendix

Guidelines for Nonsexist Use of Language in NCTE Publications (Revised, 1985)

Introduction

During the 1971 Annual Convention of the National Council of Teachers of English in Las Vegas, Nevada, the Executive Committee and the Board of Directors approved the formation of an NCTE Committee on the Role and Image of Women in the Council and the Profession. As the result of a resolution passed by the members of NCTE at the 1974 Annual Convention, one of the committee's responsibilites was to assist in setting guidelines for nonsexist* use of language in NCTE publications.

Suggestions were elicited from editors of Council journals and from professional staff members at NCTE, as well as from members of the Women's Committee. Copies of the guidelines also went to all members of the Board of Directors. At the 1975 Annual Convention, the Board of Directors adopted a formal policy statement that read in part: "The National Council of Teachers of English should encourage the use of nonsexist language, particularly through its publications and periodicals."

Ten years have passed since these guidelines were created, and although language usage has begun to change, the importance of the guidelines has not diminished. Because language plays a central role in the way human beings think and behave, we still need to promote language that opens rather than closes possibilities for women and men. Whether teaching in the classroom, assigning texts, determining curriculum, serving on national committees, or writing in professional publications, NCTE members directly and indirectly influence thought and behavior.

As an educational publisher, NCTE is not alone in its concern for fair treatment of men and women. The role of education is to make choices available, not to limit opportunities. Censorship removes possibilities; these guidelines extend what is available by offering alternatives to traditional usages and to editorial choices that restrict meaning.

---

*Although *nonsexist* is the word traditionally used to describe such language, other terms have come into common use, namely, *gender-neutral, sex-fair, gender-free.*

Language

This section deals primarily with word choice. Many of the examples are matters of vocabulary; a few are matters of grammatical choice. The vocabulary items are relatively easy to deal with, since the English lexicon has a history of rapid change. Grammar is a more difficult area, and we have chosen to use alternatives that already exist in the language rather than to invent new constructions. In both cases, recommended alternatives have been determined by what is graceful and unobtrusive. The purpose of these changes is to suggest alternative styles.

Generic "Man"

1. Since the word man has come to refer almost exclusively to adult males, it is sometimes difficult to recognize its generic meaning.

Problems	*Alternatives*
mankind	humanity, human beings, people*
man's achievements	human achievements
the best man for the job	the best person for the job
the common man	the average person, ordinary people
cavemen	cave dwellers, prehistoric people

2. Sometimes the combining form *-woman* is used alongside *-man* in occupational terms and job titles, but we prefer using the same titles for men and women when naming jobs that could be held by both. Note, too, that using the same forms for men and women is a way to avoid using the combining form *-person* as a substitute for *-woman* only.

Problems	Alternatives
chairman/chairwoman	chair, coordinator (of a committee or department), moderator (of a meeting), presiding officer, head, chairperson
businessman/businesswoman	business executive, manager
congressman/congresswoman	congressional representative
policeman/policewoman	police officer

---

*A one-word substitution for *mankind* isn't always possible, especially in set phrases like *the story of mankind*. Sometimes recasting the sentence altogether may be the best solution.

Problems	*Alternatives*
๏ salesman/saleswoman	sales clerk, sales representative, salesperson
๏ fireman	fire fighter
mailman	letter carrier

Generic "He" and "His"

Because there is no one pronoun in English that can be effectively substituted for *he* or *his*, we offer several alternatives. The form *he* or *she* has been the NCTE house style over the last ten years, on the premise that it is less distracting then *she* or *he* or *he/she*. There are other choices, however. The one you make will depend on what you are writing

1. Sometimes it is possible to drop the possessive form *his* altogether or to substitute an article.

Problems	*Alternatives*
The average student is worried about his grades.	The average student is worried about grades.
When the student hands in his paper, read it immediately.	When the student hands in the paper, read it immediately.

2. Often, it makes sense to use the plural instead of the singular.

Problems	*Alternatives*
Give the student his grade right away.	Give the students their grades right away.
Ask the student to hand in his work as soon as he is finished.	Ask students to hand in their work as soon as they are finished.

3. The first or second person can sometimes be substituted for the third person.

Problems	*Alternatives*
As a teacher, he is faced daily with the problem of paperwork.	As teachers, we are faced daily with the problems of paperwork.
When a teacher asks his students for an evaluation, he is putting himself on the spot.	When you ask your students for an evaluation, you are putting yourself on the spot.

4. In some situations, the pronoun *one (one's)* can be substituted for *he (his)*, but it should be used sparingly. Notice that the use of *one*—like the use of *we or you*—changes the tone of what you are writing.

Problems	Alternatives
He might well wonder what his response should be.	One might well wonder what one's response should be.

5. A sentence with *he or his* can sometimes be recast in the passive voice or another impersonal construction.

Problems	Alternatives
Each student should hand in his paper promptly.	Papers should be handed in promptly.
He found such an idea intolerable.	Such an idea was intolerable.

6. When the subject is an indefinite pronoun, the plural form *their* can occasionally be used with it, especially when the referent for the pronoun is clearly understood to be plural.

Problems	Alternatives
When everyone contributes his own ideas, the discussion will be a success.	When everyone contributes their own ideas, the discussion will be a success.
When everyone contributes his own ideas, the discussion will be a success.	When all the students contribute their own ideas, the discussion will be a success.

But since this usage is transitional, it is usually better to recast the sentence and avoid the indefinite pronoun.

7. Finally, sparing use can be made of *he or she* and *his or her*. It is best to restrict this choice to contexts in which the pronouns are not repeated.

Problems	Alternatives
Each student will do better if he has a voice in the decision.	Each student will do better if he or she has a voice in the decision.
Each student can select his own topic.	Each student can select his or her own topic.

Sex-Role Stereotyping

Word choices sometimes reflect unfortunate and unconscious assumptions about sex roles—for example, that farmers are always men and elementary school teachers are always women; that men are valued for their accomplishments and women for their physical attributes; or that men are strong and brave while women are weak and timid. We need to examine the assumptions inherent in certain stock phrases and choose nonstereotyped alternatives.

1. Identify men and women in the same way. Diminutive or special forms to name women are usually unnecessary. In most cases, generic terms such as *doctor* or *actor* should be assumed to include both men and women. Only occasionally are alternate forms needed, and in these cases, the alternate form replaces both the masculine and the feminine titles.

Problems	*Alternatives*
stewardess	flight attendant (for both *steward* and *stewardess*)
authoress	author
waitress	server, food server
poetess	poet
coed	student
lady lawyer	lawyer . . . she
male nurse	nurse . . . he

2. Do not represent women as occupying only certain jobs or roles and men as occupying only certain others.

Problems	*Alternatives*
the kindergarten teacher . . . she	*occasionally use* the kindergarten teacher . . . he
the principal . . .	*occasionally use* the principal . . . she *or* principals . . . they
Have your mother send a snack for the party.	Have a parent send a snack for the party. *occasionally use* Have your father . . . or Have your parents . . .
NCTE conventiongoers and their wives are invited.	NCTE conventiongoers and their spouses are invited.
Writers become so involved in their work that they neglect their wives and children.	Writers become so involved in their work that they neglect their families.

3. Treat men and women in a parallel manner.

Problems	Alternatives
The class interviewed Chief Justice Burger and Mrs. O'Connor.	The class interviewed Warren Burger and Sandra O'Connor. or . . . Mr. Burger and Ms. O'Connor. or . . . Chief Justice Burger and Justice O'Connor.
The reading list included Proust, Joyce, Gide, and Virginia Woolf.	The reading list included Proust, Joyce, Gide, and Woolf. or . . . Marcel Proust, James Joyce, André Gide, and Virginia Woolf.
Both Bill Smith, a straight-A sophomore, and Kathy Ryan a pert junior, won writing awards.	Both sophomore Bill Smith, a straight-A student, and junior Kathy Ryan, editor of the school paper, won writing awards.

4. Seek alternatives to language that patronizes or trivializes women, as well as to language that reinforces stereotyped images of both women and men.

Problems	Alternatives
The president of the company hired a gal Friday.	The president of the company hired an assistant.
I'll have my girl do it.	I'll ask my secretary to do it.
Stella is a career woman.	Stella is a professional. or Stella is a doctor (architect, etc.)
The ladies on the committee all supported the bill	The women on the committee all supported the bill.
Pam had lunch with the girls from the office.	Pam had lunch with the women from the office.
This is a man-sized job.	This is a big (huge, enormous) job.
That's just an old wives' tale.	That's just a superstitition (superstitious story).
Don't be such an old lady.	Don't be so fussy

Sexist Language in a Direct Quotation

Quotations cannot be altered, but there are other ways of dealing with this problem.

1. Avoid the quotation altogether if it is not really necessary.

2. Paraphrase the quotation, giving the original author credit for the idea.

3. If the quotation is fairly short, recast it as an indirect quotation, substituting nonsexist words as necessary.

Problems

Among the questions asked by the school representatives was the following: "Considering the ideal college graduate, what degree of knowledge would you prefer him to have in each of the curricular areas?"

Alternatives

Among the questions asked by the school representatives was one about what degree of knowledge the ideal college graduate should have in each of the curricular areas.

Sample Revised Passage

Substantial revisions or deletions are sometimes necessary when problems overlap or when stereotyped assumptions about men and women so pervade a passage that simple replacement of words is inadequate.

Problems

Each student who entered the classroom to find himself at the mercy of an elitist, Vassar-trained Miss Fidditch could tell right away that the semester would be a trial. The trend in composition pedagogy toward student-centered essays and away from hours of drill on grammatical correctness has meant, at least for him, that he can finally learn to write. But Macrorie, Elbow, and Janet Emig could drive the exasperated teacher of a cute and perky cheerleader type to embrace the impersonal truth of *whom* as direct object rather than fight his way against the undertow of a gush of personal experience. As Somerset

Alternatives

The trend in composition pedagogy toward student-centered essays, represented by such writers as Ken Macrorie, Peter Elbow, and Janet Emig, has meant that some students are finally learning to write. Yet the movement away from hours of drill on grammatical correctness has brought with it a new problem: in the hands of the inexperienced teacher, student essays can remain little more than unedited piles of personal experiences and emotions.

Maugham remarked "Good prose
should resemble the conversation
of a well-bred man," and both
Miss Fidditch and the bearded
guru who want to "get inside your
head" must realize it.

Representation of Men and Women

Important as language is, striving for nonsexist usage is to little purpose if the underlying assumptions about men and women continue to restrict them to traditional roles. If women never enter an author's world, for example, it little avails a writer or editor to refer scrupulously to students as "they" and prehistoric people as "cave dwellers." Thus, teachers and other professionals must be alert to the possible sexist implications of the content as well as the language of educational materials.

It has been enheartening to note that in the last ten years, trade publishers, textbook publishers, and publishers of reference works have become acutely aware of sexist language, thus largely alleviating the problem of discriminatory reference. Still, vigilance must be exercised.

The following recommendations concerning educational materials are made to correct traditional omissions of women or perpetuations of stereotypes.

Booklists

1. Items for a booklist should be chosen to emphasize the equality of men and women and to show them in nontraditional as well as traditional roles. Many children's favorites and classics may contain sexist elements, but books that are valuable for other reasons should not be excluded. The annotations, however, should be written in nonsexist language.

2. Picture books should be chosen showing males and females actively participating in a variety of situations at home, work, and play.

3. Booklists should be organized by subject headings that do not assume stereotyped male and female interests.

Problems	*Alternatives*
Books for Boys	Arts and Crafts
Books for Girls	Sports
	Travel

Teaching Units

1. The topic and organization of teaching units should be carefully considered to avoid sexist implications. Literature by and about both women and men should be included wherever possible.

2. When materials are chosen that present stereotyped assumptions about men and women, they should be balanced by others that show nontraditional roles and assumptions. *Jemima Puddle-Duck* and *Peter Rabbit* read together, for instance, show foolishness is not a sex-linked characteristic. Vera Brittain's *A Testament of Youth* and Ernest Hemingway's *The Sun Also Rises* present the aftermath of World War I from provocative perspectives. Placing a book in the proper historical context and using discussion questions that reflect an awareness of the sexist elements are good strategies.

3. Activities suggested in teaching units should not be segregated by sex: boys can make costumes and girls can build sets.

Reference Books and Research Materials

Reference books can be implicitly sexist in their titles, organizations, content, and language. Editors of such books should folow the suggestions in this publication to ensure nonsexist language in bibliographies, indexes, style manuals, and teacher's guides. In research works, if both males and females were studied, references to individual subjects should not assume that they are all one sex.

Implementation of Guidelines

These guidelines for nonsexist language are suggestions for teachers, writers, and contributors to NCTE publications. For the editors of NCTE publications, however, they are a statement of editorial policy.

Traditionally, editors have set the style for their publications—deciding, for example, whether there should be a comma before the conjunction in a series or whether the first item in a list after a colon should begin with a capital letter. Style decisions have sometimes been made in response to public pressure. Writing *Negro* with a capital letter instead of a lowercase letter and, later, using *Black* instead of *Negro* were both style decisions of this sort for many publishing houses, newspapers, and magazines.

It is an editor's job to rewrite whenever necessary to eliminate awkward language, inconsistency, or inaccuracy. If a job title is inaccurately identified in an article as Director of Public Instruction but the title is actually Supervisor of Public Instruction, the editor changes the wording as a matter of course and without asking the author's approval. If the subject matter or tone of an article is totally inappropriate for the particular publication, it would also be the editor's prerogative to return the manuscript to the author. In the case of language inconsistent with the guidelines, it is the editor's duty to question the author's use of a particular term; on the other hand, the author has the right to insist on its use, but a footnote will be provided to reflect such insistence.

The choices suggested in these guidelines are intended as additions to the style sheets and manuals already in use.

References

Authors and editors who would like to see further suggestions for creating a graceful, nondiscriminatory writing style should refer to these publications. (Note that many of the publishers' guidelines are in the process of being revised.)

American Psychological Association Task Force on Issues of Sexual Bias in Graduate Education. "Guidelines for Nonsexist Use of Language." *American Psychologist* 30 (June 1975): 682-84.

Editorial and Art Content Criteria for Treatment of Minorities and Women. Lexington: Ginn and Company. (Available from the publisher, 191 Spring Street, Lexington, MA 02173.)

Fairness in Educational Materials: Exploring the Issues. Science Research Associates, Inc. (Available from the publisher, 155 North Wacker Drive, Chicago, IL 60606.)

Guidelines for Bias-Free Publishing. New York: McGraw-Hill Book Company. (Available from the publisher's distribution center, Princeton Road, Hightstown, NJ 08520.)

Guidelines for Creating Positive Sexual and Racial Images in Educational Materials. New York: Macmillan Publishing Company, 1975. (Available in limited quantities from the publisher, 866 Third Avenue, New York, NY 10022.)

Guidelines for Developing Bias-Free Instructional Materials. Morristown: Silver Burdett Company, 1979. (Available from the publisher, 250 James Street, Morristown, NJ 07960.)

Guidelines for the Development of Elementary and Secondary Instructional Materials. New York: Holt, Rinehart and Winston School Department, 1975. (Available from the publisher, 383 Madison Avenue, New York, NY 10017.)

Miller, Casey, and Kate Swift. *The Handbook of Nonsexist Writing: For Writers, Editors and Speakers.* New York: Barnes and Noble Books, 1980. (Available from Harper and Row, 10 East 53rd Street, New York, NY 10022.)

Nilsen, Alleen Pace. "Editing for Sex." *Idaho English Journal* 6 (Spring 1983): 12+.

———. "Winning the Great *He/She* Battle." *College English* 46 (February 1984): 151.

Statement on Bias-Free Materials. New York: Association of Ameican Publishers. (Available from AAP, One Park Avenue, New York, NY 10016.)

Additional copies of *Guidelines for Nonsexist Use of Language in NCTE Publications* are available from NCTE, 1111 Kenyon Road, Urbana, Illinois 61801. Single copies are available free upon request, and may be copied without permission from NCTE. Please enclose a self-addressed, stamped envelope. Multiple copies are available in groups of 100 at a bulk rate, prepaid only. Ask for Stock No. 19719-012.

Resources for Liberating the Curriculum

Barbara Withers

Withers is concerned with the detrimental effect of sex-role stereotyping on the social development of both males and females. She notes briefly some of the more subtle ways in which a tradition of gender inequity may be passed on through words, images, and actions in education settings. The author views parents, teachers, and children as potential agents of change in reversing this long tradition of gender exclusiveness. The major part of the chapter suggests curricular tools which educators and religious personnel may use to make their professional environment more gender inclusive.

Feminist research begun in the 1970s highlighted some of the ways in which words, images, and actions perpetuate a tradition of sex bias and inequity through the process of socialization. There is now greater understanding of how children learn sex roles through the unconscious process of cultural transmission. Children form their behaviors and attitudes by participating in everyday patterns of communication and by observing the different behavioral expectations which adults have for boys versus girls. Traditional United States society often presents a set of expectations which are gender exclusive; they restrict and limit the development of the female child's full potential in life. These sex-role stereotypes are conveyed in highly unconscious and subtle ways through language, actions, and images presented to children in such contexts as the home, the school, and religious institutions. Although seldom taught overtly or directly, children learn sex roles in an almost automatic fashion through communication with parents, teachers, other family members, peers, and the media—television, books, and movies.

While young children may be adaptable and open to new types of sex roles, adults are, to a certain extent, victims of their own ways of life. Even those adults who might be open to more inclusive sex roles may not easily be able to adopt new values and corresponding ways of communicating. If sex-role stereotyping is therefore such an ingrained and unconscious part of adult life, how can new patterns which are more gender inclusive be conveyed to children? *In fact, parents, teachers, and children themselves are potential agents of change.* They can formally and informally focus on changing negative stereotypes in their language, actions, and images as they continue their everyday and professional interactions. Curricular tools are now available to aid educators and other agents of change in making social interaction more gender inclusive. The purpose of this essay is to examine some of these tools.

Awareness of Sex Role Exclusiveness

As a result of the massive push for women's equity and the social change orientation of the 1960s, the 1970s brought legislation which advocated sex equity and a heightened consciousness about sex bias. Of most notable mention is Title IX—the federal statute outlawing sex bias in schools receiving Title IX funds. Title IX was passed in 1973 to pressure schools to alter their use of language and curriculum materials so as to incorporate positive, unbiased views of female roles and identity. The goal of the legislation was to deal strongly with root causes of sex bias, especially in the socialization process of instruction. The focus was on integrating and including women into the curriculum; removing sex-role stereotyping in children's textbooks; and reducing the more subtle differences in classroom interactions between teachers and students, for example, sex-different expectations of teachers for student performance or sex-different communication strategies of teachers with students.

Feminist research on classroom interaction (e.g., student-teacher interaction) and curriculum has pointed out numerous ways in which members of certain social groups based on race, ethnicity, social class, religion, and sex are excluded through words, images, and actions. Words used to refer to women have been found to be restrictive and negative while other referential language simply suggests that females are not included. Images provided in basal readers and textbooks through pictures and main character roles again were found to focus on boys and men as opposed to females. Females were more often than not presented in passive roles or as supporters of males who played active, dominant roles. History textbooks were also found to exclude women's participation in the shaping of the past and present. Actions exhibited verbally and nonverbally between teacher and student in the classroom have been equally described as sex exclusive, even at the level of higher education. The Project on the Status and Education of Women has thoroughly detailed numerous ways in which women experience everyday inequities in the classroom, making the climate a chilly one for women.[1] They note several subtle ways in which women are excluded or discouraged in education settings through student-teacher interchanges, comments addressed to and about them, and lack of encouragement in out-of-classroom interactions. Most importantly they make a series of specific recommendations for changing everyday classroom behavior which expresses devalued and limited views of women. Helpful recommendations are specified for administrators; presidents, deans, and department chairs; faculty development programs; and so on. Appendix I lists their suggestions.

Despite the tremendous amount of progress in making the various agents of socialization more sex inclusive over the past two decades, there is still much sex inequity that remains to be changed in the 1980s.

Textbooks and Curricular Resources

Publishers of educational materials for children in the 1970s recognized the need to correct the language and images that limit a child's self-image. One of the earliest publishers to respond to the concerns about sex-role stereotyping of women and men and girls and boys in textbooks and story books was the McGraw-Hill Book Company. Their "Guidelines for Equal Treatment of the Sexes in McGraw-Hill Book Company Publications" received widespread publicity and distribution when they were first published in 1972.[2] These guidelines focused on sex-role stereotyping. Usually they provided authors with examples of stereotyped language and specific alternative ways in which to express the same image in less sex-biased ways; for example, the following possible substitutions for *man* words:[3]

NO	YES
mankind	humanity, human beings, human race, people
manmade	artificial, synthetic, manufactured
manpower	human power, human energy, workers, workforce

Other publishers soon followed with company policy guidelines on language usage, and some broadened the scope of their concern to include racial and ethnic stereotypes in language and illustrations or pictures. For a current list of guidelines for non-sexist usage, the reader is referred to *Language and the Sexes* by Frank and Anshen (1983).[4]

In addition, as a response to the socialization of stereotypes, the NCTE (National Council of Teachers of English) suggested guidelines for the non-sexist use of language to be followed in their publications. The introduction to their guidelines stated the following:

Whether teaching in the classroom, assigning texts, determining curriculum, or serving on national committees, NCTE members directly and indirectly influence the socialization of children. They help shape the language patterns and usage of students and thus have potential for promoting language that opens rather than closes possibilities to women and men.[5]

More information about the political background and the development of these guidelines is discussed in Chapter 3 of this book.

Other attempts have been made to alter the negative stereotypes applied to women through exclusionary language and terms. One such example is the latest edition of *Roget's Thesaurus*, edited by Susan Lloyd.[6] This new edition has banned, added, or reclassified more than twenty thousand words. For example, *mankind* was replaced with *humankind*; *countryman* with *country dweller*; and *rich man* with *rich person*. The phrase "God the Father" no longer headlines a section of the reference book. According to Lloyd, "Research has shown that if you say countryman, people think of a man—not a woman."[7] She adds that she isn't trying to make a feminist statement—just reflect "the language of the 80s." Some masculine words were kept in the new edition, such as, *master*, because she couldn't come up with a suitable substitute. In other cases she preserved the sex-biased words but changed the headings and key words. The aim was to make the category headings "as wide-ranging and neutral as possible."

Parents, teachers, and children themselves are potential agents of change if the necessary curricular tools are made available. Some of these tools may be games, toys, puzzles, films, nonprint materials, handbooks, and other aids. Work on changing negative stereotypes can begin with babies and extend through higher education. Appendix II includes an excellent list of resources which can be used for effecting change.

Teachers and others in the field of education are themselves a resource for change. They can help in avoiding reinforcement of sex stereotypes by analyzing the content of stories and textbooks, and by becoming more sensitive to negative sex stereotyping. In addition, negative stereotyping can be actively countered in some of the following ways:

1. Write to publishers with specific objections.
2. Lobby your curriculum selection committee for books and resources that are inclusive in language and images.
3. Search for and bring supplementary materials to your classroom (The Feminist Press is one particularly good source.)

4. Share your concerns with the children you work with and talk with them about how one can overcome sex bias.
5. Find others who are concerned and interested in doing something about sex-exclusive language. Support each other and talk over your frustrations, failures, and gains.

Church Education

At the same time that guidelines were being developed by major publishers in education, church educators began to respond to the same concerns. A partnership of twelve Protestant denominations—Joint Educational Development—was in the process of developing new curricular resources for a holistic approach to education in the church.[8] There was a strong push from Christian feminists to monitor the resources for inclusive language and images. In 1975, a statement of intention and guidelines was officially approved and distributed to all editors, writers, and reviewers of manucripts. This document, *Liberating Words, Images, and Actions: Guidelines to Alleviate Stereotyping*, goes beyond sex-role stereotyping to deal with human beings as whole persons.[9]

Initially conceived during the period of 1974 through 1978, this document is an ongoing statement describing the specific intentions and commitments of Joint Educational Development to model positive human values in all of its communications, programs, and resources.

The church engages in education as a means of helping persons achieve full humanness. This involves: (1) a sense of individual dignity, capacity, and worth; (2) interpersonal relations of trust, freedom, and love; and (3) a society that enhances freedom, justice, and peace for all people.[10]

To pursue the 'humanness' intention involves both an avoidance and an affirmative stance. On the one hand, it means developing leadership approaches and media which avoid discrimination and negative images related to age, race, or sex. On the other, it involves affirmative action by which a full humanness may be portrayed, understood, and pursued.[11]

The biblical foundation of church educators' concern for inclusive language and images is based on the vision of *shalom*—of wholeness. Whole persons, whole people, whole world—that is God's ultimate intention for the world. The theological understanding is that girls and boys, women and men ought to be treated as "whole," as persons of dignity and worth, created in the image of God. Therefore, the concern for the effects of stereotyping grows out of our understanding of the nature of persons.

The church is concerned not only about language as it relates to human beings but how language expresses and reflects our concept of God. Therefore, the guidelines proposed spell out concerns about the predominantly masculine images of God in liturgy and scripture.

Language about God is especially problematical. The Bible was written in a patriarchal time. Biblical and theological language has traditionally used masculine pronouns for the deity in English, often when the original language was not gender-specific or may even have been feminine. The result of this tradition, on the one hand, is to limit feminine identification with the deity; on the other, it is to limit the definition of God to masculine attributes, a form of idolatry.

With regard to God language, Joint Educational Development has two intentions: (a) to be faithful to biblical material, seeking at the same time to get as accurate a translation as possible to overcome sexist biases; and (b) to use a variety of images of God which are not limited to one gender. This involves using both feminine and masculine words to describe God's being. It also involves the intentional use of such diverse descriptive words as love, ground of being, hope and wisdom.[12]

Conclusion

We are beginning to make progress in the use of inclusive language, thereby alleviating stereotyping in language and images in printed resources used in education settings. At the same time, we must recognize that what happens in the classroom, church, and society has more impact than printed resources. Educators and others need to be sensitive to how their behavior affects those to whom they relate—teacher to student, parent to child, youth leader to adolescent, adult to adult, and clergy to congregation.

For example, in the classroom, does the female teacher always ask for a "strong boy" to help move the furniture? Why not ask for "strong, ablebodied children or young people" to help? Does the male teacher ask the girls to help with housekeeping chores, such as serving refreshments and cleaning up afterward? Is it assumed that boys will be discipline problems and girls will be docile? Children and young people are well-known to behave in ways they know the adult expects them to. Therefore, we must examine our own assumptions and values about appropriate roles and behavior, and how these expectations affect our relationship with others. Educators not only have the option but the responsibility to help all people—young and old; male and female; black, white, brown, yellow, and red; with disabling conditions or not—develop their potentials to the fullest and to be thinking, feeling persons open to new roles and lifestyles.

In today's world, stereotypes are reinforced by television and advertising that reach a wide audience. The images portrayed in media play a large role in how children and adults interpret appropriate behavior. Even though some stereotyped images do develop out of real-life situations, most often they are based on fiction. It is important not to make generalizations about people, usually in negative ways, from individual, isolated experiences. It must not be assumed that the images on television, in advertising, and in our own mental pictures are the only reality. Once stereotyping behavior and language is recognized by individuals in themselves, it is possible to comment about such images in the environment and in the behavior and language of others.

However, recognizing stereotypes is not enough. We must seek ways to counter the destruction of whole persons that has already occurred and find ways to change attitudes and institutions so that the future may be different— a society in which everyone can experience wholeness and well-being.

Notes and References

1. From Roberta Hall and Bernice Sandler. "The Classroom Climate: A Chilly One For Women?" Project on the Status and Education of Women. Association of American Colleges, Washington, D.C., 1982, pp. 1-23.

2. *Guidelines for Equal Treatment of the Sexes in McGraw-Hill Book Company Publications*, New York: McGraw Hill, 1975.

3. *Ibid.*

4. "A Selected List of Guidelines for Non-Sexist Usage." In Francine Frank & Frank Anshen, *Language and the Sexes*, 1983. Albany, N.Y.: SUNY Press, pp. 115-119.

5. *Guidelines for Nonsexist Use of Language in NCTE Publications* (adopted in 1975) and published for the membership in the March 1976 "NCTE to You" sections of the Council journals.

6. Mentioned in an Associated Press Featurescope, April 20, 1982. The edition referred to is: *The New Roget's Thesaurus*. New York: Putnam Publishing Group, 1981.

7. *Ibid.*

8. The Christian Church (Disciples of Christ), Church of the Brethren, Cumberland Presbyterian Church, Episcopal Church, The Evangelical Covenant

Church, The Moravian Church (North and South), the Presbyterian Church in Canada, Presbyterian Church in the United States, The Reformed Church of America, United Church of Canada, United Church of Christ, United Presbyterian Church in the USA.

9. Joint Educational Development, *Liberating Words, Images, and Actions: Guidelines to Alleviate Stereotyping*, 1975.

10. *Ibid.*

11. *Ibid.*

12. *Ibid.*

Appendix I

Recommendations For Selected Groups to Liberate the Curriculum

The following excerpt is taken from Roberta Hall and Bernice Sandler, "The Classroom Climate: A Chilly One for Women?"—developed with a grant from the Fund for the Improvement of Postsecondary Education of the U.S. Department of Education, 1982. For a copy of the entire twenty-three page paper, write to: Project on the Status and Education of Women, Association of American Colleges, 1818 R St., N.W. Washington, D.C. 20009.

Facilitating Change

Changing everyday classroom behavior that expresses devalued and limited views of women is a difficult challenge—especially because much differential treatment that may occur in classroom and related interaction is inadvertent, and often below the level of consciousness of both faculty and students. However, although this kind of change is elusive and difficult, it is already underway on many campuses, and directions for future changes are being charted by ongoing projects and research.

Many faculty, for example, have recognized the importance of classroom language, and are attempting to identify and to change language that excludes or disparages women.[1] Experts in teacher education at the elementary and other levels are engaged in ongoing research to isolate the small behaviors by which teachers may treat males and females differently, and to devise observation and training techniques to help teachers change. Leaders in faculty development are aiding teachers who want to become more aware of their own subtle behaviors that may discourage minority college students, and many of these strategies are also useful in identifying behaviors that expess different attitudes and perceptions based on sex. Others are exploring the complex connections between sex-of-student and sex-of-teacher in order to isolate those verbal and nonverbal classroom behaviors that may facilitate women students' class participation. Indeed, the impact of sex on interactions in school and in society is becoming a major focus for research on many fronts, both outside and within academe.

Inseparable from this focus are the growing number of academic courses and programs which incorporate perspectives on or emphasize women as subject. These include women's studies courses, and other courses which incorporate content about women, as well as information about female development, sex roles, and women's contributions to the disciplines. Some women students have reported that after taking such courses they have felt more included in the academic enterprise, and have "not only learned new facts, theories and approaches, but also . . . gained new perspectives on themselves as women and as scholars and were much more ready to assume responsibility for their educations."[2] As one student notes, "When I became a women's studies major . . . I began taking myself seriously as a science major. I'm going to graduate school in genetics."[3] Others have indicated the more immediate effect of women's studies courses in leading them to be more assertive in the classroom.[4]

In addition to citing the benefits of courses which include women as subject, women students on all levels and in virtually every study and survey reviewed for this report have emphasized their need for more women faculty at every level of postsecondary education to serve not only as teachers but also as role models, mentors and colleagues.

Women and men faculty alike—as well as students of both sexes—can benefit from strategies to help them become aware of and change behaviors that may discourage women students. A variety of recommendations for increasing such awareness and facilitating change follow. While some are designed primarily for faculty, some for students, and some for institutional administrators and others who can offer assistance and support, many recommendations may be useful to all members of the academic community.

Recommendations

Policy Recommendations for Administrators

- Issue a policy statement which makes it clear that overtly biased comments, use of sexist humor, and related behavior on the part of faculty are not appropriate in the classroom or in related learning situations. Distribute the statement to faculty and students, publish it in the student newspaper, the faculty bulletin, etc. Include it in materials distributed to new faculty and new students. The University of Miami (FL), along with other institutions, has issued such a statement.
- Incorporate the institution's policy on classroom climate issues in statements about good teaching.

- Determine how a concern with classroom climate can best be integrated into the mission, priorities and style of your institution. For example, if your mission emphasizes student development, one appropriate focus might be how classroom climate affects women's learning potential. If faculty are primarily oriented toward teaching, in-class questionnaires or class interviews, class videotaping, etc., may be more readily adopted; if faculty are more research-oriented, suggestions for research projects into classroom climate may increase awareness of and spark interest in this area.
- Include information on classroom climate issues in workshops for all faculty, including teaching assistants. It is important to make this information available to teaching assistants since they often handle many introductory courses, especially at large institutions. Thus, their behavior may establish the classroom climate for incoming women students. The Commission on the Status of Women at the University of Delaware developed behavioral guidelines on sexual and gender harassment which were included in an annual teaching effectiveness workshop for TA's.
- Ensure that all new faculty are informed of institutional commitment to an equitable classroom climate. Use workshops, seminars, informal meetings with members of their department, etc.
- Develop criteria about providing an equitable learning climate for women to be used in evaluating applicants for faculty and staff positions.
- Include classroom climate issues as a factor in merit evaluations.
- Develop a grievance procedure that can accommodate everyday inequities in classroom and related learning situations (nonactionable discrimination) as well as discrimination that is illegal. Emphasize establishing a confidential forum for airing concerns and a means of providing informal feedback to faculty whose behavior is objectionable or discouraging to women. The Massachusetts Institute of Technology is one of several institutions that have devised a model procedure of this sort.[5]

General Recommendations

- Include classroom climate issues in student evaluations. Questions might include items such as the following: Does this teacher call on women students as often as on men? Recognize women as readily as men when women raise their hands? Treat men's and women's comments with the same degree of seriousness? Make disparaging comments or use sexist humor? Make a special effort to treat women and men equally—e.g., by avoiding sexist language, using sex-balanced class examples, etc.?

- Hold informal meetings to discuss classrom climate and to stimulate awareness of the issues. Invite men and women students, faculty, student affairs and faculty development staff, and others. Use problems based on experiences at your own campus to encourage discussion.
- Set up a committee of women and men students to develop a questionnaire or survey geared to those climate issues of greatest concern on your campus. Issues might be clarified (in a non-threatening way) by using anonymous examples based on experiences at your own institution, or by citing incidents that have occurred at institutions similar to your own.
- Evaluate results of the survey, publicize where appropriate and develop plans for further activity.
- Use a survey (by department) for men and women undergraduate and graduate students to evaluate classroom, departmental and institutional climate and to determine if women find the climate less congenial than men do. Items that might be appropriately included are questions about classroom climate adapted from the Student Perception Questionnaire and questions about the broader learning climate, such as the following:
- Did your faculty advisors encourage you in your academic and career goals?
- Were men and women students within your department equally considered for assistantships, research appointments, and collaboration with advisors on research and writing projects?
- Has a faculty member ever offered to write a letter of recommendation for you, or suggested you should try to publish your research?
- Evaluate whether women transferring from "traditionally male" to "traditionally female" fields have done so because of an inhospitable classroom or departmental climate.
- Form an information-sharing network with other institutions—both coeducational and single sex—that are evaluating their learning climate for women. Members of already-established consortia might serve as a starting point.
- Use a new or already-established committee to evaluate classroom climate issues in the institution. (Existing committees might be those that deal with teaching policy or the status of women.) Involve faculty, administrators, student affairs staff and students—including women and minority students, and representatives from all concerned student groups.

- Hold meetings geared to male students (possibly led by male faculty and/or student affairs staff) to discuss male roles, attitudes, speaking styles, etc. in terms of their impact on the classroom climate.

Recommendations for Presidents, Deans and Department Chairs

- Utilize the active support of respected faculty who share the objective of improving the learning climate for women. Their willingness to publicly recognize the issue and to take initiatives (such as having a "class interview" [see below]) can help legitimize a concern with climate and set an example for others within their own departments.
- Ask heads of units, either formally or informally, what they are doing/ have done to ensure an equitable classroom climate. This will provide you with information and also indicate your concern about the issue.
- Mention classroom climate in speeches to reinforce its importance as an institutional priority.
- Circulate materials about classroom climate, such as this paper, to members of the academic community.
- Discuss classroom climate informally at parties, luncheons, meetings, etc. Informal discussion can air the issues in a nonthreatening way and allow for faculty and student commentary and feedback.
- Sponsor workshops, seminars or other sessions on classroom climate. Have your office send letters inviting faculty and staff to attend.

Recommendations for Student Affairs Personnel[6]

- Establish a workshop for all faculty who are academic advisors to increase their understanding of the classroom climate issues (as well as the traditional societal expectations and personal conflicts) that can limit women students' academic and career choices.
- Familiarize residence hall advisors with aspects of the learning climate that can discourage women students, as well as with existing channels for seeking counseling, exploring grievance procedures, etc.
- Collaborate with faculty on research concerning the learning climate for women at your institution.
- Interview or survey women and men students to determine whether they perceive overt and/or subtle discrimination in their classes.
- Hold workshops for faculty about classroom climate issues.
- Indicate your availability to meet with individual faculty to discuss classroom climate issues. (Put notices in the faculty bulletin, make a presentation at a faculty meeting, etc.)
- Establish a procedure to get feedback from each department about current classroom climates, areas which need improvement, and departmental goals you can help to facilitate.

- Work with staff of the continuing education or re-entry programs, minority center, etc. to plan workshops or group counseling sessions that focus on the climate problems special groups of women may face.

Recommendations for Faculty Development Programs

- Establish workshops, seminars or individual consultation sessions designed to help faculty become aware of classroom climate issues. Emphasize activities [7] which provide a personal frame of reference for data presented, such as:
  - role-reversal activities specially connected with classroom speaking, etc. (for example, have male faculty attempt to argue a point effectively while "talking like a lady");
  - case studies, especially those based on experience at your own campus.
- Aid faculty members in using audiotape, videotape and other devices to identify ways in which they may treat men and women students differently. (See the Student-Faculty Communication Checklist). Outside funding may be available to support such efforts. The American University (DC) for example, received a grant to provide classroom videotaping for instructors requesting it.
- Encourage faculty to keep journals, student contact logs[8] or other records to keep track of the frequency and nature of their interactions with women and men students.
- Bring students and faculty together to discuss the climate of a given classroom. Staff of the Center for Improving Teaching Effectiveness at Virginia Commonwealth University will hold a one-session "class interview" when invited by a faculty member. While geared mainly to helping white faculty understand subtle behaviors that may discourage black students in the classroom context, this method could be adapted to focus on behaviors that may discourage women. An open-ended question might be simply "What stands out to you as a woman in this class?
- Set up "micro-teaching" workshops to help faculty identify and change differential patterns of interaction with women and men students. Staff of Project INTERSECT at The American University (DC) have devised a program for elementary school teachers which could be adapted for postsecondary faculty. Each teacher presents a brief lesson plan and conducts a five-minute discussion with a "class" of two girls and two boys. The interaction is recorded on videotape and a trained observer suggests changes. The teacher than conducts the session again, paying particular attention to differential treatments (such as calling more

often on boys, encouraging the comments of boys but not girls, etc.)
(For additional information, see Resources.)

- Help faculty identify ways in which they respond to differential inter-actions between men and women students in the classroom. (For ex-ample, do they discourage, ignore, or encourage sexist humor on the part of male students? How do they handle interruption and/or triviali-zation of women's comments by male students?)
- Train faculty to conduct classroom climate workshops, seminars, etc. for their colleagues and/or for students.
- Train interested faculty to be observers in colleagues' classes.

Publicizing Classroom Climate Issues

- Use the student newspaper and faculty newsletter or bulletin to help make students and faculty more aware of classroom climate issues. Some campus groups have taken out advertisements and others have provided articles or information to campus media. The Commission on the Status of Women at the University of Delaware, for example, included in its newspaper ad a series of questions about potential sexism in the classroom, and urged students to comment either posi-tively or negatively via their course evaluation forms.
- Use the student newspaper to conduct a classroom climate survey. The Committee Against Sexual Harassment at Washington University (MO) ran a survey in the student paper which asked for information about whether women felt they were taken seriously, ignored or excluded, subjected to sexist humor and sexist comments, etc. as well as about their personal, academic and career responses to such experiences.
- Distribute an informational flyer on classroom climate issues which includes suggested actions and resource persons to contact. The Utah State University Committee on the Status of Women prepared and distributed a flyer entitled "What Can Students Do About Sex Discrimi-nation?"[9]
- Use campus media to combact "humor" with humor. The *Women's Forum Quarterly* at Seattle Central Community College (WA), for ex-ample, publishes a "Sexist Remark of the Quarter Award" to raise awareness about sexist humor and overtly biased comments in the classroom. Each "award" reprints the offending comment.

Promoting Institutional Research

- Offer incentives, such as summer funding, release time, support per-sonnel, etc. to encourage research and planning in improving the learning climate. (Such support also serves to legitimize the issues explored.)

- Establish awards for on-campus research in classroom climate issues. (See also "Recommendations for Professional Associations and Organizations.")
- Publish a catalogue of research on campus climate and related issues done by staff at your own institution. The Women's Resources and Research Center at the University of California. Davis, publishes an annual "Catalogue of UCD Faculty Research on Women and/or Sex Roles," which informs the campus community, interested scholars, and the general public of research by UCD faculty and helps to develop a network of interested scholars. Publications of this sort help stimulate further research.

Curriculum

- Include in required introductory courses, where appropriate, a unit on sex/status differences in verbal and nonverbal behavior and the valuation of behaviors by sex. Such a unit might be included in courses in several fields, including Speech/Communications, English Composition, Psychology, Sociology, Linguistics, and Women's Studies. (Some departments, such as Linguistics or interdisciplinary programs such as Women's Studies, might offer a separate course in this area.)
- Offer a speech/communications workshop in intellectual argumentation skills geared specifically to the difficulties some women (and men) students may experience regarding class participation.
- Incorporate classroom climate issues in teacher-education programs and emphasize practical skill-building techniques designed to identify and overcome subtle differential treatment of students on the basis of sex. (Course materials might include texts such as *Beyond Pictures and Pronouns: Sexism in Teacher Education Texts* and *Sex Equity Handbook for Schools* [see Resources].)

Recommendations for Faculty

Evaluating the Classroom Climate

- Use whatever means are available (audiotape, videotape, a colleague, faculty or student development staff, or student observer, etc.) for observation of your own classes to determine whether you inadvertently treat women and men students differently. The Student-Faculty Communication Checklist suggests behaviors to watch and listen for, and questions to ask.

- Administer a survey to your students to determine whether women and men students find the climate of your classroom equally hospitable, and to measure men's and women's perception of sex-based differences in classroom interaction. The "Student Perception Questionnaire" from *Sex and Gender in the Social Sciences* might serve as a model. (In some cases, students may be more comfortable responding to such a questionnaire if it is administered by a proxy.)
- Where appropriate, devise assignments in which students learn research methods by collecting data concerning the classroom climate. Students in some classes, for example, have been assigned to analyze patterns of interruption in class participation.

Questions for Faculty: Awareness and Attitudes

- Which students can you envision as potential colleagues? Are there any women included?
- Which students would you choose (or have you chosen) to work with as laboratory, teaching or research assistants? Are women and men both represented according to their abilities?
- Which students do you consider most original and creative? Are women included?
- List the names of the students in your classes. Do you know the names of more students of either sex in disproportion to their number?
- Are you as likely to offer to write letters of recommendation for women as for men students? Do your letters for women more often include extraneous comments about appearance, or marital or parental status?
- Which students have you nominated for fellowships, awards and prizes? Are outstanding men and women students equally represented?

Avoiding Behaviors That Can Create a Cold Climate for Women

Some faculty behaviors can directly discourage women students. Behaviors to avoid include:

- disparaging women in general, women's intellectual abilities, or women's professional potential.
- using sexist humor as a classroom device.
- making seemingly helpful comments which imply that women are not as competent as men (e.g., "I know women usually have trouble with numbers, but I'll be glad to give you extra help . . .").
- turning a discussion of a women student's work toward a discussion of her physical attributes or appearance.
- discussing women faculty in terms of their sex rather than their professional status.

- grouping students according to sex in a way which implies that women are not as competent or do not have status equal to men (for example, in setting up laboratory or field-work teams).
- disparaging scholarship on women, or ridiculing specific works because they deal with women's perceptions and feelings.
- questioning or disparaging women students' seriousness of purpose and/or academic commitment.

Creating a Climate That Can Encourage Women's Full Participation

Faculty can take many steps to identify and change subtle patterns in classroom and related interactions that may discourage women students. Several of the following recommendations are based on those in *Sex and Gender in the Social Sciences: Reassessing the Introductory Course.*[10]

In Class

- Pay particular attention to classroom interaction patterns during the first few weeks of class, and make a special effort to draw women into discussion during that time. Participation patterns are likely to be established during this period, and often continue throughout the term.
- Set aside a class session early in the semester for discussion of anxieties students might have about participating in class. One professor, who as a student suffered from fear of classroom speaking, found that airing the issue not only increased her students' awareness, but helped ease women (and men) students' concerns about participating.
- Tell your classes you expect both women and men students to participate in class discussion.
- Make a specific effort to call directly on women as well as on men students.
- In addressing the class, use terminology that includes both men and women in the group.
- Respond to women and to men students in similar ways when they make comparable contributions to class discussion by:
  - crediting comments to their author ("as Jeanne said . . .")
  - "coaching" for additional information, etc.
- Notice whether the "feminine" or "masculine" style of a student's comment, question or response affects your own perception of its importance.
- Intervene in communication patterns among students that may shut out women. For example, if men students pick up on each other's points, but ignore an appropriate comment offered by a woman, slow the discussion, and pick up on the comment that has been overlooked.

- Note patterns of interruption to determine if women students are interrupted more than men—either by yourself or by other students. Make a special effort to ensure that all students have the opportunity to finish their comments.
- Ask women and men qualitatively similar questions—that is, ask students of both sexes critical as well as factual questions.
- Give men and women students an equal amount of time to respond after asking a question.
- Give women and men the same opportunity to ask for and receive detailed instructions about the requirements for an assignment.
- Use parallel terminology when addressing women and men students in class, or referring to men and women in classroom examples.
- When talking about occupations or professions in class discussion, use language that does not reinforce limited views of men's and women's roles and career choices. Often, examples can be effectively cast into the "I"/"You" form with the instructor taking the role of one party and the class the other (e.g., "Suppose I am a doctor and you come to me because . . ." rather than "The woman went to the doctor and he told her . . .). Additionally, use examples with feminine pronouns, such as, "Here is a geologist who finds herself with the following discovery."
- Avoid using the generic "he" whenever possible.
- Avoid placing professional women in a "special category," for example, "woman (or worse, 'lady') accountant."
- Avoid reference to women students' appearance, family, etc., without similar reference to men students' appearance or family.
- Experiment with language that reverses expectations based on sex. One teacher, for example, used "she" as the generic form for one semester and asked her students to evaluate its impact on their perceptions and feeling.[11]
- Make eye contact with women as well as with men students after asking a question to invite a response.
- Watch for and respond to nonverbal cues that indicate women students' readiness to participate in class, such as leaning forward or making eye contact.
- Use the same tone in talking with women as with men students (for example, avoid a patronizing or impatient tone when speaking with women, but a tone of interest and attention when talking with men.)
- Ensure that women are not "squeezed out" by male classmates from viewing laboratory demonstrations or engaging in other group assignments.
- Assume an attentive posture when responding to women's questions or listening to their comments.

Encouraging Women Outside The Classroom

- Meet with women students to discuss academic and career goals.
- Encourage women students to pursue traditionally "masculine" majors and subspecialities when these areas reflect the particular student's interests and abilities.
- Consider women as well as men students when choosing classroom, teaching and research assistants.
- Ensure that women and men assistants have equally independent responsibility for their classes, and equal opportunities to pursue their own research.
- Make a special effort to consider women for teaching and research assistantships in traditionally "masculine" fields.
- Offer to write letters of recommendation for women students.
- Consider women as well as men students when making nominations for fellowships, awards and prizes.
- Include women graduate students in the "informal" interactions that can be important in communicating support and acceptance as a colleague—for example, by inviting women, as well as men, to share authorships or attend professional conferences. If you are male and uncomfortable inviting a female for lunch or other informal occasions, invite two or three women at a time.
- Provide women with informal as well as formal feedback on the quality of their work.

Recommendations for Women Students

(Some of the recommendations specifically directed to faculty and administrators may also be appropriate for student organizations which can help press for their adoption.)

- Do an informal "tally" of patterns of interruption, successful introduction of topics, development of comments, etc. during a typical class session to see if they break down along sex lines. (See the Student-Faculty Communication Checklist and the Student Perception Questionnaire for behaviors to watch and questions to keep in mind.)
- If you seem to be disproportionately interrupted in a given class, discuss your perception with other women students to see if their experience coincides with your own. If so, you may wish to get together and bring your concern to your teacher's attention.

- Give credit or "authorship" to comments made by women classmates ("as Mary said . . .")—especially if credit has not been properly given during the course of the discussion.
- Give your professors positive feedback for efforts to create an equitable learning climate. For example, if a professor makes it a point to use sex-balanced classroom examples and/or avoid the generic "he," show your attention and approval by making eye contact, nodding, etc.—or by telling the professor that you recognize and appreciate his or her efforts.
- Familiarize yourself with your institution's grievance procedure for sexual harassment. If it does not include a mechanism for airing concerns and providing feedback to faculty about overtly biased comments and sexist humor in the classroom, work to have it changed.
- Use your student evaluation form to comment—positively or negatively—on the climate of your classes.
- Where appropriate, discuss problems of classroom climate with the department chair or dean. Raising these issues as a group may be helpful.
- Encourage student publications such as the school newspaper to write about the subject of classroom climate.
- Hold meetings, workshops or hearings about classroom climate in order to bring about awareness of the subject.
- Encourage student organizations to press for inclusion of classroom climate issues in faculty development programs and in official statements relating to teaching standards.
- Recognize features of your own speaking and nonverbal style that may be counterproductive in a classroom setting. You may wish to ask classmates for their observations on your in-class style.
- If you feel you would benefit by modifying your own speaking style to enhance your effectiveness in the classroom, check with appropriate academic departments (e.g., Speech/Communications) and the student service offices (e.g., Student Affairs) to see if your institution offers workshops to help women—and men—develop intellectual argumentation skills.
- Hold meeting or workshops on class participation anxiety. Invite experts in the field, faculty and/or alumnae who successfully overcame their own reticence about speaking in public and others to participate.

Recommendations for Special Groups of Women Students

- If you find your department's climate unsupportive, seek out professional organizations for women in your field. The Association of Women Geoscientists, for example, has chapters around the country and offers membership to students as well as to practicing professional women. Such organizations can offer both role models and informal support.

- Encourage the organization of a support group comprised of women students majoring in your area. Such a group can be of special help to women in traditionally male fields by providing a setting in which women from different class years, (i.e., sophomore, junior, senior) can learn from each other's experiences and ovecome the isolation women in traditionally masculine majors often feel.
- Establish an organization for graduate women, older women, minority women, etc. where problems concerning lack of support and other climate issues, can be aired and strategies devised to deal with them. The attrition rate of graduate women dropped following the formation of a women's caucus at the University of California, Berkeley.[12]
- If your campus has a minority student center, alert staff to classroom climate issues that may affect minority women. Set up workshops, seminars, or informal meetings to discuss these issues. If your institution has no such center, establish your own informal group.

Recommendations for Professional Associations and Organizations

- Include sessions on classroom climate issues at your annual meeting. The Association of American Colleges, for example, included a session on these issues at its annual meeting. The South Atlantic Modern Language Association and the American Educational Research Association featured panels on related issues at their regional and mid-year meetings.
- Identify sub-groups within your organization that might be especially appropriate for considering classroom climate issues. These might include faculty development or student development programs, women's caucuses or commissions.
- Work with other organizations and associations such as the Special Interest Group: Research on Women in Education of the American Educational Research Association.
- Stimulate research on issues related to classroom climate by calling for papers for presentation and/or publication.
- Offer awards for innovative ideas in faculty/student development that focus on classroom climate issues.[13]

Selected List of Areas for Further Research

Many of the elements that create classroom climate have been investigated by researchers in diverse areas. Additional research is especially needed on the following:

- the effect of education climate on women's choice of academic majors
- The relationship of findings about sex-based differences in student-teacher interaction at the elementary level to classroom and related interaction in postsecondary institutions
- the relationship of the sex-ratio of a given class to patterns of interaction
- the factors (aside from proportion of men and women students) that make some classes highly sex-differentiated, others less so
- the effect of women students' interaction with male and female peers on women's perception of climate in college and in graduate school
- the differentiation of verbal and nonverbal patterns by race and by age both within and between the sexes
- the similarities between subtle differential treatment of students based on sex and based on race
- the relationship between sex-of-teacher and sex-of-student as it may affect both classroom behavior and education and professional outcomes
- the impact of courses incorporating content on sex roles and/or women, on women's classroom behavior and educational and career ambitions
- the potential value of women's speaking styles in providing a "cooperative" alternative to the "competitive" male style associated with classroom interaction at the postsecondary level
- the development of well-designed intervention studies in the postsecondary setting
- the steps women students can take to respond effectively to subtle differential treatment
- the effect of interaction between men and women faculty on men and women students
- the identification of those areas in which women students may most benefit from special efforts in creating a learning climate to counter the effects of prior experiences in school and society (for example, increasing women's class participation, ensuring women's full inclusion in field work, laboratory research, and other "hands-on" experience; or enhancing women's opportunities for collaborative work with graduate faculty)

Notes*

1. See, for example, Barbara Bate, "Nonsexist Language Use in Transition," *Journal of Communication*, Winter, 1978, pp. 139-49.

2. See, for example, student evaluations for course concerning women's achievement motivation as summarized in Nancy M. Porter and Margaret T. Eileenchild, in *The Effectiveness of Women's Studies Teaching*, Women's Studies Monograph Series, National Institute of Education, Washington, DC, 1980, pp. 33-34.

3. Senior, San Francisco State University, quoted in Lorna Sage, "Women on Course," in "Living," *The London Observer*, August 2, 1981.

4. See, for example, study by Allana Cummings Elonson and Irene Crockcroft, San Diego State University, as reported in *On Campus With Women*, Project on the Status and Education of Women, No. 20, June 1978, pp. 5-6.

5. Mary P. Rowe and Clarence G. Williams, "The MIT Non-Union Grievance Procedure: An Upward-Feedback, Mediation Model," MIT Press, Cambridge, MA, 1980. For other model procedures, see, "Appendix: Codes of Conduct and Grievance Procedures" in Phyllis Franklin et al., *Sexual and Gender Harassment in the Academy*, The Modern Langauge Association of America, New York, NY, 1981, pp. 55-74.

6. Several of the recommendations in this section are based on more general strategies outlined by Joseph Katz in "Collaboration of Academic Faculty and Student Affairs Professionals for Student Development," David C. Tilley, et al., *The Student Affairs Dean and the President: Trends in Higher Education*, Ann Arbor, MI, ERIC/CAPS 1979, pp. 33-54; and in Marjorie Abrams, "Preparing Men and Women Students to Work Together: A New Student Development Challenge," *Journal of the National Association for Women Deans, Administrators and Counselors*, Summer 1981, Vol. 44, No. 4, pp. 3-8.

7. Many sources for activities that can be used to help faculty increase their general awareness of sex-role stereotyping, sex-based expectations, etc., are now available, such as E. Nickerson, et al., *Intervention Strategies for Changing Sex-Role Stereotypes: A Procedural Guide*, Kendall-Hunt, Dubuque, 1976; C.G. Carney & S.L. McMahon, eds., *Exploring Contemporary Male/Female Roles: A Facilitator's Guide*, University Associates, San Diego, CA, 1977; *Participants Notebook for Training Sessions on the Social/Educational Context of Title IX*, Title IX Equity Workshop Project, Washington, DC, National Foundation for the Improvement of Education, 1977, pp. 17-23.

8. For the use of faculty-student contact logs in related research, see Sheila Kishler Bennett, "Student Perceptions of and Expectations for Male and Female Instructors: Evidence Relating to the Question of Gender Bias in Teaching Evaluation," unpublished paper. (Requests for reprints should be sent to Sheila K. Bennett, Dept. of Sociology, Bryn Mawr College, Bryn Mawr, PA 19010.)

---

*In the original document, footnotes 1-4 appear as 110-113 respectively.

9. This flyer and related materials are available from the Project on the Status and Education of Women in an informational packet concerning sexual harassment on campus. (For ordering information, see Resources.)

10. For ordering information, see Resources.

11. Cathryn Adamsky, "Changes in Pronomial Usage Among College Students As a Function of Instructor Use of *She* As the Generic-Singular Pronoun," paper presented to the American Psychological Association, September 1976.

12. Lucy Sells, "Convention Notes," *Sociologists for Women in Society Newsletter,* February 20, 1972 as cited in Adler, p. 217.

13. For a brief description of how to set up an awards program see "Giving Prizes and Awards: A New Way to Recognize and Encourage Activities that Promote Equity for Women in Academe," Bonny Lambert and Bernice Sandler, Project on the Status and Education of Women, Association of American Colleges, Washington, DC, 1981. (Available from the Project.)

Selected List of Resources

PUBLICATIONS

Bogart, Karen; Flagle, Judith; and Jung, Steven. Institutional Self-Study Guide on Sex Equity, Washington, DC: American Institutes for Research, 1981. Contains five separate sections and a brief introductory user's guide designed for institutional or departmental self-evaluation. One section focuses on general social-educational climate including subtle behaviors that may discourage women. Each of the other sections focuses on specific conditions, policies and practices affecting sex equity for students, faculty, administrators, and staff. Arranged as a checklist with suggestions as to which personnel might respond to questions in each area, the Guide can be used as a diagnostic tool in identifying barriers to equity, and as an educational tool to familiarize administrators, faculty and others with the needs of women on campus. Approximately 100 pages. Available from the Project on the Status and Education of Women, Association of American Colleges, 1818 R St., NW, Washington, DC 20009.

Bogart, Karen. Technical Manual for the Institutional Self-Study Guide on Sex Equity. Washington, DC, American Institutes for Research, 1981. Describes the critical incident technique and other aspects of the methodology employed in development of the Self-Study Guide. Includes illustrative problems and proposed solutions for inequities, including those stemming from subtle differential treatment of women students, faculty, administrators and staff. 55 pages and appendices. Available from: American Institutes for Research, 1055 Thomas Jefferson St., Washington, DC 20007.

Eakins, Barbara; Eakins, R. Gene and Lieb-Brilhart, Barbara, eds. SISCOM '75: Women's (and Men's) Communication, Proceedings of the Speech Communication Association's Summer Conference XI. Includes an overview of research and resources on women's communication, suggestions for workshops and courses, and list of resources for research and instruction. 208 pages. Limited number of copies are available from: The Speech Communication Association, 5105 Backlick Rd., Suite E, Annandale, VA 22003.

Franklin, Phyllis, et al., Sexual and Gender Harassment in the Academy: A Guide for Faculty, Students and Administrators, Commission on the Status of Women in the Profession. New York: The Modern Language Association of America, 1981. Explains gender as well as sexual harassment. Includes a chapter on problems of graduate women in the modern languages, and outlines steps for establishing definitions, determining codes and standards, and developing grievance mechanisms. Also includes bibliography and appendix with model codes and procedures. 75 pages paperbound, available from MLA, 62 Fifth Ave., New York, NY 10011.

Gappa, Judith M. and Pearce, Janice. Sex and Gender in the Social Sciences: Reassessing the Introductory Course. Set has three volumes with content guidelines for sociology, psychology, and microeconomics; each volume also contains "Guidelines for Student-Faculty Communication" (major contributing author, Mercilee M. Jenkins) which include specific recommendations for change and set out in chart form faculty verbal and nonverbal behaviors that may reinforce stereotypes and/or discourage women's class participation. Also included are the "Student-Faculty Communication Checklist" and the "Student Perception Questionnaire" reproduced in this paper. Introductory Sociology (major contributing author, Barrie Thorne), 175 pages; Introductory Psychology (major contributing author, Nancy F. Russo), 152 pages; and Principles of Microeconomics (major contributing author, Barbara B. Reagan), 120 pages. Prior to publication and dissemination by the Women's Educational Equity Act Program, a limited number of copies are available from Judith M. Gappa, Associate Provost, Faculty Affairs, San Francisco State University, 1600 Holloway Ave., San Francisco, CA 94132. The complete text of Introductory Sociology will also be available from the Teaching Resource Center, American Sociological Association, 1722 N St., NW, Washington, DC.

"Guidelines for Nonsexist Language," American Psychologist, June 1975, pp. 682-84 and "Guidelines for Nonsexist Language in APA Journals," American Psychologist, June 1972 (Publication Manual Change Sheet 2). Available free from the American Psychological Association, 1200 17th St., NW, Washington, DC 20036 (send stamped self-addressed envelope).

Henley, Nancy M. Body Politics: Power Sex and Nonverbal Communication, 1977. Identifies and analyzes sex/status differences in nonverbal behavior and explores ways in which everyday nonverbal communication expresses and maintains an established hierarchy in social and personal interactions. 214 pages paperbound. Available from Spectrum Books, Prentice Hall, Inc., Englewood Cliffs, NJ 07632.

Howe, Florence, et al. Everywoman's Guide to Colleges and Universities, forthcoming. Scheduled for publication in fall, 1982. The Guide is designed to aid women students in the college-selection process. Institutions listed responded to a questionnaire covering a range of items— such as curricular offerings, educational climate, sports, health and counseling services, financial aid and scholarships, child care facilities, services and centers for re-entry women, etc. For further information, contact The Feminist Press, State University of New York/College at Old Westbury, Box 334, Old Westbury, NY 11568. (516) 997-7660.

International Association of Business Communicators. Without Bias: A Guide book for Nondiscriminatory Communication, 1977. Gives specific guidelines for avoiding bias on the basis of race, sex or disability in verbal communication, in visual media, and in meetings, conferences and workshop settings. Includes list of resource publications and organizations. 77 pages paperbound. Available from the International Association of Business Communicators, 870 Market St., Suite 940, San Francisco, CA 94102.

Kramarae, Cheris and Treichler, Paula, eds. Women and Language News. Newsletter on six differences in language use, attitudes and acquisition. Includes information on new research and resources, courses and conferences. Published twice a year. Available at yearly subscription rate from Cheris Kramarae, Speech Communications Dept., 244 Lincoln Hall, University of Illinois, Urbana, IL 61801.

Lakoff, Robin. Language and Woman's Place, 1975. Discusses language used to describe and define the sexes, and identifies features of "women's language" in the context of women's devalued status and society's prescription that women be polite and deferential. 83 pages paperbound. Available from Harper and Row, Publishers, Inc., Attn: Order Dept., Keystone Industrial Park, Soranton, PA 18512.

Men and Women Learning Together: A Study of College Students in the Late
70's, Report of The Brown Project. Originally conceived as an assessment of the merger of Brown University and Pembroke College (1971)
with a special focus on the situation of women in co-educational
institutions, the study was expanded to include survey data from over
three thousand undergraduates, classes of 1978-81, from Barnard,
Brown, Dartmouth, Princeton, SUNY at Stony Book, and Wellesley, as
well as interviews with current students and alumni/ae. The Report
includes working papers on aspects of the undergraduate experience;
two analyses specific to the Brown-Pembroke merger; proceedings of
the conference Women/Men/College: The Educational Implications of
Sex Roles in Transition; and a series of specific recommendations
prepared for Brown University. 295 pages. (A limited number of copies
are available from Cynthia Steere, Box 1945, Brown University, Provi-
dence, RI 02912.)

Perun, Pamela. ed. The Undergraduate Woman: Issues in Educational Equity, forthcoming. Provides an overview of current research for administrators, faculty and counselors. Topics include critical aspects of pre-
enrollment years such as sex-bias in testing, and the college selection
process; elements of the college experience including department climates, curricula, evaluation, and teaching styles; aspects of cognitive,
moral and psychosexual development; educational outcomes such as
impact on career commitment and family roles; and objectives for
research and policy in the coming decade. Will be available from
Lexington Books, D.C. Heath & Co., 2700 N. Richardt Ave., Indiana-
polis, IN 46219. For additional information, call 800-428-8071.

Project on the Status and Education of Women, Rape and Sexual Harassment
Packet. Includes "The Problem of Rape on Campus," 1978, 8 pages;
"Sexual Harassment: A Hidden Issue," 1978, 7 pages; "Sexual Harass-
ment" (selected articles from previous issues of the Project's newsletter,
On Campus With Women), 4 pages; "Title VII Sexual Harassment
Guidelines on Educational Employment," 1980, 4 pages; and "What
Can Students Do About Sex Discrimination," (reprint, Utah State Uni-
versity), 1981, 1 page. Available from the Project on the Status and
Education of Women, Association of American Colleges, 1818 R St.,
NW, Washington, DC 20009. (A list of all Project publications is
available free with a stamped, self-addressed envelope.)

Project on the Status and Education of Women, Re-entry Women (3 packets
of 5 papers each), 1980. Papers focus on institutional barriers returning
women students often face when they enroll—or attempt to enroll—in
postsecondary programs. Each paper discusses a specific problem

(such as recruitment and admissions, financial aid, transfer policies
and graduation requirements, support services, graduate study), offers
specific recommendations for institutional change, and cites adaptable
model programs. Set also includes a paper on special programs for
special populations, an introductory paper, a paper compiling current
national statistics on re-entry women, and a list of bibliographies.
Packets are available from the Project on the Status and Education of
Women, Association of American Colleges, 1818 R St., NW, Washington DC 20009. (For a complete listing of contents of each packet as
well as a list of all other Project publications, send a stamped, self-
addressed envelope to the Project.)

Project on the Status and Education of Women, "Working Bibliography for
Classroom Climate Issues," 1982. Informal selected bibliography of
sources consulted for this report. Briefly annotated entries with an
addendum of more recently received materials. For further information, contact the Project on the Status and Education of Women, Association of American Colleges, 1818 R St., NW, Washington, DC
20009.

Sadker, Myra P. and Sadker, David M. Sex Equity Handbook for Schools, and
companion Guide for Sex Equity Trainers by Joyce S. Kaser, Myra
Sadker and David Sadker, 1982. The Handbook includes chapters on
sex bias in instructional materials and in teacher-student interaction;
field-tested strategies for nonsexist teaching; lesson plans for elementary and other courses; a resource directory, and related materials. It
also can be used as a college text for methods and for other preservice
courses, or as a training text for inservice workshops. The Guide gives
detailed instructions for designing, implementing and evaluating conferences, and for conducting two specific workshops. Available from:
Longman, Inc., College and Professional Book Division, 19 West 44th
St., New York, NY 10036. Handbook (331 pages), Guide (108 pages).

Sadker, Myra P. and Sadker, David M. Beyond Pictures and Pronouns: Sexism in Teacher Education Textbooks, 1979. Identifies types of sex bias
in the most widely-used teacher-education texts; includes guidelines
for the development of sex-fair textbooks; lists supplementary materials that can help teachers remedy biases in existing texts. (Also discusses bias concerning racial and ethnic groups.) 70 pages. Available
from Education Development Center, 55 Chapel St., Newton, MA
02160.

Silberstein, Sandra. Bibliography: Women and Language. Michigan Occasional Papers in Women's Studies., No. XII, Winter, 1980. Includes
references to unpublished as well as published works on gender differ-

ences in language; a representative sample of guidelines for nonsexist language use; articles concerning the issues such guidelines raise; and applications of the guidelines (i.e., teaching nonsexist language). (Also lists works on gender differences in nonverbal communication.) 67 pages and addenda. Available from Women Studies Program, University of Michigan, 354 Lorch Hall, Ann Arbor, MI 48109.

Thorne, Barrie and Henley, Nancy, eds. Language and Sex: Difference and Dominance, 1975. Includes articles drawn from a variety of disciplines—such as linguistics, sociolinguistics, speech communication, English, psycholinguistics, and child development—which examine the relationship between language and sex in a variety of social and educational contexts. Contains an extensive annotated bibliography, "Sex Differences in Language, Speech and Nonverbal Communication" (also published under separate cover as She Said/He Said, Know, Inc., Pittsburgh, PA, 1975). 311 pages, paperbound. Available from Newbury House Publishers, Inc., 54 Warehouse Lane, Rowley, MA 01969.

Till, Frank J. Sexual Harassment: A Report on the Sexual Harassment of Students. National Advisory Council on Women's Educational Programs, Washington, DC, August 1980. Discusses subtle and overt sexual harassment in the postsecondary setting and examines short- and long-term educational consequences for women students. Includes analysis of legal issues and a technical supplement to aid institutions in establishing definitions, setting up grievance procedures, understanding liabilities and legal remedies. Single copies are available free from NACWEP, 1832 M St., NW, Suite 821, Washington, DC 20036.

ORGANIZATIONS

American Educational Research Association's (AERA) Special Interest Group: Research on Women and Education (SIG: RWE). Founded in 1973, SIG:RWE publishes a quarterly newsletter featuring information of interest to scholars and researchers concerned with women's issues; holds a mid-year research conference: offers symposia and presentations at AERA annual meetings; and co-sponsors activities with the AERA Women's Committee and with Women Educators. For further information, contact Susan Klein, National Advisory Council on Women's Educational Programs, 1832 M St., NW, Suite 821, Washington, DC 20036, (202) 653-5846.

American Personnel and Guidance Association, Committee on Women. The Committee on Women works to increase the awareness of APGA's members about issues of concern to women and to facilitate networking. Publishes a newsletter. For further information, contact Myrna C. Tashner, Chair (612) 874-4114 or Judith Rosenbaum, Associate Executive, APGA (703) 820-4700.

Center for Improving Teaching Effectiveness, Virginia Commonwealth University. Projects undertaken by the Center include identification of subtle behaviors by which faculty may discourage minority students, and techniques to enhance faculty and student awareness. For further information, contact John F. Noonan, Director, 901 West Franklin St., Richmond, VA 23284, (804) 257-1121.

Informal Network of Researchers and Practitioners Interested in Sex Equity in Classroom Interactions. For information, contact Susan Klein, National Advisory Council on Women's Educational Programs, 1832 M St., NW, Suite 821, Washington, DC 20036, (202) 653-5846 or Barbara Richardson, Teaching and Instruction, Teaching and Learning, National Institute of Education, 1200 19th St., NW, Washington, DC 20208, (202) 254-5407.

Mid-Atlantic Center for Sex Equity. One of 10 regional centers that provide technical assistance and other resources to school systems, including training on how to avoid sex bias in student-teacher interaction. For further information, contact David Sadker, Director, Mid-Atlantic Center for Sex Equity, The American University, Foxhall Square Building, Suite 252, 3301 New Mexico Ave., NW, Washington, DC 20016, (202) 686-3511.

National Association for Women Deans, Administrators and Counselors (NAWDAC). Publishes a quarterly newsletter and journal as well as mailings throughout the year. Journal articles often focus on issues in women students' development. For further information, contact Patricia Rueckel, Executive Director, 1625 Eye St., NW, #624-A, Washington, DC 20006, (202) 659-9330.

National Association of Student Personnel Administrators (NASPA). For general information, contact Jane Howard-Jasper, Assistant Executive Director, NASPA, One Dupont Circle, NW, Washington, DC 20036, (202) 833-4660. For information on professional development assistance for women, contact Nancy Turner, Coordinator for the Women's Network, Florida State University, Tallahassee, FL 32306, (904) 644-3206.

National Council for Staff, Program and Organizational Development (NCSPOD). A national organization for those active in faculty development in two-year colleges. NCSPOD publishes a newsletter and refers consultants specializing in a variety of faculty development areas. For additional information, contact Maureen Lukenbill, President, Miami-Dade Community College, South Campus, FSPD Office, Room 3336, 11011 Southwest 104 St., Miami, FL 33176, (305) 596-1366.

National Institute for Staff and Organizational Development (NISOD). A national faculty development organization, NISOD focuses on creating a positive learning environment in community colleges and other two-year institutions. Affiliated with the North American Consortium, NISOD serves non-member as well as member institutions. It provides publications, workshops and consultants with a focus on classroom dynamics. Many offerings emphasize ways in which faculty can best serve nontraditional students. For further information, contact Nancy Armes, Executive Director, NISOD, 348 Education Building, University of Texas at Austin, Austin, TX 78712, (512) 471-7545.

Professional Organizational Development Network in Higher Education (POD). A national professional organization for those involved in faculty development at all levels of postsecondary education, POD offers a referral service to institutions seeking faculty development consultants. For further information, contact. Michael Davis, Executive Director, Office of the Academic Vice President, University of the Pacific, Stockton, CA 95211, (209) 946-2551.

Women Students Leadership Training Project. Designed to arm students with information, training and leadership skills to combat sex discrimination in postsecondary education, the project held a national conference and distributed a resource manual to student leaders in 1980. It is currently developing regional information and support networks. For further information, contact Donne Brownsey, National Student Educational Fund, 2000 P St., NW, Suite 305, Washington, DC 20036, (202) 785-1856.

Student-Faculty Communication Checklist*

It may be difficult for an instructor to be consciously aware of the interactional dynamics in the classroom, while at the same time transmitting the

(*Reprinted from Sex and Gender in the Social Sciences: Reassessing the Introductory Course)

content of the lecture of guiding a discussion. For this reason, the following techniques are suggested to help faculty with an analysis of the interaction in their classes.

A. Classroom Observation

Having a friend, colleague, or teaching assistant observe some of your classes on a random basis can be helpful. Classroom observation can be used to answer questions such as:

1. What is the number of males versus females called on to answer questions?
2. Which students (male or female) participate in class more frequently through answering questions or making comments? Is the number disproportional enough that you should encourage some students to participate more frequently?
3. Do interruptions occur when an individual is talking? If so, who does the interrupting?
4. Is your verbal response to students positive? aversive? encouraging? Is it the same for all students? If not, what is the reason? (Valid reasons occur from time to time for reacting or responding to a particular student in a highly specific manner.)
5. Do you tend to face or address one section of the classroom more than others? Do you establish eye contact with certain students more than others? What are the gestures, postures, or facial expressions used and are they different for men, women, or minority students?

B. Audio Taping of Class Section

A student could tape record some of your class sessions. Self-analysis of the tapes could provide answers to questions such as:

1. Which students do you call by name?
2. What language pattern are you using? Is there a regular use of male referencing? or the generic "he"? or the universal "man"? Are stereotypical assumptions about men and women revealed in your classroom dialogue?
3. Are examples and anecdotes drawn from men's lives only?
4. Can differential patterns of reinforcement be detected from the tapes?

Curriculum Analysis Project for Social Sciences
Student Perception Questionnaire*

Directions: Answer each of the following questions. Give only one answer to each question. Place the number corresponding to your answer on the blank to the left of the question.

_____ 1. Age at present time:
   (1) 17-20
   (2) 21-24
   (3) 25-30
   (4) 31-40
   (5) 41 or more
_____ 2. Citizenship:
   (1) Citizen of the USA
   (2) Noncitizen of the USA
_____ 3. If U.S. citizen, what is your race: (If not U.S. citizen, do not answer.)
   (1) Caucasian (White American)
   (2) Black American
   (3) Hispanic (Mexican-American, Puerto Rican, Cuban, etc.)
   (4) Native American (North American Indian/Alaskan)
   (5) Asian American
_____ 4. Sex of student
   (1) Male
   (2) Female
_____ 5. This course:
   (1) Required for my academic major
   (2) Not in my academic major
_____ 6. Does your instructor know you by name?
   (1) Yes
   (2) No
   (3) Don't know or uncertain
_____ 7. How often do you voluntarily answer questions or contribute to class discussions in this class?
   (1) Never
   (2) One to three times during the course
   (3) An average of once a week

---

* Reprinted from Sex and Gender in the Social Sciences Reassessing the Introductory Course.

(4) An average of two or three times a week

(5) An average of one or more times a day

_____ 8. How often does the instructor call on you or ask you to respond to a question or comment?

(1) Instructor does not call on anyone

(2) One to three times during the course

(3) An average of once a week

(4) An average of two to three times a week

(5) Never

_____ 9. How does the instructor most frequently call on you?

(1) By name

(2) By pointing with hand

(3) By eye contact/looking directly at me

(4) Instructor never calls on me

_____10. Are there times when you raise your hand to ask a question or make a comment but do not get called on by the instructor?

(1) Once or twice

(2) Three or more times

(3) I am called on when I raise my hand

(4) I never raise my hand

_____11. Why do you think the instructor does not call on you when you raise your hand? (Select the one answer which best reflects your opinion.)

(1) Too many students want to respond

(2) Others beat me to it

(3) Instructor does not see or hear me

(4) Instructor ignores me

(5) This situation never occurs

_____12. Are there times when you want to participate in class by asking a question or making a comment but choose not to do so?

(1) Once or twice

(2) Three or more times

(3) Nearly every day

(4) No, because I participate when I want to

(5) I do not want to participate

_____13. If you have wanted to participate in class by asking a question or making a comment but did not do so, what was your reason for not doing so? (Select the one response that most closely corresponds with your feelings.)

(1) Felt insecure, inadequate, or uncertain

(2) Another student asked question or commented first

(3) Too many students in class

(4) Disagreed with instructor but chose not to speak out

(5) This situation never occurs

_____14. In your opinion, which students most frequently participate in class? (Select the one answer that best represents your opinion)

(1) Those who are most knowledgeable or most interested in the subject

(2) Those who are seeking clarification or want more information

(3) Those who are trying to show off or get attention

(4) I have not noticed

_____15. In your opinion, which students ask the most questions and make the most comments in class?

(1) Male student(s)

(2) Female student(s)

(3) Male and female students equally

(4) Have not noticed

_____16. How does the instructor react to the questions you make in class?

(1) Encourages me to question or comment again

(2) Discourages me from commenting or asking a question again

(3) Neither encourages or discourages me

(4) I never participate

_____17. In your opinion, how does the instructor react to opinions and comments given by other students in the class?

(1) Respects the opinions of students in the class

(2) Does not respect the opinions of students in this class

(3) Embarrasses or "puts down" students for their opinions

(4) I did not notice

_____18. Does your instructor use humor or make humorous references that you feel are offensive, embarrassing, or belittling to any individuals or groups?

(1) Never

(2) One time

(3) Occasionally

(4) Frequently

_____19. How often do students articipate in this class by asking questions or making comments?

(1) Never

(2) Rarely

(3) Occasionally

(4) Frequently

Sources for Quotations

Ad Hoc Committee on the Education of Women at Oberlin, "The Education
of Women at Oberlin," Office of the President, Oberlin College, Oberlin, OH, April 1980.

Karen Bogart, Technical Manual for the Institutional Self-Study Guide on Sex
Equity, Appendix C, "Illustrative Problems and Proposed Solutions for
Inequities," American Institutes for Research, Washington, DC 1981
(cited as "Illustrative Problems").

Phyllis Franklin et al., Sexual and Gender Harassment in the Academy: A
Guide for Faculty, Students and Administrators, Commission on the
Status of Women in the Profession, The Modern Language Association
of America, New York, NY, 1981 (cited as MLA).

Ira M. Heyman, Women Students at Berkeley: Views and Data on Possible
Sex Discrimination in Academic Programs, Office of the Chancellor,
University of California, Berkeley, June 1977 (cited as Berkeley).

John F. Noonan, "White Faculty and Black Students; Examining Assumptions and Practices," unpublished paper, The Center for Improving
Teaching Effectiveness, Virginia Commonwealth University, Richmond, VA, 1980 (cited as "Assumptions and Practices").

Project on the Status and Education of Women, "Call for Information on
Classroom Climate Issues," published in the Project's newsletter. On
Campus With Women and in a number of other publications, 1980-81
(cited as Project Call for Information).

Sara Ruddick and Pamela Daniels, eds., Working It Out: 23 Women Writers,
Artists, Scientists and Scholars Talk About Their Lives and Work, Pan-
theon Books, New York, NY, 1977 (cited as Working It Out).

Adelaide Simpson, "A Perspective on the Learning Experiences of Black
Students at VCU," unpublished paper, The Center for Improving
Teaching Effectiveness, Virginia Commonwealth University, Rich-
mond, VA, 1979 (cited as "Learning Experiences").

Frank J. Till, Sexual Harassment: A Report on the Sexual Harassment of
Students, National Advisory Council on Women's Educational Programs, Washington DC, August 1980 (cited as Sexual Harassment).

Women Student's Coalition, "The Quality of Women's Education at Harvard
University: A Survey of Sex Discrimination in the Graduate and Professional Schools," Cambridge, MA, June 1980 (cited as Harvard).

This paper was developed under Grant #G008005198 from the Fund for the Improvement of
Postsecondary Education of the U.S. Department of Education. Opinions expressed here do not

necessarily reflect the position of the policy of the Department of Education, or the Association of American Colleges. The Project is funded by Carnegie Corporation of New York and The Ford Foundation. Additional copies of this paper may be obtained for $3.00 from the Project on the Status and Education of Women, Association of American Colleges, 1818 R St., NW, Washington, DC 20009, (202) 387-1300. (A list of all Project publications is available free with a stamped, self-addressed envelope.) Bulk rates are available.

Appendix II

Resource Tools for Parents, Teachers, and Kids to Liberate the Curriculum

The following article is reprinted from Eileen Abrams, Anne Chapman, Lauri Johnson, and Sally Smith, "Tools for School: A *Ms.* Checklist for Parents, Teachers, and Kids." *Ms. Magazine*, October 1982, pp. 81-84. Used by permission.

Preschool

To begin at the beginning, consider the books, games, puzzles, and toys for pre-kindergarten children. Despite some gains, most manufactured materials still depict stereotyped, rigid female and male roles. However, there are some excellent, inexpensive materials that reflect the range of options open to women and men, as well as the ethnic and racial diversity of people in the United States. *Books for Today's Children*, by Jeanne Bracken and Sharon Wigutoff (1979), provides a guide to more than 200 nonsexist books for the very young. (*The Feminist Press*, Box 334, Old Westbury, N.Y. 11568.

Teaching Aids

Teacher's guides accompany most of the curriculum resources, which have been developed by, and are available from, the Nonsexist Child Development Project of the Women's Action Alliance. (370 Lexington Ave., New York, N.Y. 10017; 212-532-8330)

Our Community Helpers Play People; My Family Play People. Each set contains 12 full-color sturdy cardboard figures with plastic stands. Community Helpers include six men, six women—each representing occupational roles. My Family Play People are black and white extended families dressed in practical, contemporary clothes. *(Produced by Milton Bradley.)*

People at Work. Twenty-four black-and-white photographs. Women and men in nontraditional roles. For classroom display and teacher/child-made books. *Produced by Instructo/McGraw-Hill.)*

Men in Nurturing Roles. Eight black-and-white photographs of men interacting with infants and young children. Poster of child with grandfather included.

Mainstreaming Photographs. These are materials from the Women's Action Alliance's Project REED (Resources on Educational Equity for the Disabled). Eight black-and-white photographs.

Mainstreamed disabled children in nonsexist school settings, plus poster of interracial family with a mother in a wheelchair.

Puzzles

Judy "Occupational Series." Eight sturdy wooden puzzles depict women and men at work. Some women in non-traditional jobs. Multiracial, easy to do. *Judy Puzzles, 310 North 2nd Street, Minneapolis, Minn. 55401.)*

Galt "Just Like Us." Six attractive color-photograph jigsaw puzzles show girls and boys in active and quiet play. Puzzles range in difficulty, but for the more experienced child.

Galt "Dressing and Undressing Puzzle." Wooden puzzle of girl and boy in peasant clothes. When pieces are removed, anatomically correct bodies are revealed. Easy to do. *(Galt.)*

Childcraft "Nurturing Puzzles." Eight puzzles depict men, women, and children hugging, bathing, feeding, nursing, playing, teaching, walking, fishing. *(Women's Action Alliance, distributed by Childcraft.)*

Play Materials

Brother and sister. Anatomically correct vinyl dolls. 11 inches, dressed in diaper, hooded jacket, with bottle. White only. *(Teft.)*

Occupational Hats. Six sturdy plastic hats for the dress-up corner. *(Childcraft.)*

Stethoscope. An alternative to plastic doctor's and nurse's kits. Sturdy metal and rubber. It really works. *(Bowles.)*

Films

Beginning Concepts: People Who Work (Unit 1). Preschool kit containing five 10-minute color filmstrips with tape cassette (or LP record). In each filmstrip, a worker describes her or his job. Of these simple, beautifully photographed presentations, the best by far is *Say Ah!*—Dr. Helen Rodriguez Trias's description of her day as a pediatrician. *(Scholastic Book Services, 904 Sylvan Ave., Englewood Cliffs, N.J. 07632; call 1-800-631-1586 for educational discount).*

A Nonsexist Curriculum for Early Childhood. Full-color filmstrip shows development of a nonsexist emphasis in multicultural daycare selling. Good training film for parents, teachers. *(The Women's Action Alliance; 20 minutes; sale only.)*

The Sooner the Better. Beautifully photographed, upbeat film explores the problems of stereotyping in a variety of preschool settings. Parents and teachers talk about their concerns. *(Third Eye Films, 12 Arrow St, Cambridge, Mass. 02138; 27 minutes; purchase or rental.)*

The Time Has Come. A companion film designed for parents of preschool children. Explores ways culture and the media inhibit or expand a child's growth.

(Third Eye Films; running time 20 minutes, purchase or rental).

Elementary and Middle Schools

Awareness Activities

TABS: Aids for Ending Sexism in School. A quarterly magazine that is probably the best single source of practical nonsexist ideas for the classroom. Each issue contains lesson plans, a biography of a women of achievement, curriculum reviews, and two posters. *(Organization for Equal Education of the Sexes, Inc., 744 Carroll St., Brooklyn, N.Y. 11215.)*

Boys and Girls Together: Non-Sexist Activities for Elementary Schools, by Mary Alexander Cain (1980), provides imaginative, easy-to-use lesson plans in all subject areas. Noteworthy are activities that help teachers examine their "hidden curriculum"—the way girls and boys are socialized into traditional sex roles by classroom interactions. Also includes practical teaching aids such as story starters, task cards, word searches, crossword puzzles, and nonsexist games. *(Learning Publications, Inc., P.O. Box 1326, Holmes Beach, Fla. 33509.)*

Nonsexist Curricular Materials for Elementary Schools, by Laurie Olsen (1977). Collection of checklists, bibliographies, a student workbook, and model curricular units that provide consciousness-raising activities for upper elementary students. Also included is a Susan B. Anthony Day kit with biographical sketches of famous women. The loose-leaf format makes to easy to reproduce for classroom use. *(The Feminist Press, Box 334, Old Westbury, N.Y., 11568.)*

A Curriculum Guide to Women's Studies for the Middle School, Grades 5 to 9, by Eileen Abrams (1981), is a how-to-guide for teaching about women in history and society. The 20 lesson plans include activity supplement sheets that can be reproduced for student use. The curriculum guide can be used as an entire course, or single activities can be excerpted for use in related courses. Easily adapted for use with students in lower or upper grades. *(The Feminist Press.)*

Student Textbooks

History
Women's Rights, by Janet Stevenson. Well-illustrated history of the movement for women's suffrage in the United States. *(Franklin Watts, 1972)*

Black Foremothers, by Dorothy Sterling. Biographies of Ellen Craft, Ida B. Wells, and Mary Church Terrell. *(The Feminist Press, 1978).*

Career Education
New Women in Art and Dance; New Women in Entertainment; New Women in Media; New Women in Medicine; New Women in Politics; New Women in Social Sciences, by Kathleen Bowman. Series of books on contemporary career women; illustrated with photographs *(Creative Education, Inc., P.O. Box 227, Mankato, Minn. 56001; 1976.)*

What Can She Be? by Esther Goldreich and Gloria Goldreich. Series of eight books that follow a woman through a day in her career; includes such occupations as police officer, lawyer, architect, veterinarian, newscaster; illustrated with photographs. *(Lothrop, Lee, and Shepard, New York, N.Y.; 1972-1979.)*

Nonprint Materials
(See also listings under "Preschool.")

Supersisters. A feminist answer to baseball cards. Each of the 72 cards in the set features a photograph of a contemporary woman on one side, and information about the achievements on the other. Teacher's guide included. *(Supersisters, 230 Park Ave., Dept. T. N.Y., N.Y. 10017)*

Great Women: A Biographical Card Game, Set 1. Foremothers: Set 2, Founders and Firsts: Set 3. Poets and Writers. Rummy-type card game includes picture cards and fact cards for the women featured. *(Great Women Cards, 310 East 46 St., Box 1, New York, N.Y. 10017.)*

Films

Happy To Be Me (1979). Candid interviews with K-12 New York City students reveal their views on topics such as the differences between males and females, working women, male homemakers, and the Women's Movement. A good introduction for both elementary and secondary students on sex-role expectations. *(Arthur Mokin Productions, Inc, 2900 McBride Lane, Santa Rosa, Calif. 95401; call 707-542-4868)*

Once Upon a Choice (1981). A humorous, original fairy tale. When an unconventional princess is faced with the dilemma of deciding which prince to marry, she decides to take a year off and travel instead. For elementary and junior high students. *(New Day Films, P.O. Box 315, Franklin Lakes, N.J. 07417; call 201-891-9240)*

Other Women, Other Work (1973). This documentary showing women working in nontraditional jobs is worth a thousand words. Profiles include a veterinarian, truck driver, pilot, carpenter, roofer, and television reporter. They discuss the problems and satisfactions they find in their work. *(Churchill Films, 662 North Robertson Blvd., Los Angeles, Calif. 90069; call 213-657-5110)*

"She's Nobody's Baby," a Peabody Award-winning documentary produced by Ms., is now available in two half-hour color segments with a teaching guide from ABC Wide World of Learning. "She's Nobody's Baby" documents the changing images of American women in the 20th century and the struggle to take control of our own lives. Narrated by Alan Alda and Marlo Thomas. (ABC Wide World of Learning, 1330 Sixth Ave., New York, N.Y. 10019.

Curriculum Resources

Careers:

The House That Jill and Jack Built. A challenging career-education program developed by the Berkeley Women's Studies Program and Advocates for Women that teaches K-3 girls and boys basic carpentry skills. Lesson plans, excellent illustrations, and photographs provide step-by-step instructions on basic skills like sawing and hammering. Available for the cost of postage only, the manual provides a good beginning for an activity-centered nonsexist curriculum. *(Contact Susan Groves, 99 Plaza Dr., Berkeley, Calif. 94705.)* Among other materials produced by the Berkeley Women's Studies Program that are available for the cost of duplication and postage are fourth-to-sixth grade-lesson plans on exclusion; biographies and essays on working women, Chicanas, and Asian Women; a unit on slavery; and a bicycle repair manual for students).

Careers To Explore, developed by the Girl Scouts, highlights more than 40 women who are working successfully in traditional and nontraditional jobs. The conversational style and photographs help personalize this career education program for first-to-fifth-grade students. *From Dreams to Reality: Adventures in Careers* provides more awareness activities for secondary students. There is also a packet of career cards. *(Girl Scouts of the U.S.A., National Equipment Service, 830 Third Ave., New York, N.Y. 10022; prices: "Careers To Explore"—Student Book—2813, "From Dreams to Reality: Adventures in Careers"—2814, "Career Cards."*

Many Thousand Words—Work Pictures Book. Collection of 8-inch-by-10-inch laminated photographs of children and adults involved in nontraditional activities. Ideal for language experience activities and bulletin board displays. Preschool and elementary level. *(Project Equality, Highline School Dist. 401, 15675 Ambaum Blvd. S.W., Seattle, Wash. 98166.)*

Math:

Math for Girls and Other Problem Solvers, by Diane Downie, Twila Slesnick, and Jean Kerr Stenmark (1981), offers fun, creative activities to win over six-to 14-year-old girls who are scared, mystified, or bored by math. Games stress cooperation, and puzzles and problems challenge students, but don't overwhelm them. Awareness activities encourage girls to consider math- and science-related careers. Teachers will find that Math for Girls makes learning math joyful and exciting for both girls and boys. *(Lawrence Hall of Science, University of California, Berkeley, Calif. 94720. Attn: Equals.)*

Social Studies:

Winning Justice for All is a social studies and language arts curriculum, developed by the Council on Interracial Books for Children to create an awareness of institutional sexism and racism. This curriculum guide uses biographical sketches and primary source material to honestly depict the struggles of white women and people of color for full and equal rights. Also includes three filmstrips, "The Secret of Good As Me," "Equal Change," and "Fighting Discrimination," Designed for the fifth and sixth grade, the reading level and conceptual difficulty make it easily adaptable for use with junior high students. *(Council on Interracial Books for Children, 1841 Broadway, New York, N.Y. 10023. Cost of entire program, teacher's manual.)*

In Search of Our Past: Units in Women's History, developed by the Berkeley Unified School District (1980), represents a pioneering effort to create a multi-ethnic women's history for junior high school students. Short stories, essays, poetry, and letters are used to portray women's involvement in U.S. and world history, *(WEEA Publishing Center/EDC, 55 Chapel St., Newton, Mass. 02160.)*

High School

A comprehensive guide to just about everything of possible use to high school teachers in this subject area is Gleanings from a Wide Field: U.S. Resources Focusing on Women That Could Be Made Useful in the High School Classroom, by Anne Chapman. A review of bibliographies, abstracts, curricula, periodicals, and services that both describes and evaluates. *(Resources for Feminist Research, Department of Sociology, Ontario Institute for Studies in Education, 252 Bloor St., W., Toronto, Ontario, Canada M5S1V6.)*

Seven interdisciplinary courses in women's studies are described in Breaking the Silence, developed by the Goddard-Cambridge Graduate Program in Social change (1979). The "short and basic" women's history unit is unusual in its concentration on the experience of "neglected" (Third World, ethnic, working-class) women. *(WEEA Publishing Center/EDC, 55 Chapel Street, Newton, Mass. 02160).*

Socialization, the female role, sexuality, and work are covered in Changing Learning, Changing Lives, by Barbara Gates, Susan Klaw, and Adria Steinberg (1979). Developed for working-class women but valuable in almost any setting. Unusually imaginative and detailed teaching strategies accompany more than 100 activities and suggested student readings. *(233 pages; from the Feminist Press, Box 334, Old Westbury, N.Y. 11568)*

Integrating women into history and social studies courses is the focus of Approaches to Women's History, edited by Anne Chapman (1979). Seven interdisciplinary curriculum units present substantial content about U.S. women's history. Detailed lesson plans, activities, chronological charts, more than 50 brief, interest-provoking documents, and an annotated resource list accompany the units. *(From Publications, American Historical Association, 400 A St., S.E., Washington, D.C. 20003).*

A cross-cultural study of women in African, Chinese, African-American societies is effectively presented in Sources of Strength: Women and Culture. Created by the Far West Laboratory for Educational Research and Development (1979), it provides background in the history and culture of each society, imaginative teaching strategies, and suggested learning materials. *(701 pages; separate bibliography, 171 pages; two oral history tapes from WEEA Publishing Center/EDC, 55 Chapel St., Newton, Mass. 02160).*

Two resource books for Chicana studies, for use in U.S. history and multicultural courses, are Profile of the Mexican American Woman, by Martha Cotera (1976), and Chicana Studies Curriculum Guide, Grades 9-12, by Odlamira L. Garcia (1978). Both are teacher-oriented. Profile provides a narrative of Chicana history, a socioeconomic profile of Chicanas, a discussion of contemporary Chicana accomplishments, and a bibliography. The Guide covers the Chicana in history, society, literature, and the arts and outlines objectives, activities, readings, and audiovisual materials for each topic. *("Profile" 367 pages; "Guide" 150 pages—from National Education Laboratory Publishers, Inc., 813 Airport Blvd., Austin, Tex. 78702)*

"Women in World Cultures," a series suitable for ninth- and tenth-graders, includes volumes on women in the U.S.S.R., in traditional and modern Africa, China, India, Israel, and Islam, each by Susan Hill Gross and Marjorie Wall Bingham (1980). Sensitive to issues of class and ethnicity, the easy-to-read narrative texts are liberally laced with quotations from original sources. The teacher's guide is brief but sound on concepts, routine on activities and testing. *(Books are typically some 120 pages; guides, 20, from GEM Publications, Inc., 411 Mallalieu Dr., Hudson, Ws. 54016; 715-386-5662)*

A textbook that spans Colonial times to the 1970s, We, the American Women, by Beth Millstein and Jeanne Bodin (1977), is chronologically arranged, well illustrated, attractive, and substantial. Less so are the separate, rather elementary activity book and the teacher's guide with routine discussion questions, projects, and a 153-item annotated bibliography. *(From Science Research Associates, 15 N. Wacker Dr., Chicago, Ill. 60606)*

Effects of language on the self-image and roles of women and men is the focus of Changing Words in a Changing World, by Alleen Pace Nilsen (1980). With its useful instructor's guide, this appealing curriculum unit would work well in almost any high school English or language arts course. (68 pages, teacher's guide, 32 pages from WEEA Publishing Center/EDC, 55 Chapel St., Newton, Mass. 02160)

Varied activities to encourage young women's interest and competence in mathematics are featured in Equals, by Alice Kaseberg, Nancy Kreinberg, and Diane Downie (1980). Although it is primarily a handbook for organizing workshops for educators, most of the projects, games, teaching strategies, and resources are directly applicable in high school classes. *(134 pages; from Lawrence Hall of Science, University of California, Berkeley, Calif. 94720. Attention: Equals)*

Resources

Sex Equity Handbook for Schools, by Myra and David Sadker (1981). Destined to become a desk reference for all teachers committed to nonsexist education, this handbook combines research on sex bias in instructional materials with the classroom model lesson plans for K-12 students, and a resource directory of sex-equity organizations. The chapter "The Two-Edged Sword: Men as Victims" is one of the few sources of learning activities to combat male sex-role stereotyping. *(Longman, Inc., 19 West 44 St., New York, N.Y. 10036)*

Guidelines for Selecting Bias-Free Textbooks and Storybooks, by the Council on Interracial Books for Children (1980). Recommended as mind-stretching reading and a model of respect for human dignity and diversity, this clear, concise, and thoughtful guide explains how to detect bias and what to do about it. *(Council on Interracial Books for Children, 1841 Broadway, New York, N.Y. 10023)*

How High the Sky? How Far the Moon? (1979). This teaching aid is designed to expand students' interests in scientific and technical careers. Outstanding accomplishments of women in science are highlighted in seven short biographies and supplemented by taped interviews. Extensive information about careers in science and an annotated listing of print and audio-visual materials appropriate for each grade level are provided. *(WEAA Publishing Cente/EDC, 55 Chapel St., Newton, Mass. 02160)*

Spotlight on Sex Equity: A Filmography (1982). Susan Morris Shaffer has compiled a concise, well-annotated bibliography of audio-visual materials appropriate for the classroom. Categories include sex roles, career development, sex equity in athletics, and ethnic women in history. Complete ordering information is provided. *(The Mid-Atlantic Center for Sex Equity, The American University, Foxhall Square Bldg., Suite 252, 3301 New Mexico Ave., N.W., Washington, D.C. 20016).*

Positive Images: Non-Sexist Films for Young People (1976), by Susan Wengraf and Linda Artel. Critical reviews of more than 400 films, videotapes, filmstrips, and slide shows for preschool through high school. *(Booklegger Press, 555 29 St., San Francisco, Calif. 94131)*

Eileen Abrams, who teaches in Philadelphia, is a middle school specialist: Anne Chapman teaches at Western Reserve Academy in Hudson, Ohio; Lauri Johnson, whose speciality is elementary school, and Sally Smith, early childhood, both work at the Feminist Press on a project for the New York City Board of Education. This panel of experts was coordinated by Florence Howe, publisher of the Feminist Press.

Part II

Identity
Creation

Surnaming: The Struggle for Personal Identity

Joyce Penfield

For at least three centuries, women have faced sexist customs and traditions in their struggle for the right to name or rename themselves. The author suggests that surname changes in fact have participated in the formation/construction of women's identity because they represent self-definition in its most symbolically meaningful form. Using data from her pilot survey of women who had created totally new surnames in the 1970s, Penfield provides insight into how women have created new surnames and why.

My Name

my name is me
a mirror
i can look in
proudly
head held high
it bears none
of my hairy
scary past
it remembers no one
who has held
or hurt me

i found my name
in a book
when i discovered
i'd been misled
i found it in myself
when i discovered
i am beautiful
i gave it to myself
a token
of my esteem   by *Pat Malcolm*

The use of last names or surnames in Western culture is a particularly interesting topic for women's studies. Nothing is more personal and more closely related to identity than one's name—be it surname or given (first) name. And equally, nothing is more symbolically attached to one's social image than one's name. Yet women in the United States have had to struggle continuously to obtain the legal right to name themselves or rename themselves for as long as this country has existed. At critical points in women's history, the legal right to use the name of one's choice has been a key issue at women's rights conventions as far back as 1848, when women signed the Declaration of Sentiments with their own first name (Stannard 1977:271).

The basic civil liberty to call oneself what one chooses has been an aspect of gender equity debated for over two centuries and is still in the process of clarification. Since surnaming practices parallel the historical struggle for gender equity, the critical examination of such efforts reminds us of the gains which have been achieved, as well as the struggles that remain. More significantly, an examination of surnaming practices among women today can provide insight into women's view of themselves. It also offers a key to uncovering a specific aspect of language use. A name is a powerful symbol, and one might argue that a name helps to create the bond between one's self-image and one's social image even more than other aspects of language. *It is argued here that surname changes made by contemporary women are not merely a reflection of changes in identity but rather an actual participating part of the process of identity-creation itself.*

Historical Context

In her book, *Mrs. Man*, Stannard (1977) documents with thoroughness the historical struggle of women to achieve what she calls "nominal sexual equality" or simply the right to name themselves. The title of the book itself refers to the common practice of taking a husband's surname at marriage and thereby becoming "Mrs. Man." In the words of one nineteenth-century woman, "A woman was expected to achieve her identity not by developing herself but by becoming a *man/wife*, i.e., marrying her ideal self" (Stannard 1977:11). Marriage was a means by which a woman took on a male identity and consequently submerged or buried her own identity. Somewhat akin to current practice in some folk societies of the world, a name was believed to be identical with a person's self, and a change of name at some initiation ceremony transformed a person into a new self. For nineteenth-century women, this ceremony was the wedding and the "new self" was Mrs. /*husband's first name*/ *husband's surname*—e.g., Mrs. John Blake. It was obvious that by giving up their female names and acquiring male ones, wives accepted anonymous identities.

An obvious disadvantage of always accepting a husband's surname at marriage and losing one's prior surname—whether the surname was given at birth (a birthname) or the surname was acquired from a previous marriage—lay in the fact that women could pass through many identity changes as their husbands died and they remarried. This might have caused few problems for housewives whose social identity involved only a small group of friends and relatives, but for those women whose identity was attached to a profession where name recognition was important, such practices were delimiting. Women who acquired a professional identity in public, such as actresses and authors, and whose surname became well-known soon discovered the disadvantages of changing their surname at marriage. They were the first to realize that part of their identity was their name and erasing their surname meant erasing their professional trademark and the remarkable achievements with which they were associated.

The solution to the conflict between maintaining a professional surname and conforming to social custom resulted in the pattern of triple names. Two well-known examples are the ardent feminist, Elizabeth Cady Stanton (Cady = birthname) (Stanton = husband's birthname), and the well-known author, Harriet Beecher Stowe (Beecher = birthname) (Stowe = husband's birthname). And so the custom of retaining a patronymic naming system was adapted to feminist purposes of the time. This change in surnaming practice symbolized a woman's new sense of herself as an individual and not merely as a wife (Stannard 1977:83). Of course, the triple name solution still meant that the actual surname used remained the husband's; and for a woman who had more than one husband in her lifetime, the previous husband's surname replaced her birthname altogether, thereby deleting her original identity. An alternative solution used to preserve identity was the use of hyphenated birthnames, thereby creating a double surname (e.g., if Martha Blake married John Green, she called herself "Martha Blake-Green.") A few braver souls reversed the order to "Martha Green-Blake." The advantage of a hyphenated surname was that a woman could hold on to part of her name in case of marriage or divorce without losing her identity.

A few feminists in the mid-nineteenth century, like Lucy Stone, rejected all of the previous alternatives to surnaming. To them, having a double surname or a hyphenated name meant having a dual identity: a personal/professional one and a marital one. Using a husband's surname still conveyed the notion of being an extension of one's husband or, to some, another part of a man's property. No matter how extensive a woman's achievements, she was still required to be identified with her husband by virtue of her surname. This practice often meant having more than one identity throughout life.

The option of using *only* one's birthname and maintaining this practice even after marriage was debated in 1848 at the Women's Rights Convention during a discussion of equality in marriage. While the men present agreed to the principle of "equal wages for equal work," they felt that equality in marriage was sacrilegious and therefore impossible. Elizabeth Cady Stanton made the following plea for retention by married women of their birthnames:

When a slave escapes from a Southern plantation, he at once takes a name as the first step in liberty—the first assertion of individual identity. A woman's dignity is equally involved in a life-long name, to mark her individuality. We cannot overestimate the demoralizing effect on woman herself, to say nothing of society at large, for her to consent thus to merge her existence so wholly in that of another (Stannard 1977:95).

It is clear from the above that while profeminist males were ready to accept the principle of gender equality in the economic realm, they were unprepared to accept it in more personal domains, namely, marriage. It is no surprise then that when Lucy Stone, in 1879, in the state of Massachusetts, tried to vote using her birthname only, she was prevented from doing so even though no law required a wife to use her husband's surname when voting. Her personal reason for refusing to use her husband's surname was profoundly significant: "My name is a symbol of my identity which must not be lost." Lucy Stone is known in feminist history for her insistence on keeping her birthname in both private and public life. Years later, when a group of women organized in 1921 to retain their birthnames after marriage, they called themselves the Lucy Stone League.

The issue of gender equity in surnaming arose again almost three decades later when in 1948 a *new* Lucy Stone League was formed which dedicated itself not merely to advancing the cause of a married woman's right to continue using her own name but also to fighting against sex discrimination in general. In fact, the new League was a forerunner of the National Organization for Women (NOW). By the 1960s, it had become less and less involved in the right of women to use the name of their choice, because by then it was a legal fact that no state except Hawaii had a statute compelling women to adopt their husbands' names. As Stannard (1977:264) points out, the new Lucy Stone League was ignoring policies imposed by case decisions, Attorneys General opinions, and voter and motor vehicle registration laws which perpetually refused to grant married women the right to use their birthnames or the surname of their choice. This trend continued in the 1960s; even as the National Organization for Women (NOW) was formed, the right of married women to a name of their own was not among those rights being demanded.

But by the 1970s NOW was forced to deal with the name issue as a result of pressure brought to bear at a grass-roots level, as many women throughout the United States decided they did not want to be nominally one with their husbands. Thousands of women decided to retain their birthnames at marriage or retain them after having been married. A few hundred women even created entirely new surnames, unaware that others were attempting to do likewise. The most important point about this transformation is that these women acted individually rather than collectively. For the most part, their motivation was primarily personal rather than ideological. Unlike the previous cases in women's history, these women were not ardent feminists. Indeed, many of these individuals did not align themselves with the ideology of, nor identify with, Women's Liberation. It is ironic, then, that relatives and public officials often took offense at these individuals' personal decision to name themselves, viewing it as militant, feminist, and radical.

As women began using their birthnames after marriage or attempted to return to their birthnames after taking their husbands' birthnames during a part of their marriage, they were immediately faced with just how permanent, enduring, and sexist the social custom of adopting the husband's name was. For it was here that the male-dominated social system showed itself most clearly. Because official agencies often refused to permit women to use or return to their birthnames, women began first to introduce their surname choices in social and professional domains where they could rarely be prevented from calling themselves what they chose. Sometimes they had to endure the negative reactions of family members, such as in-laws and mothers. But to most women who broke with the traditional patronymic system of surnaming, the question of identity was much more important than the negative attitudes of family members or colleagues.

Even though the common-law right to change one's surname without intent to defraud existed in various states during the 1970s, not only were many women unfamiliar with regulations governing surname changes, but agencies and official institutions—and even trial judges—were unaware of this common-law right. As a result, agencies and official institutions repeatedly denied women the right to use the surname of their choice on documents and official records, such as passports, mortgages, driver's licenses, deeds, and grade transcripts. This was especially true in those cases where a surname change was involved. This condition still exists today, in some degree, in a number of states. For some women, the inconsistency in laws, policy, and practice resulted in their temporarily having a shared identity, as reflected by a chosen surname for personal, social, and professional uses and another surname—that of their father or husband—for official use. The fact is that they continued their struggle individually to maintain the basic civil liberty of naming themselves, because, as one woman put it, "Part of my identity was my name." (Wen 1983: 60).

Several outcomes may be identified as a result of the attempts of women of the 1970s and 1980s to achieve this "basic civil liberty." The first is the effect that the struggle had on those most personally involved— the surname changers themselves. It may be suggested that some women became involved in issues of gender discrimination and the women's movement in general as a result of their personal decision to change their surname. The difficulties they encountered with official institutions and the emotional responses of members of the public made them more and more aware of just how sexist society really was. Idealism tempered with cold reality propelled them to not only participate in this facet of women's rights but to become leaders in the overall struggle for equality.[1] Yet another product of the surname struggle is related to social change and legal definitions. As centers for women were established, more women learned how to establish the name of their choice—in or out of court. As women chose to establish their name choice in court, and as trial judges continually denied them this right because of their own prejudices or whims, appeals were made and more and more cases were successful at affirming this basic civil liberty. Cases involving surname changes were almost always reversed without the necessity of appealing to the higher courts. As a consequence, the legal right to choose one's surname gradually emerged as a reality.

Legal Strides

No one has challenged the legal aspects of the patronymic naming system more than Priscilla Ruth MacDougall, an attorney with the Wisconsin Education Association Council. She notes that all states recognize the common-law right of any adult to adopt any name for nonfraudulent or noncriminal purposes without the necessity of obtaining a court order. Moreover, no state requires a married woman to use her husband's name or a divorced woman to use her ex-husband's name. She writes, "Women's right to retain or change their names irrespective of their marital status on the same basis as men in the United States is all but a universally recognized legal right" (MacDougall 1981:7).

In 1974, MacDougall founded one of the only existing clearinghouses in the United States on surname options and legal issues—The Center for a Woman's Own Name, located in Barrington, Illinois. She clarified the Center's initial position as follows:

It is the position of the Center for a Woman's Own Name that the name(s) a woman chooses to use is her *own* name. It may be the name given her at birth, a name assumed during childhood, assumed at marriage, assumed at a previous marriage, a hyphenated name or a name made up by herself at any time (Center for a Woman's Own Name 1975 Supplement:6).

The need for such a clearinghouse has been very great. For example, in the past ten years the Center has sold over twenty-four thousand booklets entitled

"Booklet for Women who Wish to Determine Their Own Names After Marriage."

For more than ten years MacDougall has argued in various court cases throughout the country for women's legal right to their own surname. More specifically, she has insisted on the common-law right to change a surname in contrast to a court-ordered change[2]. The legal turning point in this struggle came in 1982, when the Alabama Supreme Court unanimously agreed to overturn its earlier decision and support women's right to use their own surnames after marriage[3]. To date, a vast amount of progress has been made, comprising court cases, legislative actions, and Attorneys General opinions. One may affirm MacDougall's conclusion that "No woman has to go to court to have her name changed (MacDougall 1981:7).

A surnaming issue even more unsettled legally, and one yet to be resolved in most states, is the mother's right to give her child a surname which may be different from the father's. The cases most typically at issue are those in which parents disagree—usually after a divorce—over the child's surname and the mother has custody of a child who had initially been given the father's surname. MacDougall argues that just as common law never required married women to use their husbands' surnames, neither has it required parents to name their children with any particular surname. She views the issue as parallel to the basic civil right for women. Some states have followed this viewpoint. For example, the California Supreme Court in 1980 overruled all previous cases or policies not permitting common-law rights in surnaming children. However, for the most part, women's naming rights of children are still being litigated in most states (Zivanovic 1982:10).

In regard to the issue of child surnaming, the state of New Jersey passed legislation which would allow a mother to give her child any surname she wished. Basically, the bill (NJ-2119) allows the mother to put the name she thinks appropriate on the birth certificate, even if the co-parent (biological father) refuses to admit parentage. Such a bill not only allows for single mothers to choose the surname they wish for their children but also permits a married woman to name a man other than her husband on the birth certificate (Sunday Star Leger, 1983:52).

The Personal Struggle

Despite the vast legal territory gained in surnaming rights, women continue to encounter difficulties in naming themselves, both in common law and court decrees. Even technical experts, namely, lawyers, are often uninformed about legal matters regarding surnaming. Male lawyers who typically carry a male view of the world and, consequently, of law may advise clients incorrectly.

In 1982, the author conducted an open-ended pilot survey (see Question-naire) of a select few feminists who had created or re-created their names. They were asked to indicate how they had tried to change their surname and what difficulties they had encountered, if any. Of special interest in the survey were the personal reasons for surname changing and the bases on which they chose their new surname. The primary focus of the questionnaire was on the adoption of created surnames.

Only a handful of questionnaires (twenty) were returned, but even this small number indicates the amount of inconsistency encountered in dealing with agencies and institutions throughout the country which often follow customary procedures historically founded on sexism. Most of those who responded to the questionnaire had made their surname change in the late 1970s. Those who had tried a common-law change invariably had encoun-tered resistance from official agencies as they tried to change their name on documents. Many women had convinced agencies that a common-law change was legal by getting the Attorney General to write a letter endorsing the procedure or by sending the agency a notarized Affidavit of Name Change[4].

Even so, some agencies—e.g., university transcript offices or Social Securi-ty—continued to refuse a surname change without a court order. Those who did follow the procedure of applying to the courts mentioned few problems in dealing with agencies thereafter. But obtaining the court order was often linked entirely to the whims of the trial judge. Male judges frequently revealed their bias by denying surname changes on the grounds that "it would be bad for your children to have a different last name; they would be confused" or "Why do you choose this name, are you ashamed of your heritage?"

Many responses to the questionnaire reflected an awareness of the conser-vative and sexist reaction of trial judges. A well-known feminist scholar who obtained a court-ordered surname change admitted that "at the time I took the easy way out, and said the change was to make it easier to pronounce and spell, rather than for the real feminist reasons motivating me." Several respon-dents mentioned that their lawyers cautioned them not to make surname changes for ideological reasons or feminist causes, for the courts would deny them. Even female lawyers provided such counsel, as one respondent wrote: "The only thing she advised me of was not to seem too *political* because the entire success of the name change depended solely on the judge." This advice may not have been misplaced, since this respondent mentioned that the judge asked her if her parents knew that she was changing her name—even though she was twenty-five years old at the time and had been supporting herself since age nineteen.

What patterns did women follow in selecting their new names? The survey uncovered a variety of creative methods which women used in creating sur-names. Some combined part of their father's birthname and part of their mother's birthname. Others chose one or more syllables of their father's birthname to create an entirely new surname, or added middle names to existing birthnames. Still others abandoned their birthnames altogether and used their middle names as new surnames. Some women rejected all portions of their birthname, as well as their given name. Several fabricated new names after months of soul-searching for words which symbolized their new identity in encapsulated form. A few had rather mystical associations with the choice of their surnames. One, for example, mentioned that her choice came purely from her imagination, "as if descended from another level of (my) consciousness."

Yet despite all of the problems that women have encountered, the struggle to change surnames has continued for thousands of women around the country. Most of the women surveyed are perhaps somewhat unique, since they chose to CREATE a new surname. In this sense, they may be the leaders of a new trend in women's surnaming practices. Their decision not to use the birthname of any male (be it their husband or father) but to CREATE entirely new surnames propels women toward a new sense of identity. This may be contrasted with the sense of identity mentioned by Stannard. For these women, surnames were more than a part of individual identity; indeed, they played a key role in the formation of a new self. One respondent underlined this conclusion by noting that "To me it [a surname change] felt like claiming my own identity." To all of the women in the survey, the old adage "you are who you say you are" rings true. And as they decided who they were and changed their surnames accordingly, traditional society was forced to accept their definition of themselves.[5]

Conclusion

For at least three centuries now, women have struggled to answer the simple question "What's in a name?" with the answer "My identity." Although their answer has remained invariably the same, it has been translated into different surnaming practices from one point in history to another. However, the underlying issue captured so well by Lucy Stone's words has remained: "My name is the symbol of my identity." Women of today, women of the past, and women of the future will continue to struggle with this overriding issue—one of self-definition in its most meaningful form. The conflict between women and the courts or women and institutions in using the surname of their choice exemplifies a significant struggle—the conflict between women's definition of self and society's definition of them, which is too often based on sexist customs and traditions. In many senses, women's struggle to define themselves by selecting the surname of their choice has resulted in a gradual social change which began at a highly personal level. This essay has illustrated how customs involving language use began at the individual level and were initiated by women for highly personal and individual reasons. Women are changing customs involving language use and, consequently, forming a new social image of themselves.

There are some important theoretical lessons to be learned from the surnaming struggles of women in the past two decades. Perhaps it can no longer be argued simplistically that language is only a REFLECTION of social change and can never itself be a motivator of change. Surnaming struggles should force us to reconceptualize the relationship between language use and social change. Surnaming is but one example where patterns of language usage have preceded social change. Society has been forced to change its patterns of language use as women demanded that they be "called what they wish to be called." All of this has happened despite society's resistance against changing many of its attitudes towards women. Taken in this newer theoretical perspective, the implications for women are obvious. Perhaps the lesson is that women should recognize the need to first liberate themselves and their use of language in everyday life before demanding a similar response from society.

Questionnaire

Dear Colleague,

I am currently preparing an article on SURNAME CHANGING practices of women in the U.S. or women residing in the U.S. I am interested in the various ways in which women have changed their last name other than the traditional adopting of their father's or husband's surname. Could you please take a few minutes to supply as much information as possible regarding your own surname change. Thanks.

1. If you have not personally changed your surname, do you know someone else who has done so that I might contact:

Name _____ Address _____

2. Do you use a surname which is NOT that of your father or husband? In what circumstances do you do so? Explain.

3. How was your changed surname (non-traditional method) arrived at or composed? PLEASE EXPLAIN AND ILLUSTRATE (two names combined, part deletion, addition of a syllable or ending, hyphenation, etc.)

4. Was or is your SURNAME CHANGE carried out through legal means (the courts)? If so, in what state?

5. What LEGAL difficulties did you encounter in making your surname change? (Did the lawyer advise you of restrictions in doing this?)

6. May I have permission to quote your case and name as described above? _____ yes _____ no

   If you don't want me to quote your name, may I use the general information mentioned above in my article without citing your own personal surname? _____ yes _____ no

7. Additional comments of relevance:

   Do you know of any scholarly references on the above topic which I might consult? individuals?

Notes

1. See pp. 124-125 of this essay, which summarize results of a brief open-ended survey of women who created their surnames. Most women commented that the problems they encountered in using their surnames had launched them into fighting more openly for women's rights or made them even more ardent political activists for women's rights.

2. To make a common law name change, MacDougall advises that one simply contact any agency with which her "old" name is listed and inform it of the change. For those women residing in Wisconsin who are unsure of what to do, they can call the University of Wisconsin-Extension Dial-a-Tape, which tells them how to retain or change a surname, or they can contact the Wisconsin Attorney General's office for advice.

Perhaps the most eloquent resource which MacDougall has produced is a brief presented in a Florida name-change case in which she outlined the law of women's names (*In re Hooper,* 20 Fla. App. 2d 83,288 P9, 370 (1983). This document cites numerous court cases, state statutes, federal statutes, constitutional provisions, Attorneys General opinions, and references which are extremely helpful for future court cases. More importantly, her brief addresses each argument against the common law right to choose one's own surname.

3. In 1982, in *State vs. Taylor,* the Alabama Supreme Court unanimously overturned its ten-year-old decision in *Forbush vs. Wallace,* which had denied women the right to use their own surnames.

4. The following is an example of An Affadavit of Name Change:

I, *JANE A. SMITH,* the undersigned, do hereby give notice that, from this day forward, I shall be exclusively known by the name, *JANE A. PROOF,* and that official signature for the same shall be (signed)

_____

(*JANE A. PROOF*).

_____

JANE P. SMITH (signed)

5. A similar phenomenon of name changing is to be found in the practice adopted by the Zionist pioneers who began to return to Palestine in 1882 and which continues to the present. No sooner did the feet of these immigrants tread the soil of the Holy Land than they changed their names from a typical east European variety to a Hebrew surname which drew upon the natural features of the Holy Land or some historical moment in the past history of the Jewish people. The adoption or creation of this new name signified a spiritual rebirth which symbolized psychologically the termination of a persecuted and oppressed identity which they had inherited. This name changing practice continues to the present day and involves many thousands of individuals. For more details, see especially Amos Elon, *The Israelis: Founders and Sons* (1971).

The same practice is followed among the Black Muslims in the United States.

References

Appellate Brie by Petitioner Kerry Mack Hooper (also as Florida Association for Women Lawyers) an amicus curiae in the 2nd District Court, 20th Judicial Circuit, Charlotte County, Florida, Dockett #83-288. (Initially presented May 17, 1983)

Center for a Woman's Own Name. *Booklet of Historical News Sources* (1974). Barrington, Illinois.

_____. *Bibliography of Historical News Sources* (1974). Barrington, Illinois.

_____. 1975 *Supplement to Booklet for Women Who Wish to Determine Their Own Names After Marriage* 6 (1975). Barrington, Illinois.

Elon, Amos. 1971. *The Israelis: Founders and Sons*. NY: Holt, Rinehart & Winston.

Forbush v. *Wallace*, 344 F. Supp 217 (M.D. Ala 1971), 405 U.S. 970, 92 S. Ct. 1197, 31 L.Ed.2d 246 (1972).

Kramarae, Cheris. 1981. *Women and Men Speaking*. Rowley, Mass.: Newbury House.

Letter from Priscilla Ruth MacDougall to Sen. Orrin G. Hatch, August 5, 1983.

Mazur, Janet. "Husband's Name Optional for Contemporary Women," *Asbury Park Press* (New Jersey), Friday, Nov. 26 (1982).

MacDougall, Priscilla Ruth. "Women's Name Rights," *Spokeswoman* August (1981), p. 7.

Ms. "What's in a Name?" July (1983), p. 29.

Stannard, Una. 1977. *Mrs. Man*. San Francisco, California: Germainbooks.

Stanton, E., S. Anthony, and M. Gage. 1881. *History of Woman Suffrage*. p. 80.

State v. *Taylor*, 415 So. 2d 1043 (Ala. 1982).

Sunday Star Ledger (Newark, NJ). "Measure Lets Single Parent Pick Surname", Feb. 6 (1983), p. 52.

Wen, Patricia. "Married Women Discovering What's in a Name?" *Sunday Star Ledger* (Newark, NJ), May 22, (1983), p. 60.

Zivanovic, Crista. "Lawyer's Plan to Settle Names Issue Took 10 Years," *The Capital Times* (Madison, Wisc.) Monday, November 15 (1983), p. 10.

Renaming: Vehicle for Empowerment

Nan Van Den Bergh

In this chapter the author argues that collective redefinition or "renaming" is a powerful tool of empowerment which minorities have successfully used as well as women. She takes the ideological stance that language change should be an integral part of feminist activism and develops the idea that certain types of language change can in turn introduce social change. Van Den Bergh forces us to consider language theoretically as more than a set of symbols with referents. Language also fulfills evaluative and social funcitons in the lives of the users and consequently plays a key role in forming positive and negative perceptions of individuals and social groups. It is these functions of language which may participate in and trigger changes in the social order.

As a result of the civil rights movement and feminist activism in the last two decades, ethnic minorities and women have exerted an impact on language usage by demanding the right to "rename" themselves and their experiences. For feminists, the path toward liberation has included collectively redefining what it means to be female. Redefining personal and collective experiences by changing the labels used to refer to these experiences has been one way to gain power. In other words, ethnic and feminist renaming may be considered a vehicle for empowerment.

Perhaps the core issue addressed by civil rights proponents and feminists has been the redistribution of power to provide equal access to rights, resources, and opportunities. Powerlessness or the inability to obtain and use resources to achieve individual or collective goals is perpetuated by the negative evaluation of those in power towards the powerless group (Solomon 1976).[1] Although women constitute a numerical majority (51% of the U.S. population), when issues of power and its distribution are considered, they are as powerless as other minorities.

Empowerment

Empowerment strategies assist persons who belong to a stigmatized social category to develop and increase their ability to influence the world around

130

them (Solomon 1976: 12–28). One such strategy is the individual and collective redefinition of self.[2] Such relabeling is psychologically powerful for the powerless group in at least two ways. It gives them a sense of control over their own identity, and it raises consciousness within their group and that of those in power. Redefining one's experiences by changing language serves to alter the perspective and attitudes of the society-at-large. This affective dimension can pave the way for possible social changes. Social change involves an extensive and enduring reordering of society, usually preceded by a tension between forces seeking to alter the existing arrangements and forces desiring to maintain the status quo (Olsen 1968: 137). Empowerment thus holds implications for social change, as powerless groups seek to gain power over societal resources through collective and/or self redefinition.

Researchers in various disciplines have noted that language is related to the way society functions. But while there seems to be consensus that language change and social change are related to one another, there appears to be variance in the proverbial chicken and egg syndrome. Can language really cause or initiate social change, or is language change an effect of societal changes? Such discussions hinge on the notion of the Sapir-Whorf Hypothesis.[3] The less extreme version of this hypothesis—linguistic relativity—holds that language is a reflection of reality and, therefore, any changes in this reality must precede language changes rather than vice-versa. Lakoff (1975) reflects this view when she argues that language change invariably reflects social change. Therefore, feminists should focus on social change rather than on language change.

The Whorfian discussion may be oversimplistic when applied to the feminist struggle to achieve power and equality. In fact, changing attitudes through conciousness-raising is the indispensable intermediary between the transformation of reality and the corresponding alteration in language. Consequently, there are two key questions which redefinition introduces: (1) What effect does redefinition have on the self-perception and attitudinal perspective of the powerless group and those in power? (2) What impact do social attitudes eventually have on social change?

One period in United States history can offer insight into these interesting theoretical issues. An initial strategy used by civil rights and feminist activists in the 1960s and 1970s to uproot institutionalized racism and sexism was to alter racist and sexist language. These activists did not wait for the ultimate goal of a nonracist and nonsexist society before they began to challenge oppressive language. Rather, the act of confronting racism and sexism which were reflected in word usage became one of several approaches to empowerment.

Why should language change be such an integral component of social change agendas? Language is social behavior. Language functions not only to communicate cultural values but serves also to define and maintain social roles (Warshay 1972: 3–9). In other words, language places an individual within a given social stratification, class, or caste, and it suggests how a person is to be evaluated by others. *Language, then, is not neutral or value-free; it can embody negative value stances and valuations related to how certain groups within society are appraised.* To this extent, social identity is inextricably tied to language. All the negative associations society imposes on a social group are carried by the symbols of language.

Language also plays a key role in reflecting society's dominant group ideology and the composite belief system which epitomizes the needs and aspirations of society or a social group.[4] For example, the belief that women are inferior to men is suggested in the conventional practice of addressing adult females as *girls* and adult males as *men*. Quite basically, language embodies cultural values which in turn have a profound effect in determining one's quality of life.

It may be argued that linguistic imbalances based on gender or ethnicity are worthy of study because they bring into sharper focus the inequities of the real world. That is, sexist language provides clues about the extent of social discrepancy between men and women. Language, then, is a mirror of power imbalances and, as such, it is capable of becoming one weapon or instrument for social change. In what ways might language function as a vehicle for creating a nonsexist or nonracist world?

To change language may not be to embark on drastic social changes directly, but it does involve consciousness-raising; that is, bringing awareness of a problem to the public's attention. The assumption underlying consciousness-raising is that before a behavior can be changed, there must be awareness that a situation exists warranting alteration.[5] The consciousness-raising function of redefinition is somewhat analogous to legislation. Although the enactment of a law may be considered the expression of social custom at some point in time, law can also be used as an impetus to change social behavior in the future. For example, during the 1960s, civil rights legislation served more to prod the citizenry into accepting a social reality of equality apart from race or skin color than it did to indicate that the United States was no longer a nonracist society.

Link to Empowerment

Ethnic renaming has been linked to empowerment historically. In great part, the evolution of ethnic renaming can be attributed to the politics of ethnic classification. In the 1960s ethnic groups rejected being classified as NONWHITE, since this term masked significant differences between them.

Blacks were no longer satisfied with being referred to as *colored, Negro,* or *Afro-American.* The Black power movement adopted the term *Black,* making a statement about their identity to society and elevating pride in their ethnic members.

The pattern of renaming was followed by other ethnic groups. Chicano/Chicana was reclaimed as a label potentially better able to symbolize an active political ethnic identity for persons of Mexican ancestry. *Native American* is the designation used by the federal government; however, the National Tribal Education Association uses the term *American Indian.* This is because it serves to remind the government of its treaty obligations to Indians.[6] It is also true that many American Indians prefer to be named only by their individual tribal designation, of which there are 487 (Hartley 1981: 3).

Renaming as Feminist Ideology

The inadequacy of conventional language in addressing the gamut of women's experiences was articulated by Betty Friedan two decades ago when she described women's powerlessness as the "problem which has no name" (Friedan 1963).[7] A name, *sexism,* was subsequently applied to that problem. Within language, sexism has manifested itself in two important ways. First there are differences between how women and men speak.[8] Second each sex tends to be spoken about in different ways.

Not only can language serve to reflect sexist attitudes toward women, but it also reinforces and perpetuates them. Sexist language has been named as an instrument of power in maintaining gender apartheid. Feminists, including many nineteenth-century suffragettes, have been clear about the dynamic. In fact, Elizabeth Cady Stanton rewrote the Bible in 1895 to eliminate its sexism (Beardsley, 1977:105–8). Before delineating ways in which feminist renaming has exerted its impact on social change, it is appropriate to indicate the ideological stance within which language change has been articulated as an integral component of feminist activism.

Feminism is primarily concerned with the creation of new cultural forms allowing for a more equitable quality of life for all. Creating a new social order entails the formulation of new ideas, new attitudes, and new forms of organization which will affect economic, physical, and psychological survival (Daly 1978: 1–34). In order to embark upon such a venture, "old realities" need to be challenged, including that of language. Daly speaks of challenging conventional language as a process of exorcism "peeling off the layers of mindbindings . . . movement past . . . an imposed sense of reality and identity . . ." (Daly 1978: 1–34). She maintains that deceptive perceptions are implanted throughout language so that the way to begin spinning new realities is to alter—or, in her words, "dis-spell"—the sexism embedded in words.

In a similar vein, Rich (1978) suggests that since naming has been a male prerogative, then *re-vision* or the art of looking back, seeing, and naming is an act of survival for women. Because language is power and has been used to keep people silent who have been least able to articulate their suffering, being "released into language . . . is learning that it can be used as a means of changing reality" (Rich 1979: 51–68).

Feminist ideology, therefore, has incorporated the principle of renaming, since language is so intimately entwined with the distribution of power in society. Changing language raises consciousness. It brings to public attention the deceptions inherent within words in order to dis-spell them. Through such an exorcism, renaming makes public a political statement, and it empowers the group by giving it a sense of control over life. Renaming is the politics of personal experience. Therefore, the way in which one names one's experiences has profound implications extending beyond the individual.[8]

Conclusion

Altering language and naming one's own experiences have been integral facets of feminist activism. This is so because being able to exert control over language as illustrated in the act of naming and renaming constitutes power. The extent to which terms which were unheard of two decades ago are used in commonplace fashion today seems to serve as testimony that renaming can be an empowering vehicle for women.

Notes

1. Although it seems quite clear that persons of color will constitute minority groups, it may be less obvious as to how that label could be applied to women. There are three basic components necessary for a group to be considered a "minority": (1) identifiability—i.e., physical characteristics; (2) differential and pejorative treatment in terms of receiving necessary rights, resources, and opportunities; and (3) a consciousness of oppression (Dworkin and Dworkin 1976: 17).

2. See Penfield in this book for a discussion of the impact of renaming as part of forming individual rather than collective identity.

3. The Sapir-Whorf Hypothesis has at least two versions: "linguistic determinism," which holds that language not only reflects cultural perceptions but in fact determines and prescribes them, and "linguistic relativity," which holds that language only reflects the cultural reality of its speakers. The first version of the hypothesis might be translated to mean that changing language can in fact change cultural perceptions. The second version suggests that language changes occur only after social or cultural changes have taken place.

4. See Deckard (1975: 7) for further discussion of the formation of a dominant group ideology.

5. See Sarachild for a discussion of the importance of language awareness before change.

6. Medicine in this book elaborates on the imposition of white culture and English on American Indians.

7. More recently Friedan (1985:26–28, 66–70) notes that feminism has spread to many parts of the world while it has quietly crept away in the United States. She calls for approaches to "get the women's movement moving again."

8. At least four linguistic processes have been used by feminists in renaming themselves and their experiences. The first—creating new terms—includes using words seemingly nonexistent before feminism's resurgence (e.g., *sisterhood, sexism,* and *Ms.*). The second renaming process—altering the format of words—entails changing meanings through hyphenation and using slashes. This allows for the dis-spelling of sexist deception within language, as well as for the creation of more inclusive terms (e.g., *s/he*). The third renaming process involves reclaiming archaic meanings. By uncovering original intent, images of strength and power can replace those of ugliness and evil. The fourth renaming process entails the expansion of the conceptual boundaries of words.

(See Henley in this book for further examples of these and other processes.)

References

Beardsley, Elizabeth. 1977. "Traits and Genderization." In *Feminism and Philosophy,* edited by M. Vetterling-Braggin et al. Totoway, N.J.: Rowman, pp. 124–136.

Daly, Mary. 1978. *Gyn/Ecology: The Metaethics of Radical Feminism.* Boston: Beacon.

Deckard, Barbara. 1975. *The Women's Movement.* New York: Harper and Row.

Dworkin, Anthony, and Rosalind Dworkin. 1976. *The Minority Report.* New York: Holt, Rinehart and Winston.

Friedan, Betty. 1963. *The Feminist Mystique.* New York: Dell.

————. "How to Get the Women's Movement Moving Again," *New York Times Magazine* Nov. 3 (1985).

Hartley, Jo. "A Minority Report," *Comment,* 13:1 October (1981), p.3.

Lakoff, Robin. 1975. *Language and Women's Place.* New York: Harper Colophon Books.

Olsen, Marvin. 1968. *The Process of Social Organization.* New York: Holt, Rinehart and Winston.

Rich, Adrienne. "Teaching Language in Open Admissions." In *On Lies, Secrets and Silence,* edited by Norton. New York: W.W. (1979) 51–68.

Sarachild, Kathie. "Who are We? The Redstockings Position on Names." In
    Feminist Revolution, edited by Restockings. New Paltz, N.Y.: Redstock-
    ings.
Solomon, Barbara. 1976. *Black Empowerment*. New York: Columbia Univer-
    sity Press.
Warshay, Diana. 1972. "Sex Differences in Language Style." In *Toward a
    Sociology of Women*, edited by Constantina Safilios-Rothschild. Lexing-
    ton, Mass.: Xerox.

Women Take Back the Talk*

Cheris Kramarae and *Mercilee M. Jenkins*

This chapter provides an apt summary of the direction of research in women's language for the 1970s and 1980s. Kramarae and Jenkins address the role of the feminist radical leaders in recovering and constructing women's language and culture. Their work focuses on a necessary stage in the process of feminist nationalism, the shaping and creating of language. They demonstrate with precision how feminist leaders are breaking the unnatural silences imposed on women by taking back the power of language and talk.

The assault systems which work against women's freedom are composed of links among hierarchies based on class, race and sex, and economic imbalances supported by the verbal threats and the verbal and physical attacks made by males—often on those who are nearest and supposedly dearest to them. Much of feminist scholarship, as well as other forms of activism, reflects an exploration and breaking down of these links. For decades, women have sought remedies for men's verbal street hassling and physical assaults on them. In many countries, women have organized Women Take Back the Night marches to call attention to men's resistance to their freedom of movement on so-called public streets and to illustrate a technique of collective resistance to these verbal and physical assaults.

This chapter documents some of the strategies women are using to take back some control of language and talk. The ways that women can be, and have been, *voleuses de langue*, thieves of language (Claudine Hermann's phrase), is explored both indirectly and boldly in much of women's talking and writing. This invasion of what men so often tell us is their property can be traced in many places. While men continue to present their deeds and titles, women continue to seize the language to try to make it say what they mean.

At a six-day Feminist Scholarship Conference at the University of Illinois

*We thank Ann Russo for her helpful comments on an earlier version of this essay.

at Urbana-Champaign in 1978, the authors began to document some of women's efforts to take control of talk by analyzing what participants said about language and how they said it (Kramarae and Jenkins 1985). At that time, the following categories of language innovation were derived from the discussions: (1) talking about "the problem"—analyzing women's relationship to language—and naming what we discovered; (2) making negative words, such as "spinster" and "bitch," positive by redefining them; (3) making positive words negative, such as turning methodology into methodolotry, to challenge male authority; (4) coining new expressions, such as "gaslighting", which means to drive someone crazy by denying her reality, as the doctor/husband did to his young wife in the move, *Gaslight;* and (5) using metaphors, stories, jokes, and analogies to depict aspects of women's experience for which there are no words in a patriarchal language. Since this conference, women have continued to use these methods of making maledominated language their own and have identified new ways to challenge the patriarchal communication complex and resist the "malestream" response to these efforts.

In this brief review, the authors focus on feminist activities in the United States and Britain which have affected the English language. Some attention is also given to related activities of women speaking and writing in several other languages and locations. Many women have talked and written about the ways in which English, as it is represented by most dictionaries, has been taken away from them. They have spoken and written about the problems with the magisterial, hierarchical, authoritative style accepted as normal for the pulpit, legislative floor, classroom, and much interpersonal exchange. Some are making serious play with the conventions and pointing out alternatives. Such activities are called radical—and have been for more than one hundred years.[1] They *are* radical and they have been actively resisted for all these years.[2] Radical activities include recognizing women's rich oral tradition, the power of feminist humor, and personal-experience storytelling to transform their lives and thereby change the world.

All of these actions are part of a search for what sociologists refer to as identity, and what Judy Grahn (1978: 14) calls "the reclamation of ideas, political directions, culture [to] make it possible for women to speak honestly, and in a whole voice, to say what we actually see and think in a tone of voice and language." This statement is appropriate to the lives of all women. As Rayna Green (1984: 7) writes, "identity" is not a matter simply of genetic makeup or natural birthright. "For people out on the edge, out on the road, identity is a matter of will, a matter of choice, a face to be shaped in a ceremonial act." It will be created *for* us unless we try to shape our places ourselves.[3] Journeying is a central metaphor of many myths, folktales, and personal-experience stories, but the quest is different for women. Men seek to find their rightful place in society but women seek to break out of theirs (Zimmerman 1985).

Today women are taking back the talk. They are still reclaiming, naming, and changing language categories in addition to "writing the body"—creating their own connections and telling what formerly has been taboo. Women are recognizing the value and art of their interactions as they laugh and tell stories. They are developing strategies for overcoming male resistance and assessing the damages of past linguistic transgressions.

Labeling

Changing the Categories

Rosario Morales (1981), objecting to the labels often appled to her ("white" and "middle-class") and the political assumptions made on the basis of those labels, writes that she wants to challenge the ready application of those labels and the beliefs that go with such divisions. Others may label her simply "white" or "middle-class", but she wants to claim herself as Puerto Rican, United States American-born, working-class, married, middle-class, housewife, intellectual, feminist, Marxist, and anti-imperialist.

I am a whole circus by myself   a whole dance   company with stance and posture for being in middle class homes   in upper class buildings   for talking with blacks
      for carefully angling and directing   for choreographing my way thru the maze of classes of people and places thru the little boxes of sex   race   class   nationality
      sexual orientation   intellectual standing   political preference   the automatic contortions   the exhausting camouflage with which I go thru this social space called

CAPITALIST PATRIARCHY

a daunting but oh so nicely covering name   this is no way to live . . . (Morales 1981: 92).

Many other new labels are offered. In fact, a major activity of contemporary feminism is relabeling.

Talking New Names

Some women rename themselves by discarding their "married name" and retaking their "birth name" or another name of their choice, such as an important symbolic last name (e.g., Judy Chicago or Olivia Freewoman) or the first name of their mother or other close woman friend as a new last name (e.g., Sarah Elizabeth) (Spender 1980; Stannard 1977; Lassiter 1983).[4] For some women, the taking of new names and the reshaping of old names is a continuing part of existence. Native American women know the empowerment which can come from adopting names from their ancestors, from mythical forbears, and from social and political events. For Native people, taking new names and giving names are part of a religious process. Thus, by invoking powers of female spirits, and by giving themselves and others power to speak, remember, create, and endure, women can help chart their position in society (Green 1984: 7–8).

Making Reversals

One of the strategies employed by feminists is to make the negative positive. Mary Daly (1978) calls herself a *hag*, which formerly meant "an evil or frightening spirit." She asks, evil and frightening to whom? Others make positive reference to themselves as witches and spinsters, to stress the importance of their having control over what they are called and how they are treated. Some of these women have made etymological searches to resurrect old meanings of these terms. This can be done successfully with most of the words men use to describe women because the majority of these words have slid semantically to a derogatory sexual meaning.[5]

"Old women" and "fat women" have been defined as "unfit," "powerless", and "lacking will power" by patriarchal, aesthetic, and erotic standards. Feminists are still working on reversals of these definitions which have in the past been so influential in limiting the ways women can identify themselves. In discussing these male-defined words which we have too often used as "default standards," Baba Copper (1985) points out that "one of the primary definitions of patriarchy is the absence of old women of power." In the next decade, women will continue work on new words of female empowerment to replace the male-defined words for "old" and "fat", which reflect men's loathing of women who are not sex-objects, breeders, or caretakers.[6]

Still other women make the positive negative, thus transforming reality. For example, some experiment with the division of the world into "women" and "non-women," a reversal, of course, of the category scheme which has been used by non-women. Most women do not regard this as a valuable permanent solution to sexism, but it nevertheless highlights the imposed category system which begins with the assumption that there are two hierarchical categories of humans. In Western English, there are women and non-women, masters and touchables. Scrutinizing and altering the system itself directs our attention to the category rules and the goals of the originators of those rules.

Naming/New Expressions

Most gender-related dichotomies are not of our making, but we can use them strategically. Some women at United States universities have recently announced completion of spinster's rather than master's degrees, making obvious the traditional attention accorded the male side of the gender-linked terms.

Some of the coinages are now well known: "male chauvinist," "sexism," "sexist," "Ms.," [7] and "herstory." They are so well-established that some people are making revisions of even these new words. For example, Jo Haugerud, a cartoonist and the editor of *Flame: A Coalition on Women and Religion*, has suggested that instead of using "herstory" to refer to events of the past, "hystery" should be used because it refers to origin or womb. She adds, "If 'history' is properly 'hystery,' then the past is hysterical. Right?" (*The Flame* Dec. 1982 and Jan. 1983). She also offers the following dialogue about "chauvinist":

He: I guess you'd call me a 'chauvinist.'
She: Not any more. Now I believe in calling a bigot a bigot. (*The Flame,* March 8, 1983)

Marilyn Frye (1983) also notes that the term "male chauvinism" seems to have gone out of fashion—although the phenomenon has not. She says that it needs an "ism" sort of word to reflect its attitudinal-conceptual-cognitive-orientational complex. For her own writing she made up the words "phallism" and "phallist" for this complex, but notes that the strangeness of the terms bothers her because its novelty suggests that the phenomenon itself is novel or strange—while, in fact, it is very common. She adds that "the strangeness of the term is not an indication that the phenomenon is strange or rare but a flag notifying us that English doesn't have a word for [even such] a common and such a potent thing as this" (Frye 1983: 41–42).

Suzette Haden Elgin, a linguist and a word-maker, has analyzed the types of additions women have made to the language they have inherited, offering her own coinages. A sampler:

to ablactate	To wean others from an unwholesome and destructive dependence upon oneself or upon some other woman.
Academic Regalian	The elitist artificial language mode used in scholarly syntax, archaisms,
	gratuitous bits of foreign language, jargon . . . idioms such as "so to speak," etc; the language mode required for academic success in the United States. Analogous modes exist for other professions—for example, Medical Regalian, Forensic Regalian, etc.

aclawac (AK-luh-wak)   An advertisement or commercial that presents women
                           as ignorant, incompetent, obsessed with toilet bowls,
                           etc; an acronym from AD/COMMERCIAL/LABEL-
                           ING/ALL WOMEN/AS/CRETINS. Plural is
                           "Aclawacs."

ambigenic   Non-sexist. (NOTE: The "e" is like the vowel in "bed"
                           and the stress is on the next-to-last syllable.)

bordweal   An artificial barrier raised to keep women out of
                           things, such as an irrelevant height requirement.
                           (From O.E. "bord-weal," "a wall of shields.")

to granny   To apply the wisdom and the experience of the elderly
                           to any situation.

vironology   The science of men. (NOTE: The obvious term "viro-
                           logy" has already been taken for the study of viruses;
                           this term is therefore coined by analogy with "femino-
                           logy.")
                           (*The Lonesome Node* 1:1 (Sept/Oct. 1981,2)

But these coinages were only a start for Elgin. In writing her science fiction novel *Native Tongue*, she created Laadan, a language for women. The novel takes as its premise the view that existing human languages are inadequate to express the perceptions of women, and it then explores possible consequences of the creation of a language specifically designed to remedy such an inadequacy. In *Native Tongue*, the women linguists are not prevented from carrying out their project of creating a women's language. The men do not take them seriously because they are certain that people cannot create viable new languages (as opposed to revising existing languages), and because if anyone *were* to do successful language-making it would not be women. The book includes information on ordering a beginning grammar and dictionary of Laadan, the women's language.

Elgin's linguistic creativity has had a wide audience because of the publication of her novel and is at the moment available to speakers and writers interested in the nature, purpose, and value of English and other languages. But this certainly does not mean that it will be around very long for observation and use; the words of women of ideas disappear very quickly (Spender 1983). *A Feminist Dictionary* by Kramarae and Treichler with Russo (1986) recovers thousands of the coinages, explanations, definitions, revisions, and revelations English-speaking women have made during the past several hundred years. These were found mainly, although not exclusively, in the publications of white, middle-class women; most of the linguistic creativity of poor women and women of color is irrevocably lost. It is not available even in those books of American colloquialism in which some of the words of working-class and Black men are recorded. Although this general situation continues, one of the very healthy signs of the current women's movement is the number and circulation of publications by feminists and the continuing work of feminist presses.[8]

Writing the Body

This term is most often associated with discussions among some French feminists and has spread to England and to the United States. These French feminists argue, in part, that women need to learn to write from their bodies, their pleasures, and their experiences. Finding a traditionally American problem-solving approach inadequate, some of the French writers, such as Helene Cixous, suggest that women write with "mother's milk" or "the blood's language" rather than reconstruct a past in which women have been vocal or fill in the gaps they have discovered. Many other women have criticized this particular psychoanalytical approach and perspective for being ahistorical, and for paying little attention to or ignoring class and race differences and analyses of the institutions which support the oppression of women. On the other hand, those writers who do not subscribe to psychoanalytical approaches of "writing the body" also discuss the importance of considering the entire body as part of language. They are concerned with writing and talking of "theory in the flesh" as the physical realities—the flesh and blood experiences—of lives which are used to create a politic and to envision a healing future (Moraga and Anzaldua 1981: 23).

Cherrie Moraga (1981) discusses the importance of the rhythms closest to her—the sounds of her mother and aunts gossiping in the kitchen, half in English, half in Spanish. Listening to them, she notes the absences in her own poetry.

And the hands—I had cut off the hands in my poems. But not in conversation; still the hands could not be kept down. Still they insisted on moving (Moraga 1981: 55–56).

Also beginning with the body, Cheryl Clarke (1981: 128) identifies the lesbian as a woman who has "decolonized her body" and lesbianism as a recognition, an awakening, a reawakening of passion for each (woman) other (woman) and for the same (woman) women. According to her, this new speaking and writing of the body means an ideological, political and philosophical commitment to liberation from male tyranny at all levels. In a similar vein, Kate Clinton (1982: 38), a lesbian feminist and humorist, talks of connecting humor with the erotic. "I met a woman and we laughed and made love and we laughed as we made love and we made love as we laughed."

Other writers point out the importance of considering the rich oral legacy of Black-female storytelling, mythmaking, and music in order to understand the fiction of such writers as Zora Neale Hurston who faced daily oppression in a society full of hatred for Black skin and female bodies (Bethel 1982). Concern with "writing the body" can mean paying attention to all the socioaesthetic problems and solutions of speakers and authors.

Reclaiming Nonstandard Languages

In an important essay, "Murdering the King's English", Judy Grahn (1978) tells why she uses and encourages others to use language in ways not considered correct by academic experts. What they call nonstandard or working-class manner or illiterate English, she calls "speaking honestly, and in a whole voice . . . in a tone of choice and language which is appropriate to the writer's life and to the lives of millions of other women" (Grahn 1978: 14). For, she writes, the way truth is told determines how true it is and how useful it is. And useful to who?[9]

There are other examples of women reclaiming nonstandard languages. Zora Neale Hurston, a novelist, folklorist, and anthropologist, born in the all-Black town of Eatonville, Florida, at the turn of the century, gives us in her books "a nonstandard language"—a reality not accepted in traditional, white, modern American literature. Cherrie Moraga (1983), daughter of a Chicana and an Anglo, speaks two tongues in her writing. Irena Klepfisz (1986), who writes Yiddish and bilingual Yiddish/English prose and poetry, points out that what was once the language of an entire culture has now become a joke. Many feel free to make fun of the Yiddish accent, the inflection, and the words such as *shpil* and *shlep*. Klepfisz believes that her commitment to Yiddish supports the diversity present in the feminist community while at the same time supporting her Jewish heritage.

Verbal Art in Action[10]

Despite numerous articles and books about girls' and women's folklore or verbal art forms, such as storytelling and humor, there is the persistent belief that women do not generally tell stories and jokes as much as men do and that they do not have their own distinct strategies for using these verbal art forms in context. In 1973, Naomi Weisstein wrote that, in contrast to other oppressed groups, there was nothing that could be called women's humor. "I mean a humor which recognizes a common oppression, notices its source and the roles it requires, identifies the agents of the oppression" (Weisstein, 1973:

88). Twelve years later, Alice Sheppard (1985) says there is still confusion as to whether there is such a thing as women's humor.

Several studies done over the last ten years (Kălcik 1975; Jenkins 1984; Neitz 1980; Green 1977; Coser 1960; Eakins and Eakins 1978; Painter 1980) indicate that while women may tell fewer jokes and stories in mixed groups than men, examples are plentiful in women's same-sex groups in a variety of contexts—consciousness-raising, radical feminist, student, young mothers, and kinfolk. While some researchers have found little evidence of women telling formulaic jokes in same-sex groups (Jenkins, in press; Neitz 1980; Kălcik 1975), Carol Mitchell (1977) has collected a large number of examples of this type of joking from women through interviews and questionnaires.

Mitchell has written about the different ways women and men use humor. She found that generally women prefer jokes that pertain to their own experience (menstruation, rape, pregnancy) as do men (penis size, castration). In some cases, however, who tells the joke to whom determines how it is perceived. Even when women and men enjoy the same jokes, they often interpret them differently based on their experience. This is especially true of sexual jokes. These findings are not surprising considering what we know about the common basis of social experience necessary for humor to be shared.

These examples illustrate Mary Jo Neitz's (1980) premise concerning the social dynamic of joke-telling in her article "Humor, Hierarchy, and the Changing Status of Women."

The telling of jokes is a social relationship involving three parties: the teller, the object and the listener. The relations among these parties usually reflect the social structure often reinforcing it, but occasionally serving to rebel against it (Neitz 1980: 211).

The Western, white, feminine role dictates that women should be listeners and objects of humor, not the originators of stories, jokes, and word play. This may in large part account for their lower incidence of humor in mixed groups and their tendency not to see themselves as jokers or storytellers, or to be seen in this way by others. As Kristen Langellier and Eric Peterson (1984) point out, "the semantic space for storytelling is assumed to be occupied by men." Neitz (1980) likewise reports that folklorists have considered humor as a "male preserve." The implication that women do not tell stories or jokes is another way in which women's speech is devalued. It is part of the denial of women's culture, as well as their contribution to culture.

This situation is in sharp contrast to, for example, matrilineal ways which have survived within the Cherokee nation—despite the many years of enforced patrilineal forms of government—because of the oral tradition. Marilou Awiakta (1986) points out the continuing damage to women in the Western cultures resulting from the "Eden apple" and other powerful and destructive myths. Awiakta recites the Cherokee healing myth of the strawberry (which tells of the ways large, ripe berries were used by the Great Apportioner to bring about a reconciliation after a quarrel between the first woman and man), and talks of the importance of the oral tradition shared by both women and men (Awiakta 1986: 109–111).

A fundamental reason that white, Western women's verbal art forms have been unseen is that they occur most readily among women only, and they don't always look the same as men's do. Langellier and Peterson (1984), Jenkins (1984), Neitz (1980), and Kalcik (1975) have found similar features in women's storytelling and joking that distinguish them from the performances of men in terms of the social relationships indicated by Neitz between teller, listener, and subject of the joke or story.

Women's joking and storytelling tends to be very situation specific. That is, they more often tell personal experience stories and make witty remarks than use formulaic jokes. Rather than a "can you top this?" mode of storytelling or joking competition, there is often an "Oh, God this happened to me too!" motif. Their stories and jokes tend to flow with the conversation and the conversation flows through the storytelling and joking. Storytelling and joking are not necessarily segmented, marked, or separated from the ongoing talk. The telling can be collaborative rather than competitive. The overlaps, interruptions, and interjections which occur during the course of telling a story augment it. In addition, the point of the story and the point of view may differ from men's storytelling in a way that characterizes women's strategic use of language.

Strategically, women's stories are designed to create an atmosphere of support based on a sense of a shared social reality. This reality is not reified in the culture as men's reality is. So the point of the story or joke is created or discovered jointly in the immediate context (Langellier and Peterson 1984). We are spinning our relationships as we spin our stories as we spin our reality. Through storytelling we give our own meanings to our experience and through our joking we reverse men's reversals and turn the social order right-side up (Clinton, 1982). Bonnie Zimmerman's (1985:260) study of published lesbian personal-experience narratives illustrates this self-affirming quality and shows us the value of personal narratives to "debunk expert knowledge" and provide "alternative role models". Dorothy Painter's (1980) study of lesbian humor demonstrates how lesbians can take painful experiences in the straight world and turn them into jokes she calls "dumb things straight people say."

This view of the self-affirming quality of women's narratives and humor runs counter to the reports that women's humor is more self-deprecating than men's (Levine 1976). This is why we need to look very carefully at the issue of point of view. Neitz (1980) argues that self-deprecating humor offers a kind of release to oppressed groups that is not allowed in society and a way of dealing with role conflict. But she also indicates that there is another kind of humor which puts down the stereotypes we are forced to live by rather than women. The first type reinforces the status quo, but the second provides an opportunity for change. It is both a form of self-expression and a means of social criticism. When used by women, the first type of humor might be called "female" and the second "feminist." Both kinds of humor can promote solidarity, support, and community, but only the second can reshape our lives and our world. This is the same kind of distinction that has been made between personal experience stories told in consciousness-raising sessions and stories women tell in other contexts, where the status quo may be lamented but is accepted.

Radical laughter can reach the heart, give insight and sight, create a sense of community among diverse people, and validate a world-view (Clinton 1982; Jenkins, in press; Little 1983; and Kaufman 1980). Clinton (1982: 38-39) desribes a feminist humorist as a fumerist—"a sparking incendiary with blazes of light and insight" (38-39). She writes that feminists do not make wisecracks. They make "whys cracks". "We ask our own questions and they have the potential of splitting the world apart" (Clinton 1982: 39). Zimmerman also speaks of the radical potential of personal-experience storytelling. She describes the coming out stories of lesbians as "exuberant and unabashed political propaganda, like Cuban murals or the plays of Brecht" (Zimmerman 1985: 261). She argues for the importance of writing down our oral culture and continuing to see the connections between the personal and the political.

Malestream Response

The strategies for taking back the language and working to make our voices heard are not, of course, given credence or praise by most non-women. After all, when women pose a linguistic threat, the others are quite capable of revising the rules to support their control over language and knowledge. A part of this process of challenge and refutation was described in a nineteenth-century brochure "Woman's Rights Fables," which contained the following story:

The Crowing Hen

There once lived in a Farm Yard a great many Roosters and Hens, and it chanced one morning that a young Hen with a very fine voice began to crow. Thereupon all the Roosters hurried together and solemnly declared that there was nothing so dreadful as a Crowing Hen! Now there was in the Yard a Rooster who had always been feeble and could only cackle, but when the Hen mentioned this, the Roosters shook their heads and said: "Females do not understand Logic."

MORAL—There is a great deal of difference between a Cackling Rooster and a Crowing Hen. (Lillie Devereux Blake n.d.)

Given that women's activities are constantly restricted, no matter what strategies they use, why do they continue to use a creative variety of linguistic devices to try to change their situation? We suggest several reasons.

First, since the obstacles—material and psychological—are ever-present, working to overcome them is a necessity. Women's daily speech and writing have daily implications for our economic and psychological existence.

Second, only by using a greater variety of linguistic strategies can women build a more comfortable world/word structure for themselves. Since language systems are social constructions, they *are* open to alterations to fit our needs, although the "word experts" seldom encourage alterations by women. For example, in one survey of attitudes on issues of sexism and American English conducted in the 1970s among teachers, and editors of books, magazines, and newspapers, the members of the Linguistic Society of America were the least in favor of changes (Nilsen et al. 1977). But women are continuing to offer ideas about vocabulary, syntax, and conversation structure, in spite of the discouraging claims of so many male language experts about the ways in which language can or should work.

Talking About Damages

One of the side benefits of documenting women's linguistic innovations is the uncovering of men's past theft of language—including the specifics of their strategies to retain the power to name and their semantic derogation and exclusion of women. We give one example here.

Man Handled

In 1850, an Act of Parliament decreed that *man* should mean *woman* also. But this legislation of meaning did not immediately clarify and expand women's legal rights. For example, in 1868 in Manchester, England, women demanded to be registered as voters. Their case was taken by sympathiser and Counsel, Mr. Corbbett, before the registry board. Corbbett said that *man* must have one of two meanings—either the common acceptance of *man* as distinguished from *woman*, or the meaning of *mankind*. If the former, then it imported the masculine gender and thus, because of the 1850 Act, also included the feminine gender. If it had the meaning *mankind*, it was even clearer that it meant both *man* and *woman*. The women agreed with this argument. The men on the Board, however, did not follow the manly logic set forth in the 1850 Act and did not allow the women to register (*The Revolution*, October 29, 1868: 267).

The social injustices supported by grammar rules regarding the false generics *man* and *he* have been spelled out by many critics during the past one-hundred years, such as Charlotte Carmichael Stopes (1908) and Julia Stanley and Susan Robbins (1978). But such injustices have been denied or trivialized for as long.[11] One of the strategies women use in everyday speaking and writing is simply to use fewer false generics (Martyna 1983). They are often coerced into using them, however, in secretarial typing and academic writing. The many studies on the use of so-called generics make clear that even after more than one hundred years of legal and grammar book insistence that women are included in *man* and *he*, the truth is that they really are not.[12] In speech and writing, many people use the alternatives to the prescriptions set forth by law and grammarians.[13] As the nineteenth- and early-twentieth-century women fighting for suffrage and other legal reforms knew, the meaning and use of the so-called generic could mean the difference between economic survival and death. For many men, the generic debate is a manageable and trivial issue. They would like to focus attention on it and off other feminist issues.[14]

Uncovering men's past control of language also helps us witness their sexualizing of women's identity.[15] This uncovering can detail the kinds of ways women have been silenced. Alice Walker (1974: 66) asks, "What did it mean for a Black woman to be an artist in our grandmothers' time. . .?", that is, a time when Black women were given no books, no pens, no training in reading or writing.

Other methods have been used to silence women. Andrea Dworkin (1985) writes of the very differing responses to women's talk and screams as opposed to men's, and of the ways men's "freedom of speech" silences women. She writes that "Silence is what women have instead of speech." It is their form of relatively safe dissent.[16] But our silence does not say what is happening to us.

The revelation of the patriarchal aspects of our language and speech also helps us talk about the processes of definition and redefinition, create new expressions, and list those of our experiences which still have no name. To many women, the most difficult task is recognizing the unsaid—the lexicon gaps and the types of silences still to be broken. A short section of "love" nouns from Suzette Haden Elgin's (1985) dictionary of Laadan gives an illustration:

aayaa	mysterious love, not yet known to be welcome or unwelcome
aazh	love for one sexually desired at one time, but not now
ab	love for one liked but not respected
ad	love for one respected but not liked
am	love for one related by blood

ashon	love for one not related by blood, but kin of the heart
aye	love that is unwelcome and a burden
azh	love for one sexually desired now
eeme	love for one neither liked nor respected
oham	love for that which is holy
sham	love for the child of one's body, presupposing neither liking nor respect nor their absence

Elgin's dictionary of Laadan includes many words not easily translated into English except by lengthy definitions. Just two more examples of interest to many women: "Radiln" is defined as a non-holiday, a time allegedly a holiday but actually so much a burden because of work and preparations that it is a dreaded occasion, especially when there are too many guests and none of them help. "Ratho" is defined as a non-guest, someone who comes to visit knowing perfectly well that they are intruding and causing difficulty.

"To assess the damage is a dangerous act," Cherrie Moraga points out (quoted by Gloria Anzaldua 1981). Critics will, predictably, say that the activities we describe in this essay are not highly theoretical, that the women are ranting again, that their claims are strident, unsupported, and do not meet the authoritative aesthetic and academic standards (Spender 1986; Russ 1983). True, the work we cite will not convince those who follow highly formulaic, academic malestream (Mary O'Brien's term) research behavior, that is, people with little concern with the ways language is constructed by women and men, or with transforming gender asymmetries in talk. Many of the challenges to linguistic studies have come from the alternative visions of theorists not formally associated with any of the university research or teaching centers. These challenges combine with those of other brave people in academia who have used a variety of research and analytical techniques to contribute to an explosion of inquiry on and magnificent writing about women and language[17]; These challenges are breaking what Tillie Olsen (1979) calls "unnatural silences" imposed on those who, owing to circumstances of sex, race, and social class, have been discouraged or prevented from taking back the power of language and talk.

Notes

1. One definition of *radical*, listed in *A Feminist Dictionary* (Kramarae and Treichler with Russo 1986), comes from Kathie Sarachild, writing in 1973, who points out that the word comes from the Latin word for *root*.

And that is what we meant by calling ourselves radicals. We were interested in getting to the roots of the problems in society. You might say we wanted to pull up weeds in the garden by their roots, not just pick off the leaves at the top to make things look good momentarily. Women's Liberation was started by women who considered themselves radicals in this sense.

2. See Thorne et al. 1983 for an extensive annotated bibliography of some of these activities.

3. See Ostriker 1986 for a discussion of the struggle of women poets to achieve self-definition within literary traditions which are themselves committed to repress creative female voices.

4. See Penfield in this book for a more extensive description of surname changing by women.

5. See examples in Schulz 1975.

6. For fat women's discussion of terminology and oppression, see Schoenfielder and Wieser (1983).

7. Similar processes of renaming and creating new expressions are going on in many languages. In a letter published in *Manushi: A Journal About Women in Society* (No. 31, 1985: 26), Kalyani Chaudhuri of Calcutta states that as a government servant she is constantly cross-examined about her marital status.

I find that people will not rest without finding out the marital status of a woman they are introduced to, and, next, the occupation of her husband. It is as if the identity of the woman remains a blur without these dimensions.

The use of Ms. seems a strident declaration of foreign origin. I think the word Srimati should be used for all women, married or unmarried. In Bengali, as in the original Sanskrit, Srimati does not connote marriage. It simply means someone possessing Sri or grace, and is the feminine equivalent of Sriman, used of a man. . . . Where the person is known to be a woman, she may be addressed as Sm, without fussing about her marital status.

Incidentally, and purely coincidentally, Sm is an inversion of Ms.

8. For information about many of the publications and many of the presses—such as Shameless Hussy Press, Spinsters, Ink, and Kitchen Table Women of Color Press—see the periodical *off our back* and Hartman and Messer-Davidow, eds. (1982). These small independent presses have published major, "risky," feminist work. Many have suffered such (sometimes fatal) problems as lack of working capital or even vandalism.

9. Grahn (1978: 14) notes that *whom* is the standard form, but "to-who" is prettier and sounds like an owl—it has "fuller content."

10. This discussion combines storytelling and joking to encompass personal-experience narratives of both a serious and humorous nature, as well as formulaic jokes and spontaneous one-liners or witty remarks. We have combined discussion of these verbal art forms because of their overlapping and intermingling usage among women,

similarities in their functions in interaction, and parallel attitudes about women's use of these forms.

11. For some discussion of the use of generics by writers and researchers, see Dubois and Crouch in this book.

12. Henley, in this book, summarizes and cites numerous psychological studies confirming the exclusion of females by males in the perception of generic references.

13. See Miller and Swift 1980, Baron 1984, and other guidelines mentioned in Thorne et al. 1983 and *Women and Language*.

14. There are many jovial newspaper and news magazine columns written by men on this topic. In fact, they were so ubiquitous in the 1970s that it was difficult *not* to see those columns.

15. See, for example, *An Intelligent Woman's Guide to Dirty Words* (Todasco et al. 1973), which is a listing of definitions of women given in so-called standard dictionaries.

16. Women's and men's uses of passive sentence constructions deserve more study. Many feminists argue that men often leave the agent of such constructions unstated to make their statement more authoritive (e.g., "It is agreed that women have slower responses.")

See Christine Salem (1980) for observations on many feminists' use of passive sentence construction to avoid naming the enemy (e.g., "We are denied equality.") It might be suggested that with so few positions for women on university faculties, feminist faculty members often develop skill in the use of passive sentences as a verbal strategy of survival in the university.

17. See the bibliography in Thorne et al. 1983 for examples.

References

Anzaldúa, Gloria. 1981. Speaking in tongues: A letter to 3rd World women writers. In *This bridge called my back: Writings by radical women of color,* edited by Cherríe Moraga and Gloria Anzaldúa. Watertown, Mass.: Persephone Press, 165–173.

Awiakta, Marilou. 1986. Cherokee Eden (with aside): An alternative to the apple. *Fireweed: A Feminist Quarterly* (Native Women) 22 (Winter): 109–113.

Baron, Dennis. 1984. *Grammar and gender.* New Haven, Conn.: Yale University Press.

Bethel, Lorraine. 1982. "This infinity of conscious pain": Zora Neale Hurston and the Black female literary tradition. In *But some of us are brave: Black Women's Studies,* edited by Gloria T. Hull et al. Old Westbury, N.Y.: The Feminist Press, 176–188.

Cantor, Joanne R. 1976. What is funny to whom? *Journal of Communication* 26: 164–172.

Chapman, Anthony J. and Nicholas J. Gadfield. 1976. Is sexual humor sexist? *Journal of Communication* 26: 141–153.

Clarke, Cheryl. 1981. Lesbianism: An act of resistance. In *This bridge called my back: Writings by radical women of color,* edited by Cherríe Moraga and Gloria Anzaldúa, Watertown, Mass.: Persephone Press, 128–137.

Clinton, Kate. 1982. Making light: Another dimension some notes on feminist humor. *Trivia: A journal of ideas* Fall: 37–42.

Copper, Baba. 1985. The view from over the hill: Notes on ageism between lesbians. *Trivia: A Journal of Ideas* Summer: 48–63.

Coser, Rose L. 1960. Laughter Among Colleagues, *Psychiatry* 23: 81–95.

Daly, Mary. 1978. *Gyn/Ecology.* Boston: Beacon Press.

Dworkin, Andrea. 1985. Against the male flood: Censorship, pornography, and equality. *Trivia: A Journal of Ideas* Summer: 11–32.

Eakins, Barbara Westbrook, and R. Gene Eakins. 1978. *Sex differences in human communication.* Boston: Houghton Mifflin Company, 75–76.

Elgin, Suzette Haden, ed. *Lonesome node.* The Ozark Center for Language Studies, Route 4, Box 192–E, Huntsville AR 72740. (SASE)

————. 1984. *Native tongue.* New York: DAW.

————. 1985. *A first dictionary and grammar of Láadan.* Madison, Wisc.: Society for the Furtherance and Study of Fantasy and Science Fiction (Box 1624, Madison, WI 53701)

Frye, Marilyn, 1983. *The politics of reality: Essays in feminist theory.* Trumansburg, N.Y.: The Crossing Press.

Grahn, Judy, ed. 1978. *True to life adventure stories, vol. one.* Trumansburg, N.Y: The Crossing Press.

Green, Rayna. 1977. Magnolias grow in dirt: The bawdy lore of southern women. *Southern Exposure* 4: 29–33.

————. ed. 1984. *That's what she said: Contemporary poetry and fiction by Native American women.* Bloomington: Indiana University Press.

Hartman, Joan and Ellen Messer-Davidow, eds. 1982. *Women in print II: Opportunities for women's studies publication in language and literature.* New York: The Modern Language Assoc.

Jenkins, Mercilee M. 1984. "The story is in the telling: A cooperative style of conversation among women." In *Gewalt durch Sprache: die Vergewaltigung von Frauen in Gesprachen,* edited by Senta Trämel-Plötz. Frankfurt am Main: Fischer Taschenbuch Verlag. Also available through ERIC, ED 238 083.

————. In Press. "What's so funny?: Joking among women." *Proceedings of the First Women and Language Conference.* Berkeley, CA: Berkeley Women & Language Group.

Kălcik, Susan. 1975. ". . . like Ann's gynecologist or the time I was almost raped." In *Women and folklore,* edited by Claire R. Farrer. Austin: University of Texas Press, 3–11.

Kaufman, Gloria. 1980. Introduction. In *Pulling our own strings,* edited by Gloria Kaufman and Mary Kay Blakely. Bloomington, Ind.: Indiana University Press, 13–16.

Klepfisz, Irena. 1986. "Secular Jewish identity: *Yidishkayt* in America." In *The Jewish atribe of Dina: A Jewish women's anthology,* edited by Malanie Kaye/Kantrowitz and Irena Klepfisz. Special issue of *Sinister Wisdom* 29/30, 30–48.

Kramarae, Cheris, and Mercilee M. Jenkins. 1985. "Women changing words changing women." In *Sprachwandel und feministisch Sprachpolitik: Internationale Perspektiven,* edited by Marlis Hellinger. Wiesbaden: Westdeutscher, 10–22.

Kramarae, Cheris, and Paula Treichler, with assistance of Ann Russo. 1986. *A Feminist Dictionary.* New York: Pandora Press.

Langellier, Kristin M, and Eric E. Peterson. 1984. "Spinstorying: A communication analysis of women's storytelling." Paper given at the Speech Communication Association Convention, Chicago, Ill.

Lassiter, Mary. 1983. *Our names, our selves: The meaning of names in everyday life.* London: William Heinemann.

Levine, Joan B. 1976. The feminine routine. *Journal of Communication.* 26: 173–175.

Little, Judy. 1983. *Comedy and the woman writer.* Lincoln: Nebraska: University of Nebraska Press.

Martyna, Wendy. 1983. "Beyond the he/man approach: The case for nonsexist language." In *Language, gender and society,* edited by Barrie Thorne, Cheris Kramarae, and Nancy Henley. Rowley, Mass.: Newbury House 25–37.

Miller, Casey, and Kate Swift. 1980. *The handbook of nonsexist writing: For writers, editors and speakers.* New York: Lipincott and Crowell.

Mitchell, Carol A. 1977. "The sexual perspective in the appreciation and interpretation of jokes." *Western Folklore* 36: 303–329.

Moraga, Cherríe. 1981. "La Güera." In *This bridge called my back: Writing by radical women of color,* edited by Cherríe Moraga and Gloria Anzaldúa. Watertown, Mass.: Persephone Press, 27–34.

_____. 1983. *Loving in the war years.* Boston: South End Press.

_____. and Gloria Anzaldúa, eds. 1981. *This bridge called my back: Writings by radical women of color.* Watertown, Mass.: Persephone Press, 128–137.

Morales, Rosario. 1981. "We're all in the same boat." In *This bridge called my back: Writing by radical women of color,* edited by Cherríe Moraga and Gloria Anzaldúa. Watertown, Mass.: Persephone Press, 91–93.

Neitz, Mary Jo. 1980. "Humor, hierarchy, and the changing status of women." *Psychiatry* 43: 211–223.

Nilsen, Alleen Pace, Haig Bosmajian, H. Lee Gershuny, and Julia P. Stanley. 1977. *Sexism and language*. Urbana, Ill.: National Council of Teachers of English.

Olsen, Tillie. 1979. *Silences*. New York: Delacorte Press.

Ostriker, Alicia Suskin. 1986. *Stealing the language: The emergence of women's poetry in America*. Boston: Beacon Press.

Painter, Dorothy. 1980. "Lesbian humor as a normalization device." In *Communication, language and sex*, edited by Cynthia L. Berryman and Virginia A. Eman. Rowley, Mass.: Newbury House, 132–148.

Russ, Joanna. 1983. *How to suppress women's writing*. Austin: University of Texas.

Salem, J. Christine. 1980. "On naming the oppressor: What Woolf avoids saying in *A room of one's own*." In *The voices and words of women and men*, edited by Cheris Kramarae. London: Pergamon Press, 209–218. Also *Women's Studies International Quarterly* 3, no. 2/3 (1980), 209–218.

Schulz, Muriel. 1975. "The semantic derogation of woman." In *Language and sex: Difference and dominance*, edited by Barrie Thorne and Nancy Henley. Rowley, Mass: Newbury House, 64–75.

Schoenfielder, Lisa, and Barba Wieser, eds. 1983. *Shadow on a tightrope: Writing by women on fat oppression*. Iowa City: Aunt Lute Book Company.

Sheppard, Alice. 1985. "Funny women: Social change and audience response to female comedians." *Empirical Studies of the Arts* 3: 179–195.

Spender, Dale. 1980. *Man Made Language*. London: Routledge & Kegan Paul.

_____. 1982. *Women of ideas and what men have done to them: From Aphra Behn to Adrienne Rich*. London: Routledge & Kegan Paul.

_____. 1986. *Mothers of the novel: 100 good women writers before Jane Austen*. London: Pandora.

Stanley, Julia Penelope, and Susan Robbins [Wolfe]. 1978. "Going through the changes: The pronoun 'she' in Middle English." *Papers in Linguistics* 11: 71–88.

Stannard, Una. 1977. *Mrs Man*. San Francisco: Germainbooks.

Stopes, Charlotte Carmichael. 1908. *The sphere of "man": In relation to that of "woman" in the Constitution*. London: T. Fisher Unwin.

Todasco, Ruth, et al., eds. 1973. "An intelligent woman's guide to dirty words". Brochure published by Chicago Loop Center YWCA.

Thorne, Barrie, Cheris Kramarae, and Nancy Henley, eds. 1983. *Language, gender and society*. Rowley, Mass.: Newbury House.

Walker, Alice. 1974. "In search of our mothers' gardens: The creativity of Black women in the South" *Ms*. May: 64–70.

Women and Language. Periodicals edited by Cheris Kramarae and Paula
    Treichler, 244 Lincoln Hall, University of Illinois, Urbana, Ill. 61801.
Weisstein, Naomi, 1973. "Why we aren't laughing anymore." *Ms*. 49–51, 88–
    90.
Zimmerman, Bonnie. 1985. "The politics of transliteration: Lesbian personal
    narratives." In *The Lesbian Issue: Essays from Signs*, edited by Estelle B.
    Freedman, Barbara C. Gelpi, Susan L. Johnson, Kathleen M. Weston.
    Chicago: University of Chicago Press, 251–270.

Part III

Women of Color

The Role of American Indian Women in Cultural Continuity and Transition

Bea Medicine

The author, an anthropologist and member of the Lakota Sioux tribe in South Dakota, examines the impact of white culture and language on American Indian women. American Indian women contribute to the continuity of their ancestral culture through their role as mothers who pass on the ancestral language. They have helped to maintain the native language as story tellers and translators of native oratory. But they are also agents of change. Their skill in English has placed them in the role of *cultural brokers*—a dimension of power not held by male Indian leaders. Medicine discusses some of the repercussions of this gender role reversal.

American Indian and Alaskan Native women are perhaps the most neglected and grossly treated in the literature of minority women. This is true especially in research on speech forms and patterns of language usage in American Indian and Alaskan Native communities. Research on the language patterns of women in these communities suffers from the mistaken notion that such an entity as "the monolithic American Indian" exists. To speak of speech patterns typical of "the American Indian" and to make generalizations across tremendously complex and varied linguistic differences is obviously dangerous. There are an estimated 206 distinct languages being spoken by natives of North America which reflect totally distinct language stocks, with many of them being as dissimilar as English and Chinese (Chafe 1962). Such multiplicity of languages makes it extremely difficult to speak of the linguistic aspects of "the American Indian woman."

It is important to point out, however, that although there is great variation in American Indian languages, traditions, and customs, there is a common experience which these communities share historically as a result of language policies and practices imposed by various political institutions and education systems governing them. For example, many of the unique language systems of American Indians have been obliterated through the education policies of a federal government which often has sought to eliminate the cultural and linguistic differences of the indigenous tribes in order to pressure them into becoming part of the dominant culture. In some cases, this suppression of language has resulted in their decline or their death. Today, language retrieval and revitalization are seeking to undo the results of this linguistic oppression. In other cases, this oppression has had less devastating effects on American Indian communities and instead resulted in varying degrees of native language use among contemporary native peoples. As a result, one finds that there are extreme variations in the communicative skills in native languages from one tribal community to another on reservations or in urban areas.

The power of linguistic domination by the superimposition of an alien tongue—English—and an education system, both of which serve as instruments of social control, have markedly affected the structures, uses, and attitudes of the languages of subordination. Indian women are particularly affected by these sociohistorical circumstances for a variety of reasons to be discussed below. American Indian women perform at least three distinctive social roles through their patterns of language use in their communities. They maintain cultural values through the socialization of children; they serve as evaluators of language use by setting the normative standards of the native or ancestral tongue and English; and they are effective as agents of change through mediation strategies with the White society.

Enforcers of Tradition

The historical pattern of English language domination has been especially significant for Indian women—the primary socializers of children.

The introduction of the majority language—English—placed and continues to place a heavy burden on Indian women because adopting the English language often has meant losing linguistic symbols of culture and gaining male bias carried by the semantic system of English. One example is found in the very different way gender is handled in some American Indian languages and English.

Standard English with its male bias has often obviated the rich gender-based distinctions which exist in the ancestral language. To cite one example, Lakota Sioux, in any of its three dialects—Lakota, Dakota, or Nakota—has significant obligatory structural markers to indicate first person women's speech as opposed to men's speech. For the most part these markers consist of suffixes. For example, *Hanta yo* would be a command muttered by males to indicate "Get out!" *Hanta ye* would be the equivalent referential meaning for female speakers.

Aside from the more obvious linguistic obligatory markers which exist in American Indian ancestral languages and which do not in English, there are also an entire set of kinship terms serving to depict social and familial relationships in American Indian culture. Again, these do not exist in their English translation. Women are indirectly affected here again.

For example, in Lakota, gender-specific terms exist to indicate birth order and vocative designations, so that for females the simple English term "brother" would be distinguished in one of two ways depending on age: *tiblo* "older brother" versus *mi-sunka-la* "younger brother."* Conversely, similar terms are used by males to indicate feminine gender and age (or birth order). Moreover, in the bilateral kinship system, the terms are extended to parallel cousins or cross cousins, depending on the sex of the speaker. As a result, one can understand the confusion a superimposed kinship system, such as English, brought to social structures and reciprocal relationships in this particular American Indian culture and to others. In those cases where the ancestral language has literally died or barely continues to exist, often even linguistic marking of female-female relationships, feminine bonds, and responsive relationships have been obliterated.

Building on these ancestral kinship designations, mothers usually indicate proper behavior to daughters and other "daughters" in kinship equivalencies, such as female parallel cousins. One may commonly hear such affective assessment given to daughters as, "White persons don't have proper kinship names for brothers. But you know you respect your older brother, and take care of your younger one."

It may be that some Lakota persons as well as other American Indian groups have accepted or have been forced to accept the new kinship models imposed by the white culture and language. Although specific linguistic designations may no longer exist, other culturally revealing patterns of language usage remain. One such vestige is the "joking relationship." Such verbal interaction with its sexual connotation which an older sister's husband often extends towards his wife's younger sister or her younger female cousin reflect a language usage pattern which denotes the continuity of an ancient cultural form. Perhaps English or the ways of white people have not been effective in destroying core cultural values. In Lakota communities, women continue to participate in joking relationships, usually at public events. These jokes are always stated in Lakota, for it is felt that this type of humor is best expressed in the native tongue. Nuance and repartee reflect skillful manipula-

---

EDITOR'S NOTE:
*There are, of course, many language communities throughout the world which have been in contact with English and yet retained such distinctions as age and familial relationship in their use of English. Nigerian English "senior brother" and "junior brother" is one such example. The fact that Lakota and other American Indian communities may not retain such distinctions marks the extent of the cultural oppression which the adoption of the English language in the United States has imposed.

tion of language and add to the enjoyment of the group. Some women are known for their remarkable wit and subtlety in "joking" and "putting men down" by their verbal skills.

There are other instances where women of an older generation who stayed at home and attended local schools rather than going away to governmental or parochial boarding schools are known to have greater knowledge in oral history or knowledge of traditional techniques and material items. These women are often envied for this unique and valued information, not only by other women but by Lakota males as well. It is in the rich folklore and legendary domain that much knowledge is being lost in cultural transmission to children, especially grandchildren. These youngsters tend to be monolingual in English and thus stories detailing "how it was in the old days" are usually told in English. Folktales and proverbs which have traditionally served as prescriptive devices are not totally significant in contemporary communities in the native idiom. Cultural retrieval programs have succeeded in collecting folktales and legends in English. Folktales have also been recorded in the native language. Whether in English or the native language, these have relied heavily on women's contribution, both as storytellers and translators of native oratory.

Cultural Brokers

One particular role which women have played and continue to play in many American Indian cultures is that of mediator between their own community and White society. They are often vested with this role because of their facility with the English language. In many communities, women acquire English more readily than men, and this resulting competence often places them in the role of mediator. One can hear statements such as the following made by a Brule Sioux male from the Rosebud reservation: "*They* (BIA administrators, county welfare workers, judges, and police officers) listen to women when they talk to them."

Yet, while there is a realization of the need for such mediators on the part of Indian men, there is at the same time a great deal of dislike, criticism, and frustration. Males often criticize women for learning the English tongue "too well," since getting too close to the White society is taken as a sign of assimilation and consequent rejection of one's own cultural values. But the fact that women are put in the role of mediators becomes a point of frustration for males. They envy them for their bilingual skill and especially the power associated with it in the dominant society. In a sense, such language usage patterns make males feel helpless in the face of oppression and racism in a dominant White society. This emasculation often leads to conflict between males and females, exhibited too often toward wives in verbal or physical battering. Such conflict is an especially onerous position to men in Northern Plains Indian societies, which have been labeled "Warrior" societies. Since male self-valuation has produced a sense of male superiority, the "macho" image is eroded by such speech usage patterns, and the locus of control in male/female relationships is seen by males as being usurped.

Lakota Sioux adults can be seen in dual roles as cultural conservators and cultural innovators in the area of language use. This traditional role of cultural guardian is seen vividly in this example from Ella Deloria (1945: 43) who uses it to include all adults:

Nor was it any wonder that small children rapidly learned their social duties, since the training constantly given them was calculated to condition them and direct them in that way. All grown-ups by tacit consent seemed to "gang up" for that purpose. Even before a child was aware of his kinship obligations they make sentences and put the correct words and formal speeches into his mouth for him to repeat to this or that relative. It was their informal but constant system of education in human relations and social responsibility.

But it was acknowledged that the major socializers of children were the Lakota females, even though both men and women taught the proper kin terms which guaranteed smoothly working *tiospaye* (extended family) relationships in a traditional setting. It was this sharing of child training which was quickly submerged in a new superimposed system of patriarchal orientations, a system foisted on the Lakota in the acculturational process which held to the ideal that the training of children was entirely in the woman's domain. Along with the demolition of the warrior role among the Sioux, and the fact that women were often sent to get the rations which were doled out in the early reservation period, women began a subtle but functional assumption of the role of cultural broker or mediator. In addition, women were often recruited to work in the houses of missionaries and of other agents of change. In order to interact on this level, women learned the English language as a means of survival in a rapidly changing situation. Women also taught the children that interaction in two different worlds required entirely different languages and subsumed a new behavioral pattern.

Interestingly, women were recruited along with the men to attend off-reservation schools in such far-removed places as Hampton, Virginia, and Carlisle, Pennsylvania. It was in these schools that the native language was suppressed and both sexes learned to excel in reading and writing English. It was usually the Indian men who said that they had completely lost their ability to speak the native tongue after returning to the reservation. On the other hand, oral history accounts, such as those of the Standing Rock Reservation, substantiate that women were often called on to deliver speeches in community events such as Christmas and New Year's celebrations, weddings, and other public events.

In the public sphere as well as the private ones, Lakota women are groomed to be expressive. Even today when I return home, I am expected to address the crowds at Pow Wow celebrations and other community events. The skill of public speaking was and is now equally accessible and available to both Lakota males and females.

At the time when Tribal Councils were first functioning on reservations, some Lakota members often took their daughters to observe the meetings, and they thus became aware of the *Pogo* (political climate of a new institution). Since meetings were conducted in English and Lakota, fluency in both languages was enhanced. It was not surprising that Standing Rock had a female Tribal Chair in the 1940s and another in the 1950s. This may have been unusual, but the thrust to biculturalism and bilingualism was seen as a means to understanding the superimposed culture with a strong background in the native one. The females fulfilled both.

As mothers, women have played an important role in educating their children in the proper usage of the English language through games devised for this purpose. Such training has added a great deal to the success of their children in school. Often contextual situations were pointed out to indicate to the child the proper vernacular mode. Students who lived at home had parental surrogates within the kinship network as well as parents who supported their efforts. Speech-making was still part of the expected behavior pattern. More important, before the days of relevant Indian curricula, many of the mothers encouraged the use of oral history, legends, and native materials to write histories of the various villages or towns on the reservation as a means of interesting students in improving writing competency in English.

Evaluators of Language

Women in American Indian communities hold a wide variety of different attitudes toward language usage. They range from very traditional ones in which ancestral language and values are tenaciously adhered to, even though English is also used, to a more assimilationist one in which children are not even spoken to in their ancestral language. Some families try to maintain a truly bilingual home. As mothers, women play a decisive role in the whole matter of language choice, since it is often their decision that determines which language the child will acquire naturally. Some continue speaking the ancestral language to the child but send the child to a school in which English is the only language of instruction. Others speak English only. Still others follow a bilingual model through the use of more modern bilingual schooling. For example, some Southeastern groups such as Lumbee or Pamunkey, although claiming to be native, do not have a cultural or linguistic base which reflects a tribal character. On the other hand, such groups in the Northeast as the Passamaquody or the Penobscot have retained a native language base. In the Southwest, the Navajo evidence a high degree of monolingualism in their native language. It could be argued that women have contributed greatly to these variations in bilingualism. A long-distinguished "Indian" trait seems to center on native autonomy; the choice is usually made by the mother or maternal surrogate as to which language or languages will be used and consequently learned by the child. It is often the case, however, that one hears statements regarding the loss of language, such as, "I'm sorry that my mother did not teach me my native language."

This paper has discussed various aspects of women's role in American Indian communities as manifested by the use of the ancestral language and English. As males and females within these communities have acknowledged, the impact and importance of native women in cultural and linguistic continuity is noteworthy.

References

Chafe, Wallace L. 1962. "Estimates Regarding the Present Speakers of North American Indian Languages," *International Journal of American Linguistics* 28: 161–171.

Deloria, Ella. 1945. *Speaking of Indians*. New York: Friendship Press.

Dumont, Robert V. 1972. "Learning English and How to be Silent—Studies in Sioux and Cherokee Classrooms. In *Functions of Language in the Classroom*, edited by C. Cazden, V. John, & D. Hymes. New York: Teacher's College Press.

Hill, Ruth Beebe. 1979. *Hanta Yo*. New York: Macmillan.

Leap, William T., ed. 1977. *Studies in Southwestern English*. San Antonio: Trinity University Press.

Malancon, Richard, & Mary Jo Malancon. 1977. "Indian English at Haskell, 1915." In *Studies in Southwestern English*, edited by William Leaf. San Antonio: Trinity University Press.

Medicine, Bea. " 'Speaking Indian': Parameters of Language Use Among American Indians." FOCUS, March, 6 (1981), 1–8.

_____. 1979a. "Native American Speech Patterns: The Case of the Lakota Speakers." In *Handbook of Intercultural Communications,* edited by Molefi Ashante, Eileen Newmark & Cecil Blake. Beverly Hills, CA.: Sage Publications.

————————. 1979b. "Bilingual Education and Public Policy: The Cases of the American Indians." In *Bilingual Education and Public Policy in the United States,* edited by Raymond Padilla. Ypsilanti, Michigan: Eastern Michigan University.

————————. 1979c. "Issues in the Professionalization of Indian Women." Paper presented to the American Psychological Association, Toronto.

Metcalf, Ann. December 1978. "A Model for Treatment in a Native American Family Service Center." Oakland, CA.: Urban Indian Child Resource Center.

Phillips, Susan. 1972. "Participant Structures and Communicative Competence: Warm Springs Children in Community and Classroom." In *Functions of Language in the Classroom,* edited by C. Cazden, V. John, & D. Hymes. New York: Teacher's College Press.

Language and Female Identity in the Puerto Rican Community

Ana Celia Zentella

Puerto Rican females are on the cutting edge of language change. Their many different patterns of bilingualism and bidialectalism provide a unique understanding of the role of women in the process of language change. These issues are examined here in the context of the social dimensions of Puerto Rican identity.

Current statistics reveal that Puerto Ricans are the most disadvantaged ethnic group in the United States (Puerto Rican Forum 1981). In comparison with Whites, Blacks, Mexican-Americans and others, Puerto Ricans as a group have the highest percentage of families living below the poverty level, the highest percentage of families with children living in poverty, the lowest participation in the labor force, and the lowest median income. Instead of improving, the socioeconomic situation of Puerto Ricans over the last decade has deteriorated. In 1975, the median income of Puerto Ricans was 59% of the national median income, but in 1985, Puerto Ricans earned only 47% of the national income—a 12% drop in ten years.

The most disadvantaged members of the most disadvantaged group are Puerto Rican women, 62% of whom earn less than $5,000 per year. In the crucial area of job experience, Puerto Rican women are the least likely of Hispanic women to have had work experience. Today the number of Puerto Rican women over fourteen years of age in the labor force is roughly one-half that of other Hispanics. Compounding this lack of access to jobs is the fact that twice as many Puerto Rican families (41%) are headed by women as other Hispanic families (Hispanic Research Center 1984).

Although researchers have begun to document the desperate socioeconomic conditions that most Puerto Rican and other Hispanic women endure, they have yet to explore the reasons why these conditions exist from the point of view of a comprehensive analytical framework. Most of the scarce research available has as its point of departure a static view of Hispanic culture that is divorced from the socioeconomic realities in which the cultural group is acting and reacting. As result, study after study seems repetitively similar as each of them probes the source of the problems faced by Hispanic women (Andrade 1982). The "causes" which are frequently pinpointed include the Hispanic male's machismo, the Roman Catholic Church's focus on female self-sacrifice, and the fatalism and personalism of the Spanish heritage. The "conclusions" of these studies seem very convincing, since the structure of both the Hispanic family and the Church favor male development and female underdevelopment. At first glance, it seems logical to explain the Puerto Rican female's dismal statistics as a result of her learned gender roles.

Andrade (1982) has documented at least four recurrent problems with the research which has isolated culture as the crucial variable in the study of Latina women: the view of the culture is too homogeneous, the research is ethnocentrically biased, the samples are small and limited to single communities, and the methodology is culturally inappropriate. Moreover, it is undoubtedly true that culture does play a role, and a significant one, but *it alone* does not determine Puerto Rican behavior and conditions. Latinas in the United States do not live in test tubes isolated from the conflicting influences of the socioeconomic structures around them, as illustrated by the changing nature of the labor market and the use of welfare for social control. Neither are Puerto Rican women immune to the effects of class, race, national origin, and linguistic differences.

Identity Conflicts: Nationality, Race, Language

The problems that Puerto Ricans share with all lower working class people are exacerbated by identity conflicts which are triggered by such forces as the colonial status of Puerto Rico, racism, and feelings of linguistic inferiority. Puerto Ricans are prevented from achieving goals they set for themselves because they are made to feel in conflict with who they are, what color they are, and what language they should speak. This negative impact is likely to be more severe in each of these areas on Puerto Rican women than on men because each corresponds to a domain that is traditionally considered female.

The impact of Puerto Rican migration on national identity is central to the identity crisis. Every group of migrants suffers the trauma of uprooting and the consequences of cultural conflict, but the Puerto Rican migration is unique even among Hispanic groups in one fundamental way: the United States' control of the governmental, education, and linguistic policies affecting Puerto Ricans predates their arrival in the United States. Since Puerto Rico has been a colony of the United States since 1898, Puerto Ricans born in the United States or on the island are citizens of the United States from birth. As a result, American citizenship conflicts with Puerto Rican identity even in the native land. But as far as the definition of identity is concerned, most Puerto Rican parents raise their children to believe that those who are born in Puerto Rico are Puerto Ricans and those who are born in the United States are "American." This cleavage within families—often based on accidents of birth, given the massive back and forth migration—contribute to the confusion of the children, especially if they find that they are not perceived as "real" Americans by others. The effect on women, because they are most frequently linked in poetry and politics to the "motherland," is pronounced. Thus, there is confusion over WHAT AM I? PUERTO RICAN OR AMERICAN?

The racial aspect of the identity crisis that young Puerto Ricans in the United States face is shared by all other peoples of color, but it conflicts with traditional Puerto Rican values. Here in the United States, Puerto Ricans learn that United States racial categories convert Hispanic culture into a race—a nonwhite race—when they are asked to select among Black-White-Other, or Black-White-Hispanic, on census and other questionnaires. Such classifications ignore the fact that, unlike the United States, where genotypic theories classify persons with one drop of Black blood as Black, Hispanics are a mixture of three races. In contrast, in Puerto Rico, people with fair features are considered "blancos" ('white'), those whose features are African are considered "negros" ('Black'), and the more prevalent combinations of these groups and others, including Native Americans and Asians, are recognized with a multitude of terms, for example, "tregeño" ('olive skinned'), "indio" ('Indian'), and various mixtures of black and white, such as "grifo," "jabao," "mulato," "moreno," and so on. Whereas racial identification supercedes cultural identity in the United States, the reverse is true for Latin America, where people are identified primarily by their culture (Rodriquez 1980). This inversion of the primary factors of identification contributes to the identity conflict of Hispanics in the United States, particularly among the second generation and among females, who are more concerned about standards of beauty. A darker-skinned male is less exposed to the tyranny of "hay que mejorar la raza" ('we must better the race'), that is, by marrying a light-skinned rather than a dark-skinned female. In short, there is confusion over WHAT COLOR AM I? WHITE OR BLACK? In response to the three-way conflicting pressures they feel between their parents' cultural identity, the United States denigration of blackness, and the Afro-American reaffirmation of Black pride, many Puerto Rican youth of all complexions have chosen to identify themselves as neither White nor Black but as "nonwhite".

These identity conflicts are further exemplified by the linguistic insecurity resulting from consistent attacks on the way Puerto Ricans speak. One of the most effective lessons that Puerto Rican children learn in United States classrooms is to be ashamed of the variety of Spanish spoken both in their native land and in their home by their parents. This is achieved through such practices as constant correction and denunciation of Puerto Rican Spanish pronunciation, vocabulary, and grammar. Puerto Ricans are told that they speak a dialect of Spanish that is not "real" Spanish, harkening back to the antilinguistic postures held by the first United States colonial administrators of the island who were horrified when they did not find Puerto Ricans speaking the Spanish of Castile (Zentella 1981a).

Today's detractors are as unaware as the first colonial administrators were of basic notions of language variety and its social correlates. Speakers of every language share certain features of pronunciation, grammar, and word formation with others in their community, and these become important symbols of membership in a particular group. This variety is what is meant by the word dialect; dialects distinguish each geographical region, class, ethnic group, and race from others. Just as people of Great Britain say "flat" and "qestionnaire" for what North Americans call apartment and pronounce "questionnaire," Puerto Ricans say "china" and "graciah" instead of "naranja" and "gracias." Except in the minds of some arch anglophiles, British English is not considered superior to American English. Similarly, Puerto Rican Spanish should not be considered inferior to any other Spanish dialect.

Puerto Ricans in the United States are caught in a linguistic double bind; their Spanish is considered unacceptable and so is their English. Many New Yorkers with characteristic New York accents ridicule the Spanish accented English of island-born and island-reared Puerto Ricans, and qualified teacher applicants from this group have received poor grades on the New York City Board of Education's oral exam because of their accents. Puerto Ricans are not blind to the fact that while many North Americans consider French and other accents of English elegant, Spanish accents are often considered laughable or repulsive. Inevitably, the adults lose confidence in their ability to speak and learn English, and their children—the second generation—learn to be ashamed of their parents because of the latter's accents. Many parents, particularly mothers, must depend on young children to negotiate for them in their encounters with bureaucracies. Such experiences tear at the strong family fabric that is characteristic of Puerto Rican culture, and they help destroy traditional notions of "respeto" ('respect') in adult-child relationships. Yet another aspect of Puerto Rican English that is subjected to attack is the assimilation of the second generation's English to the surrounding Black dialect (Wolfram 1973). Many young Puerto Ricans learn to speak like the Afro-Americans with whom they share the schools and ghettoes. These Puerto Rican youngsters become the object of a new epithet: "You sound like a spic" is replaced by "you sound like a nigger." Males tend to adopt Black street speech more readily than females because of its covert prestige as rough and masculine; females tend to use the local white vernacular dialect in their formal speaking style (Poplack 1981). Thus, there is confusion over WHICH LANGUAGE SHOULD I SPEAK, SPANISH OR ENGLISH? WHICH SPANISH SHOULD I SPEAK, PUERTO RICO'S OR SPAIN'S? WHICH ENGLISH SHOULD I SPEAK, BLACK OR WHITE?

Language Socialization in El Barrio

In East Harlem, New York City—the Puerto Rican community known as El Barrio—where I conducted research between 1978 and 1981 (Zentella 1981), children are exposed to a very rich linguistic environment. There is constant activity and interaction in varieties of Spanish and English. In the midst of overflowing garbage cans, ripped out doorways, and gaping mailboxes, several intimate social networks gather against the backdrop of tenements and housing projects. Age and gender are the basic linking factors in these social networks for both children and adults, and each one is identified with Spanish or English. Each network established by age and gender has its own favorite space and time on the block for socializing, and good weather brings everyone down to "janguear" ('hangout') for a while. When the women between forty and sixty years of age take time out between their household chores to chat, they congregate in the hallway vestibules that house the mailboxes and face the street. Their conversations are in Spanish because they are Spanish dominant. Some are monolingual. The Spanish-dominant men of the same age stand or sit around a domino table and parked cars located in front of the "bodega" ('grocery store') and "banca" ('numbers parlor'). The "young dudes" in their early twenties are English dominant. Lovers of disco and salsa music, they lean against parked cars or stand outside video arcades with their "boxes" (large radios). The younger mothers are English-dominant women in their late teens and early twenties who sometimes lean against other cars or sit on the narrow stoops or steps of the tenements, or on park benches, with their baby carriages alongside. Teenagers congregate in the video arcade along with Afro-Americans or move to sit on cars during private discussions. The young children (three to twelve-year-olds) have the run of the area in front of their building. They whirl about from one area to the next and thus are always subject to the supervision of one of the networks. As a result, the children are intermittently addressed by monolingual standard or nonstandard Spanish speakers, monolingual standard and nonstandard English speakers, and by bilingual and bidialectal speakers of both languages. Because of the linguistic diversity on the block, the children grow up to be bilingual and bidialectal.

First-generation adults from the island's larger towns and from families better off than most constitute one segment of the community. Because they were privileged enough to be able to pursue their education beyond the elementary grades, they speak the standard Spanish of Puerto Rico (referred to as PRS from here on). Other block residents who were born and raised of poorer families in Puerto Rico, often from rural areas, share most pronunciation features with their more educated neighbors, along with a few nonstandard characteristics such as the substitution of "l" for "r" at the end of syllables, for example, "coltal" for "cortar" ('to cut'). The second-generation children of both groups tend to speak more English than Spanish; thus, their Spanish vocabulary and grammar are more heavily influenced by English.

There is a greater divergence in the varieties of English spoken on the block than in the varieties of Spanish. Both first and second generations speak PRS, but those who were reared in Puerto Rico speak a variety of English which is marked by Spanish-language interference phenomena, while the second generation speaks two kinds of nonstandard English: Puerto Rican English (PRE) and/or Black English Vernacular (BEV) (Wolfram 1974). PRE is the principal linguistic code shared by those who were born and raised in the United States. Despite the fact that each social network is generally identifiable by one code only, (e.g., older females with PRS, young dudes with BEV, and elementary school-age children with PRE), members often speak more than one variety, depending on interlocutors and speech situations. Dialectal variation is charactristic of many speakers on the block.

With such language diversity on the block, how do children decide what to speak to whom? Children learn to respond to older adults in accordance with the community norm "Speak the language spoken to you," which is required by both the presence of monolinguals and the cultural importance of "respeto" ('respect'). It is more likely that female children are expected to comply with this norm than males because "respeto" implies notions of politeness, and polite behavior is expected of females in most cultures (Brown 1980). Thus, it is more polite to address others, especially adults, in the language they know best. The girls who were the main subjects of my research developed fairly accurate strategies for identifying the primary or dominant language of people whom they did not know. Specifically, they used three reference points: the physical characteristics that distinguish Puerto Ricans and other Latin Americans from North Americans, the age-related classification that assumes infants and the elderly speak only Spanish and all others know English, and the gender-related patterns that link women with speaking Spanish and men with speaking English.

Differences in bilingual language behavior and proficiency can be accounted for by many variables (Zentella in press), but the socialization of Puerto Rican children into appropriate female and male roles is particularly significant. This process provides girls with more exposure to and participation in Spanish than their brothers, for example, greater restriction to the house and/

or mother, play and friendships with females, caretaking responsibilities with infants, attendance at Spanish religious services, and inclusion in female discussions and activities like cooking, cleaning, sewing, taking clothes to the laundromat, and watching the "novela" ('soap opera'). Distinct periods in the maturation process favor one language or another, or the ability to switch from one to another (Flores et al 1983). As children go through school, English becomes their dominant language; as they accompany their mother in her round of appointments at hospitals, agencies, schools, and so on they become keenly aware of the survival value of English in the world of education, housing, social services, and employment. Female teens become particularly adept at alternating between Spanish and English to maneuver in public and private domains and to accomplish varied discourse objectives (see code-switching below). Young mothers are reintegrated into the older women's Spanish-speaking network as they discuss childbearing and take up the responsibilities of home management. Thus, the older a woman gets in the community, the more Spanish she is likely to use.

Twenty-year-old Vicky was typical of many of the young women in this regard. She was born and raised in New York City and had never been to Puerto Rico, but her parents were Spanish dominant and spoke to her in Spanish. Vicky answered in Spanish and English, but was much more fluent in the latter; she spoke English to her sisters and brothers and close friends. When she met and fell in love with Tito, another Puerto Rican born and raised in New York City, she spoke English to him and his sisters and brothers, but Spanish to his monolingual mother. When they married and had children, Vicky was in daily contact with her mother-in-law because they lived in the same building, and she became a regular participant in her mother-in-law's network of older women who offered advice, recipes, first aid, and spiritual support. When their son Eddie was born, Vicky and Tito spoke to him in English, but Eddie was always around his mother when she was speaking Spanish to the older women. She believed that her children should speak the language which the person they were talking to spoke best, but because Eddie's Spanish was very limited, this was not enforced. When it became obvious that Eddie had some difficulty speaking, his mother expressed the opinion that there should be no restrictions on her son's choice of language; her overriding concern was that he speak the language that he knew best, which was English. Eddie's gender, his young age, and his speech problem absolved him from the community norm that requires children to speak the best language of their addressee.

Vicky's position may change as Eddie grows, if his English becomes clearer, and if he learns Spanish. Significantly, Vicky's own Spanish fluency is increasing as she takes on the duties of older women, for example, attending family funerals in Puerto Rico, and she gradually becomes part of their network. This, in turn, may strengthen her children's knowledge of Spanish. On the other hand, she may be joined by the mothers of other third-generation children who may reject the "best language of your addressee" norm as an imposition and/or interference with the child's linguistic development. Schools play a big role in the oration of these attitudes because, contrary to the research linking bilingualism to greater cognitive and verbal flexibility, several mothers have been told by teachers that speaking to the children in two languages will impede their language development. There are already some children on the block, like Eddie, whose Spanish is so limited that they have a hard time addressing each interlocutor in the proper language; but most make some attempt to do so. Very often children manage greetings and routine exchanges in Spanish, but switch to English shortly thereafter. What are the cultural implications of the children's increased dominance in English? Will Puerto Ricans share the fate of other linguistic minorities who have lost their mother tongue by the third generation? The preeminent role of women in child rearing, their immersion in Spanish-linked activities, their responsibility for contacts with the family in Puerto Rico, and the traditional association of the home or "we" language with feelings of personal intimacy and group solidarity, make women the culture bearers, that is, those given most responsibility for maintenance of the home language and cultural survival.

Puerto Rican Cultural Identity and Language

Principal responsibility for the maintenance of the Spanish language places a heavy burden on Puerto Rican females. Given the influence of more than four hundred years of Spanish rule, the United States' imposition of English, and the lack of other means of national identity, the survival of Spanish has become inextricably linked for many with the survival of Puerto Rican identity and that of the Puerto Rican nation itself. As one United States Puerto Rican sociologist explained it, "To be Puerto Rican is to be inseparable from your language, so it is particularly offensive to any Puerto Rican to listen to anyone who claims to be Puerto Rican and does not know the language" (Betances quoted by Ghighliotty 1983). Paralleling the consistent identification of Puerto Rican identity with the Spanish language is a concern for the repercussions of extended contact with English. Many of the island's intellectuals and others believe that English has had a continuously deteriorating effect on the Spanish of the island and that Puerto Rico's national identity itself is being threatened.

This debate is especially heated and guarded when returnees—those who have lived in the United States and returned to Puerto Rico—are considered.

The widespread interest in the returned migrant "problem" and the increased intensity of the attacks on Spanish and English in the island's media do not appear to be disconnected. The returnees too have strong views on the matter. In a recent study conducted by the author (Zentella 1986), forty-three bilingual teens (twenty-three females, twenty males) who had returned to Puerto Rico and were in high school were queried about their view of their use of Spanish. More than 87% of them rejected the idea that they are negatively influencing the island's Spanish, and 76% of them said that they were not damaging the English language either. Those who agreed that they were having a deleterious impact on the languages could mention only slang words as evidence, obviously confusing lexical variation with deterioration. Another more fundamental insight was gleaned from their position on the link between language and culture.

When interviewed about the future of Spanish in Puerto Rico, approximately 40% of the teen returnees who were surveyed agreed with the prediction that Spanish would not be spoken on the island in fifty years. The majority were not distressed by the prospect of a non-Spanish-speaking Puerto Rico in the future. Fifty-six % stated that it would not bother them if the prediction mentioned previously came true. Young Puerto Ricans in Puerto Rico have obviously extended the New York Puerto Ricans' acceptance of a Puerto Rican identity without Spanish (Attinasi 1980). This view is not popular in Puerto Rico's academic, artistic, or political circles; it is vehemently rejected by those whose every fiber cries out against the vision of a non-Spanish-speaking Puerto Rico. But any analysis of the returnee versus islander conflict must be viewed in the context of the political and economic forces that have resulted in the massive displacement and replacement of Puerto Rican people from their island. A people's language, attitudes, and behavior are shaped by the nature of their experiences with the social structure around them and the roles they are forced to play in it. Adolescents, particularly females, caught in the middle of the transfer of people and payments can be expected to reflect this conflict in their notions of identity and language. They attempt to resolve the conflict via their commitment to bilingualism and biculturalism, only to encounter hostility to this solution both in the United States and in Puerto Rico.

Our survey of language attitudes held by adolescent returnees in Puerto Rico revealed some interesting differences between males and females. Although the majority of both sexes agreed on most questions, females were more conservative in matters of language loyalty. For example, the only respondents who stated that English monolinguals could not be considered Puerto Rican were women. Also, females supported the notion that Spanish is indispensable to Puerto Rican identity more than did the males (48% versus 30%). Although the women were equally divided as to whether they would care if Spanish were spoken in Puerto Rico in fifty years, the men showed less ambivalence; 67% of them would not care.

Our sample was too limited to allow us to assert that language loyalty is stronger among Puerto Rican bilingual females than males. There is, however, enough sociolinguistic evidence about female participation in the maintenance of appropriate linguistic norms in other communities to make us confident that further investigation will corroborate our tentative findings (Labov 1972; Trudgill 1974). Sociolinguistic research on gender and language suggests that women are more aware than men of the link between social status and speech. This may be so becaue it constitutes important knowledge for those responsible for preparing children to succeed. In this way, women serve as proprietors of the standard dialect. One reflection of women's sensitivity to the issues of language and class is the fact that women are more resistant to changing their way of speaking if linguistic change in the community is moving away from the prestige norm. For example, if a community begins to pronounce a word differently, women will continue using the original pronunciation longer than men. On the other hand, women are usually the leaders of linguistic changes that correlate to prestigious ways of speaking or a prestigious language variety. As one example, educated Southern women are now using more "r's" after vowels in their speech than male Southerners—e.g., "car" (Nichols 1974). In sum, women are alert to the appropriate norms which may be the most conservative in the community or the ones on the cutting edge of change. In either case, they seem to take the language pulse of the community and guide their children accordingly. In the New York Puerto Rican community, women who are faithful to their traditional role as keepers of the culture speak more Spanish and express more loyalty to it, but they also adapt to the need of the English-dominant society by becoming fluent bilinguals and proficient code-switchers.

Code-switching is the bilingual alternation of words, phrases, and sentences. Unfortunately, it is the most misunderstood behavior in language minority communities in the United States. Perhaps the most frequent linguistic accusation hurled at young Puerto Ricans in the United States is that they speak neither English nor Spanish, but *Spanglish*, meaning a haphazard mixture of which they in turn become ashamed. In fact, as children develop the ability to switch between the sounds and grammars of the two languages which they know in order to address different people, they also learn to extend this ability to switch for stylistic purposes and to accomplish it within the boundaries of a sentence (Zentella 1983). Often code-switching is misinterpreted as evidence of a lack of linguistic knowledge, but a spate of recent research has proved that switching serves many significant social and discourse functions beyond that of filling in forgotten words or phrases (see collection in Duran 1981). Nor does code-switching signal the deterioration of one or both of the languages involved; in fact, switchers display formidable knowledge of sentence structure (Poplack 1979; Sankoff and Poplack 1980). In a bilingual community such as El Barrio, code-switching allows Puerto Ricans to make a graphic statement about the way they live with a foot in each of "Dos Worlds/Two Mundos," as the title of Padron's (1983) poem reflects. Our data and that of the Centro de Estudios Puertorriqueños (Poplack 1981) showed that the most prolific intrasentential code-switchers were also the best speakers of English and Spanish, and that these were usually women. This evidence contradicts Robin Lakoff's contention that switchers never become fluent in either of their codes and that they waste time and energy in deciding which code is appropriate for each situation (Lakoff 1975). Lakoff was referring to monolingual women who learn to switch between speech styles because they are criticized as weak when they "talk like ladies" but are in turn labeled "unfeminine" when they do not. This analogy is also applicable to bilingual code-switchers in the Hispanic community. The very survival of Puerto Rican children often depends on how they present themselves and how they speak. The responsibility for such rearing is placed squarely on the shoulders of women, both by the traditional culture and the sexist divisions of labor in the United States. The situation is aggravated by the fact that almost one-half of the families are headed by women alone. If Lakoff is right, the Puerto Rican woman's concern about maintaining the home culture and preparing her children for the dominant outside culture, about being proficient in both English and Spanish and switching between both, can be debilitating and stress producing. This is the stereotypic picture painted in the research that was discussed at the beginning of this essay. But contrary to prevalent stereotypes, the reality is that most Puerto Rican women do succeed in raising their children to be healthy people, despite the triple jeopardy of gender, race, and class, and despite the conflicts about national origin and linguistic and cultural differences. When we seek out the wellsprings of the coping strength of these women, we find that bilingualism and code-switching are vital. Neither the maintenance of Spanish nor the ability to code-switch have a noxious effect on the development of the individual or the community, except when these are accorded differential power and respect by the dominant society. Like their Taino, Spanish, and African sisters before them, today's Puerto Rican female survivors turn what others see as their liabilities into their strengths. For many of those who "make it," poverty, racial mixture, female status, and linguistic difference become sources of power and confidence. Accordingly, such women can represent a vital contribution to the achievement of greater equality in the United States. The appreciation that Puerto Rican women have of the value of bilingualism and their commitment to cultural pluralism has led them to the leadership of the movement for equity and excellence in education via the bilingual model.

Similarly, their survival in alien institutions can help to teach poor children to overcome formidable obstacles, and their mixed Indian, African, and European blood can help bridge the United States polarization between black and white. Their ability to speak both Spanish and English is an invaluable asset as they struggle to survive in their two worlds and to accomplish these laudable goals.

References

Andrade, Sally. 1982. "Family Roles of Hispanic Women: Stereotypes, Empirical Findings and Implications for Research." In *Work, Family, and Health: Latina Women in Transition*, edited by R. Zambrana. New York: Hispanic Research Center, Fordham University.

Attinasi, John. 1979. "Language Attitudes in a New York Puerto Rican Community." In *Bilingualism and Public Policy: Puerto Rican Perspectives* (reprints from a conference) New York: Centro de Estudios Puertorriqueños.

Brown, Penelope. 1980. "How and Why are Women More Polite: Some Evidence from a Mayan Community." In *Women and Language in Literature and Society,* edited by Sally McConnell-Ginet, Ruth Borker, & Nelly Furman. New York: Praeger.

Duran, Richard, ed. 1981. *Latino Language and Communicative Behavior*. Norwood, N.J.: Ablex Press.

Flores, Juan, John Attinasi, and Pedro Pedraza Jr. 1981. "*La Carreta* Made a U-Turn: Puerto Rican Language and Culture in the United States." *Daedalus,* (Spring 1981), 193-213.

Ghighliotty, Julio. "Bilingual Education Said Not a Matter of Language," *San Juan Star,* April 3 (1983).

Hispanic Research Center. 1984. "Hispanic Families in New York City." *Research Bulletin* 5:1-2, New York: Fordham University.

Labov, William. 1972a. *Language in the Inner City: Studies in the Black English Vernacular*. Philadelphia: University of Pennsylvania Press.

_____. 1972b. *Sociolinguistic Patterns*. Philadelphia: University of Pennsylvania Press.

Lakoff, Robin. 1975. *Language and Woman's Place*. New York: Harper and Row.

Nichols, Patricia C. 1976. "Black Women in the Rural South: Conservative and Innovative." In *The Sociology of the Languages of American Women: Papers in Southwest English 4,* edited by Betty Lou Dubois & Isabel Crouch. San Antonio: Trinity University.

Padron, Henry. 1982. "Dos Worlds/Two Mundos." Unpublished poem. 1982.

Poplack, Shana. 1979. "Sometimes I'll Start a Sentence in Spanish y Termino en Español: Towards a Typology of Code-Switching." Working Paper #4. New York: Centro de Estudios Puertorriqueños.

Puerto Rican Forum. 1981. *The Next Step Toward Equality*. New York: National Puerto Rican Forum.

Rodriguez, Clara. 1980. "Puerto Ricans: Between Black and White." In *The Puerto Rican Struggle in the U.S.: Essays on Survival in the U.S.*, edited by C. Rodriguez, V. Sanchez Korrol, & J. Alerds. New York: Puerto Rican Migration Research Consortium, Inc.

Sankoff, D., and Shana Poplack. 1980. "A Formal Grammar of Code Switching." Technical Report No. 495. Centre de Recherches Mathématiques. Université de Montréal.

Trudgill, Peter. 1974. *Sociolinguistics: An Introduction*. London: Penguin 1974.

Wolfram, Walt. 1974. "Sociolinguistic Aspects of Assimilation: Puerto Rican English in New York City." Arlington, Va.: Center for Applied Linguistics.

Zentella, Ana Celia. 1981a. "Language Variety among Puerto Ricans." In *Language in the U.S.A.*, edited by Charles Ferguson and Shirley Brice Heath, Cambridge: Cambridge University Press.

——————. 1981b. "Hablamos Los Dos. We Speak Both. Growing Up Bilingual in el Barrio." Doctoral dissertation, University of Pennsylvania.

——————. "Spanish and English in Contact in the U.S.: The Puerto Rican Experience." *The Spanish Language in the Western Hemisphere*. Special Issue *WORD*. 33:1-2 (April - August 1983).

——————. 1986 "Returned Migration, Language, and Identity: Puerto Rican Bilinguals in dos Worlds/Two Mundos." *Journal of International Education*.

——————. In press. "Individual Differences in Growing Up Bilingual." In *Cross-Cultural and Communicative Competencies: Ethnograpies of Educational Programs for Language Minority Students*, edited by Marietta Saravia Shore. Council on Anthropology and Education Publication. West Cornwall, Conn.: Horizon Communications.

Informal Conversation Topics Among Urban Afro-American Women

Kikanza Nuri Robins and *T. Jean Adenika*

In this segment of contemporary Black history we have an opportunity to learn what was important in the lives of three different classes of Black women in the 1950s, 1960s, and 1970s. It is basic to this anthology that one can best understand women of color by analyzing their sociopolitical and cultural context. Robins and Adenika draw on feminist activism to interpret the verbal interview data they have collected from Black women respondents. In this way, they are able to infer changes in Black women's values and belief structures over three politically intense decades.

In the literature on Afro-Americans, Black women are usually discussed in relationship to someone or something—their families, white women, or Black men (Staples, 1973; Lerner 1972; Ladner 1971). They have been examined in studies which attempted to discern their roles among other Third World peoples (Moraga and Anzaldus 1981) and their involvement in political and social movements (Sterling 1979; Wallace 1978; Salaam 1980). The world of Black women has also been portrayed in literature (Bell, Parker, and Guy-Sheftall 1979; Washington 1975), but little has been written which describes Black women's world as *they* see it. The study described in this essay attempts to see the world of Black women from their perspective as they talk about it. The reality of Black women as they define it can provide some understanding of their values and beliefs. A major premise of this study is that Black women's values and beliefs can be inferred from the way in which they talk about their past and present lifestyles and experiences.

Sociopolitical changes can impact in subtle ways on the lives of those individuals involved. Mass movements often bring gradual changes in the cultural values and belief systems of the affected individuals. This study postulates that as a result of the social upheavals in the United States during the 1950s, the 1960s, and the 1970s Black women underwent changes in their values and belief structures.

Three time periods are used here as the base sociopolitical constructs for comparing the topics of conversation of Black urban women in three socioeconomic classes. These time periods are: the 1950s—the Integrationist Period; the 1960s—the Social Activist Period; and the 1970s—the Feminist Period.

Methodology

Forty-five Black female respondents were involved in this exploratory study. All lived in the Los Angeles area at the time and had resided in major urban centers during the eras covered by the study. Eighteen had been raised in the rural South, five in the urban North, nine in urban centers of the West, and thirteen in small Midwestern towns. Respondents were selected on a random basis from social clubs and church auxiliaries representing specific socioeconomic classes.

Open-ended, unstructured interviews were used individually with each respondent to elicit comments about her life and the sociopolitical events during the three periods under discussion.[1] Drawing on the technique of guided recall, respondents were asked to recall what they were doing, who their friends and mates were, what was going on generally in their lives and what the topics of conversation were with their friends and mates during these three periods.[2] The transcriptions of these recorded comments became the primary source of data for this exploratory study.

In recalling various topics of conversation in the different sociopolitical eras, the respondents were encouraged to elaborate and clarify their comments about each different era. They commented at length on their personal relationships with men, their children, race relations, their jobs, and money. It was then possible to infer changes in values and belief structures from the differences in comments made concerning each era.

Respondents in the study were selected according to three socioeconomic categories (middle class, lower middle class, and working class) and three age groups (those currently in their fifties, forties, and thirties). Table I shows the number of respondents according to these overlapping categories.

Table I Number of Respondents by Age Groups

	Now in their fifties	Now in their forties	Now in their thirties
Middle class (n = 15)	6	6	3
Lower middle class (n = 15)	6	6	3
Working class (n = 15)	6	6	3
	T = 18	T = 18	T = 9

Age differences were used in order to obtain comments about topics of conversation in the three different sociopolitical eras. Table II depicts the crossover of age and era which the sample of Black women interviewed reflects. The members of the oldest group were in their early twenties during the era of the 1950s, in their thirties in the 1960s, and in their forties in the 1970s. The second to oldest group and the youngest group were removed by ten and twenty years respectively. Consequently, they commented on only one or two eras while the oldest group commented on all three.

Table II   Age of Respondents in Three Socio-Political Eras

	1950s	1960s	1970s
Oldest age group (n = 18)	in their twenties	in their thirties	in their forties
Second oldest age group (n = 18)	—	in their twenties	in their thirties
Youngest age group (n = 9)	—	—	in their twenties

Socio-Economic Classes

The researchers drew on observed cultural values and patterns to define the socioeconomic categories rather than on statistical data, such as income and profession. The defining cultural and historical parameters of the three categories selected are described below.

Middle-class Black women were those who had grown up not only with middle-class values but with middle class family incomes as well. They were second-generation college graduates—a rarity among Black Americans over forty-five years of age. These women were public school administrators, attorneys, physicians, or else they were married to men in these professions. They owned their own homes or other real property and their leisure activities included the theatre, travel, and charitable or service associations within and outside of the Black community.

Many women in the *lower-middle-class* category believed themselves to be members of the middle class. But while they had middle-class values, their incomes, occupations, and leisure activities resembled those of the working class. They were among the first generation of their families to graduate from college and typically held white collar jobs, such as clerks, sales people, and teachers.

Within the lower-middle-class group there were a number of Black women who were exceptions to this standard sociological classification. These women had been raised by lower-class or working-class parents but as adults lived according to middle-class values and economic standards. They too were business executives, physicians, and public school administrators. Because their parents had taught them to adhere to the work ethic and because they were academically and professionally overachievers, they were able to change their class status. They no doubt also benefited greatly from the social and economic improvements in Afro-America resulting from the social and political agitation in the 1960s. Their commitment to improve the lives of lower-class Afro-Americans was very strong.

Aside from these exceptional women, if a lower middle-class family had an income comparable to those in the middle class, it was usually the sum of two salaries rather than one. Leisure activities of lower-middle-class women were a combination of working class and middle-class leisure activities.

Working-class Black women were high school graduates who may have attended college but did not graduate, or who had participated in a post-secondary certificate program to become, for example, a dental technician. They held pink-collar and low-skill clerical positions. While working-class men in blue-collar skilled trades might earn a middle-class income, working-class women as a rule did not. Older working-class women (forty years and over) may have owned their own homes. Most, however, were renters. Leisure activities included movies, house parties, nightclubs, and rhythm and blues concerts.

Discussion of the Data

"What did you talk about with your close friends?" This question, whether asked directly or stated implicitly as we listened to and participated in interviews, yielded a list of topics of conversation common to all the women in the three classes and over the three time periods. Differences surfaced when we focused on the *primary topics* of conversation and *specific aspects* of that topic. Black women reported talking about the men in their lives, their children, jobs, money, the state of the race, their activities in the Black community, white people, their relationships with other women, their health, their church activities, and their participation in fashion trends. The following discussion analyzes these topics in relationship to the sociopolitical periods and socio-economic class differences.

The Integrationist Period (the 1950s)

During the 1950s, Afro-Americans were barred from full participation in the social, political, and economic institutions of this nation. Twentieth-century slavery, which took the form of institutional racism and segregation, fueled a nonviolent but smoldering attack on American racism by Black intellectuals and their white sympathizers. Since the lack of cultural and social development of Afro-Americans was cited as the cause for their subordinate position in society, they sought to prove themselves worthy of assimilation into the social and economic mainstream of America. During the Integrationist Period, there were a number of legal successes which eliminated *de jure* segregation, but the day-to-day behavior of whites reflected the racist facts of life in America. In spite of great evidence to the contrary, most Afro-Americans believed that through self-improvement the total integration necessary for uplifting the race was possible.

Middle-class Black women recalled talking primarily about their men, children, job, and the state of the race in the 1950s. As teens, they had assumed they would get married, so they speculated about the professions their spouses would have. Even though they were middle-class, most Black women prepared to work and expected to continue working while raising their children and building a home. However, work for the woman as well as the man was to be in the professional category. This, of course, underscored the need to attend college themselves and to instill in their children a value for education. College was expected to be the place to find a husband, so parents sent daughters to specific colleges to find promising young men. They gave strong support to the Black colleges, since attendance at most prestigious white colleges was not then an option for Black Americans.

Conversation about children always focused on the social requirement to have them and the importance of educating them well so that they would be a credit to the race. The state of the race was a very important topic; achievements and setbacks—individual and collective—were discussed constantly. Social and political organizations like the National Association for the Advancement of Colored People and Urban League were considered to be very important to the improvement of race relations. These groups were supported both by active memberships and financial contributions. Middle-class Black women discussed ways in which self-improvement could alleviate racism and the behavioral changes the Black masses had to make in order to be accepted by whites.

Lower-middle-class Black women talked primarily about family and the race issues which were becoming increasing important in this period. The paramount concern of lower-middle-class women during the Integrationist Period was how to assume a lifestyle that would lead to total acceptance by white society. They were concerned that their children become high-achievers and behave properly in school so that they could go to high school (preferably a newly integrated one) and then to college. College was their dream for self-improvement, upward mobility, and integration into the economic mainstream of white society. There were few scholarships for Black youth at that time. Thus, the topics of conversation revolved around where to go to college and how to get the money. At that time, the Black colleges were more expensive than the local public colleges and universities. Moreover, the relative merits of attending a Black school rather than a white one were heavily debated. Black schools provided nurturing role models, professional contacts, and future spouses, but white schools were white and for that criterion alone, were thought by many to be inherently superior.

The young lower-middle-class women were also concerned with their sexuality. For them, sex meant retaining virginity until marriage. Loss of virginity was a prime concern because it might lead to pregnancy which would in turn terminate education goals and limit the prospects for getting a *good* husband. So pervasive was this value that women expressed surprise later to learn that many of their friends had been sexually active before marriage. Most topics on sexuality were taboo in polite discussion in the 1950s. A *good* husband was one who had gone to college, had been successful in sports as well as academics, had a high status job as a civil servant (not, however, in the post office), an engineer, a physician, or an attorney, and who displayed that intangible trait—potential for success. Women worked, or assumed that they would, but never thought of their jobs as being anything more than a source of income. Lower-middle-class Black women were active in church and community, performing tasks designed to improve the image of Black Americans and thus making them more acceptable to whites.

Working-class Black women talked about their children, their jobs, and their relationship with women and men. Schooling and home training were important for their children. Schooling meant attendance at both elementary and secondary schools; graduation was a great accomplishment. They talked about how the children were doing in school, their achievements, and their problems. Their concern for the children at home was in raising them to be hardworking and well-behaved. Setting the behavioral parameters for being *good* children was also important.

Many women did not have jobs outside the home during the 1950s, but those who did were often domestic workers. One woman from a Northeastern city recalled that she and her friends would barter for and exchange goods and services among themselves. One would iron, another would take care of the children, a third, who worked outside the home, would pay cash for the services provided her. If they were not married, these women would talk about getting a man; if they were married, they would discuss strategies for keeping him.

The greatest difference between conversations about men among working-class women and middle- or lower-middle class women was the detail in which they discussed their sex lives. Middle-class women did not discuss it at all. Lower-middle-class women talked only of the fear of pregnancy and the consequent necessity for abstention. At the other end of the spectrum were working-class women, who did not deny that they were sexual beings. Their conversations about men included the size of the men's organs and the skill with which they used them. The major criterion for comparing men was whether they were caring and creative during the foreplay and resolution period of lovemaking, or whether they were "hit and run men."

When discussing other women, they talked about the need for, or appreciation of, trustworthy and loyal female friends. At the core of these conversations was an ever-present need to acknowledge their Black womanhood, for it altered their vision of the world and, naturally, their conversations. Their lives were not affected by the integration movement to the same degree as the lower-middle-class women, because their economic status afforded them a lifestyle that was far removed from what they considered to be real hope. They worked so that their lives would be free from hunger and cold, and they prayed that their children's lives would be better than their own. Their view of the world was provincial and a contrast of black and white. Because they felt they could not diminish white power, they viewed integration with suspicion and white people as relentless oppressors.

Comments made in the interviews about topics of conversation in the 1950s suggested that racial advancement and integration were most important to middle- and lower-middle-class women. Education and emulation of whites were seen as the primary vehicles for achieving these goals. Middle-class Black women were much more insulated from the impact of racism than the others. Women expected to marry and assumed they would work all of their lives. Great emphasis was placed on the education and upbringing of the children by all women, so that the children's lives would be better than those of their parents, and so that they could assimilate further into white society. Sex was not discussed except among working-class women, and men were topics of conversation only in regard to marriage. Middle-class women, with the greatest amount of material resources and leisure time, volunteered in organizations to advance the race. On the other hand, working-class women were too busy trying to exist on a day-to-day basis to spend time discussing the state of the race. Their conversations evolved from survival-level issues but were influenced by the reality of being Black women in Afro-America.

The Social Activist Period (the 1960s)

During the 1960s, the Social Activist Period, economic, social, political, and education segregation were still a festering reality. Blacks had become disenchanted with the passive resistance which characterized the Integrationist Period, and they were frustrated by the slow pace of social change. The 1960s gave birth to Black pride, Black demands for political and economic power, mass marches, sit-ins, race riots, and peace demonstrations. This period was the most volatile of the three examined. An increasing number of Black Americans began to resist white America's definition of Negritude and its concomitant policies of economic and political exclusion. Blacks were joined in their protests by whites who felt racial unrest endangered the nation's survival or who simply believed racism to be an immoral aspect of American society. Parallel to the Afro-American push for equality was a slow upsurge of opposition to these demands for civil and human rights by many white Americans who interpreted Afro-American achievement as a threat to their own economic security or traditional social position. White America's resistance to total integration intensified to such a level that the political forces which had once assisted Afro-Americans in their progress toward equality were quieted by the end of the decade.

The period ended with a stronger collective Afro-American self-concept. Intellectuals were clear about the ramifications of institutional racism which were designed to benefit white America. They were also clear that power does not change hands easily. Permanent change occurs only in an economic climate where there is full employment and where there are substantial numbers of majority Americans willing to examine the moral issue of institutional racism in a democratic society.

The data revealed that the 1960s brought little change to the conversations of middle-class Black women. The primary topic of conversation was still the education of their children, for education was the only way to preserve one's social class. Though they remained concerned about the state of the race, the swell of Black pride surging through Afro-America was not a primary topic of conversation. Perhaps this was so because most middle-class Black women during this period belonged to old, established families from the Southeast which had always had strong racial identification and pride. These were the families with old money—money that had supported the Black colleges and universities in the country. And these were the families which had descended from the half million free Blacks in the United States at the time of Emancipation.

The conversation topics of middle-class women reflected a passive acceptance of male dominance. The women continued to view themselves as very important in managing their families, but always second to the men in their lives. For middle-class women, the one difference between the 1950s and the 1960s was their changed attitude toward work. Work was now more than a job, for their interests had shifted to work as a means of personal development and gratification. Those who were in professions began to seek ways to demonstrate a greater social commitment through their work. They spent much time talking about new ways to use their skills to provide service for lower-income and less-advantaged Afro-Americans.

The sociopolitical milieu of the 1960s was the topic of conversation for lower-middle-class women, and it impinged on all other topics. As one respondent noted, "People were divided into two categories: those who did something about race relations and those who chose not to become active. Everyone talked about it." One of the major issues introduced was to what degree integration was desired by Black people. In the 1950s, lower-middle-class Black people had tried very hard to be as much like white people as they could. With the 1960s came discussions about the desirability of total assimilation. Integration was seen as desirable for jobs and education opportunities, but social integration was quite another issue. The lower-middle-class women were active in integrating schools, and churches, forming chapters of Black sororities on white campuses, and fighting for leadership in these and other traditionally white organizations, like the P.T.A. As a result of Civil Rights achievements, Black women felt that they were now in direct competiton with white women—on the job, for career advancement, and socially for the attention of Black men.

Conversations about men were now peppered with the shared disappointment with the behavior of Black men. It seemed to these women that Black men were marrying far too many white women. Black men also appeared reluctant to take political risks for personal career advancement or to contribute to the advancement of Black Americans. For example, it was the perception of some lower-middle-class women that once Black men held positions of status—positions which had previously been closed to Black people—they lost their pioneering spirit and did not help other Black people to take similar steps forward. The opposing argument was that Black men could not be politically active if they were to keep the jobs they had worked so hard to obtain.

Many of the lower-middle-class women who worked began to redefine their jobs as careers, but they continued to view home, husband, and children as their major responsibilities. Often, with divorce came lower incomes, but these women struggled to find ways to continue to infuse the lives of their children with middle-class ideals, pride in being Black Americans, and activities which would reinforce these values.

Women talked about the speech of their children. Academic achievement, social advancement, and general acceptance by whites was determined to a large degree by fluency in Standard English. Standard language and appropriate behavior became crucial for many lower-middle-class Black families, because this period brought them an increased degree of participation in white Ameica.

As the data reveal, many working-class women in the 1960s found themselves divorced. Those who had not worked in the 1950s had to work now to support themselves and their children. Women who were still married found it necessary to work "not just for the money, but for our sanity." They felt a need to get out of the house and do more with their lives. Many women endured discrimination at work both as women and as Black people. Talking informally at home with their friends about what was happening at work helped to diffuse tension and "helped us to keep our jobs."

Besides their jobs, working-class women talked about their money, their men, and their children. Since money was a scarce commodity, it was an important topic. Like the lower-middle-class women, many of the working-class women were now facing the problem sof single parenthood. They shared survival strategies, including "about 300 ways to prepare ground beef." Added to their conversation about men were the topics of remarriage, the loneliness of being single, and their dismay at the apparent reluctance of their male suitors to court and woo them.

In regard to children, school, and discipline, the women "bragged about the good things" the children did and "did not talk about the bad things." Working-class women were concerned with providing male models for their sons and often sought the brothers, cousins, and husbands of their friends to talk to their sons about sex and being a Black man in a white world. Unlike the lower-middle-class women, they were not very active in the movement for social equality, but they did discuss the ways in which it affected their lives. For example, they sensed the pressure placed on their children to conform to middle-class behavioral standards at school. Interview data suggest that these women worried most about the future for their children and regular employment for their men. This period saw a slow elimination of jobs for men who did not have technical skills or post-secondary education. These changes were being felt most in Black working-class communities and did not escape the watchful eye of working-class women.

The 1960s brought many Black women out of their homes into the job market in pursuit of additional income. Many middle-class and lower-middle-class women found they enjoyed the idea of a career rather than a job. Regardless of class, all the women felt that their Blackness and their womanhood uniquely shaped their lives and their views of the world. Middle-class and lower-middle-class women addressed the race problem openly. While middle-class women continued their support of established organizations, lower-middle-class women explored new avenues of service to and support of the Black community. Working-class women did not confront the issue collectively but rather dealt with situations on a personal and individual level.

The Feminist Period (the 1970s)

The Feminist Period of the 1970s was dominated by women demanding and campaigning for an equal share of the American dream. They used the same legal and rhetorical strategies developed by the social change activitists of the previous decade. Women, as defined in American culture, were the possessions of men to be cared for and protected much in the same way as children. White women fared far better than Black women economically and socially, but were perceived as inferior to white males. Without a man, their social and economic status diminished considerably.

While the masses of Black women did not join the feminist movement, many shared feminist ideals. Some of those ideals affecting their lives included a desire for better child care, child support, equal pay for equal work, potential for career mobility, assistance at home by male partners, education opportunities, and a general redefinition of stereotypical sex roles.

The comments offered by our respondents reveal that during the 1970s middle-class Black women continued to talk about those things which had dominated their conversations for the past two decades: men, children, work and the state of the race. Under pressure from Black women, Black men began to assume more responsibility for the raising of their children. Additionally, the men began to show more commitment to the Black community than they had in the 1960s. As one respondent noted, "Their actions began to catch up to their rhetoric, and we liked that."

Education remained a paramount concern. As more and more Black people were able to complete college and university programs, education at the best schools became even more important, because the competition had increased. Greater support was provided to the historically Black colleges and universities not only because the schools needed a stronger financial base but also because the young people could make important social and business connections while studying at these institutions.

While middle-class Black women continued to work, their conversations about work expanded to include discussion of their achievements in private business ventures and the increased enjoyment and satisfaction they derived from their newly defined careers. Middle-class women continued their memberships in organizations and associations which addressed racial issues. They perceived that their role in advancing the race was to serve both as models of achievement for other Afro-Americans and as examples of community stability and racial pride.

Lower-middle-class Black women continued to grow and change with the times, as well as to nurture and support one another's development through their discussions. The data show that the most frequent topic of conversation during this period was Black America and its relationship to the rest of the world. Civil Rights, the peace movement, and integration were evaluated, critiqued, and redirected countless times. Social activism and political involvement increased as the women became more aware and reached a greater understanding of institutional racism and its integral role in American society. They believed that because the degree of interracial comingling was increasing, they had to remain diligent in their fight against racial inequities. Therefore, they became involved in professional and political associations to politicize the Black people who they felt "had made it" socially or economically. These individuals thought of themselves and their families only, instead of demonstrating a strong racial commitment by supporting community endeavors and involving themselves with Black youth.

A repeated theme in the conversations of lower-middle-class Black women was how to impart middle-class values, high self-esteem, and racial pride to their children. By the 1970s, too many Black youth were blatantly unaware of or unconcerned with the battles their parents had waged to uplift the race. It was extremely important to lower-middle-class Black women that their offspring have a keen understanding of Afro-American history in order that they too would continue to struggle against American racism.

Talk about men revolved around finding, getting, and keeping a husband. Those women with husbands continued to believe one of their roles as wives was to help their husbands get ahead. This help included subordinating their careers—which continued to be a means of upward mobility and self-satisfaction—to those of their husbands and accepting relocation anywhere in the country if this led to the husband's getting a better job. They also discussed parenting and the type of fathers their husbands and ex-husbands made. For the first time, lower-middle-class Black women began to discuss their sex lives openly. They shared a growing sense of their own sexuality and the way it affected their relationships with their husbands and lovers. This openness may be seen as a response to the feminist encouragement of self-expression in such matters.

A new topic of conversation was the relationship of Black women to one another. Feminists care about other women. Women became more conscious of how they selected their friends and their relationships became deeper, more expansive, and more meaningful. Through these richer associations, they learned more about one another as women, and to their surprise, this increased their understanding of men.

Working-class Black women made only a few changes in their conversation during the 1970s. Money was still a perennial problem. The concerns they had for their children also remained the same. Even as the children grew older, "mothers still wanted their children to behave properly and to do well in school." Working-class women did find they were giving their children more serious responsibilities at home by including them in decision-making and explaining to them in greater detail the restrictions a low income creates for a family. Jobs were still jobs, so the important aspects of working were the conditions under which they labored and the relationship they had with the people at work.

With men, working-class women became more demanding and more expressive of their needs. The attitude and sexuality of men continued to be a topic of conversation. The comparison of the reactions and attitudes of their men in similar situations became important once these women began to express their feelings to their husbands and lovers, instead of merely to their friends. Reports of feminist demands by the mass media were not viewed as issues relevant to their lives.

Running through the stream of conversation from the 1950s to the 1970s was the theme of single Black womanhood. Even those women who were married shared an empathy with their single friends for the elusiveness of Black husbands. When asked directly about the apparent lack of change in conversation topics over three decades, Black working-class women invariably replied that times change but people do not. What was most important to them were the people who affected their lives, not in the future, but in the often overwhelming present.

The marital situations of women in all classes changed in the 1960s, particularly among those in the middle and lower middle classes. By the 1970s, many of these women began to consider marriage a social option rather than a necessity. The 1970s brought increased awareness of sexuality to all women. They discussed their sex lives more openly and shared their feelings and expectations with their spouses and lovers. The lives of lower-middle-class women during the 1960s and 1970s were filled with rearing children, building careers, and increasing social activism. Lower-middle-class women wanted their children to be entrenched in a middle-class lifestyle and to have a positive cultural consciousness. By the 1970s, these women were acutely aware of the impact of various movements on the social and poltiical fibers of the Black community.

Lower-middle-class women were extremely active in movements seeking social change—continually searching for the ideal relationship to white society. In the 1950s, lower-middle-class women wanted integration and total acceptance by whites. They wanted integration for jobs and economic parity in the 1960s, and in the 1970s, they still wanted acceptance, but as Afro-Americans, not as Black people trying to be white. Middle-class and working-class Black women also were influenced by the social changes over these three periods, but the conversations of working-class women did not reflect the same intensity of involvement demonstrated by lower-middle-class women.

Conclusions and Interpretation

Within the parameters defined by socioeconomic class, our exploratory study suggests that changes in topics of conversation among Black urban women in informal settings were linked to sociopolitical changes. The findings were based on a small sample of Black women residing in Los Angeles who were members of clubs and church groups. Our conclusions may not be applicable to all Afro-American women, but they do serve as a basis for the development of a full-scale study of conversation topics of urban Afro-American women.

We postulated that as a result of the social upheavals which occurred during the 1950s, 1960s, and 1970s, Black women underwent changes in their values and belief structures. It was also our premise that these changes would be detected in a content analysis of interviews which probed the conversation topics of Black women in informal settings. Our data support these premises.

Black women from the three classes over the three time periods discussed their relationships with men, money, race relations, their children, and their jobs. The sociopolitical movements were manifested in the women's conversations as they addressed and adjusted to social changes. What for years had been viewed as how to get and keep a job, now became a strategy for upward mobility in a self-fulfilling career. Children had been social requisites, but by the 1970s, women were having them or not having them by choice. Black women of all socioeconomic classes worked to insure that the lives of their children would not be tainted in the same ways that racial oppression and discrimination had affected their own lives.

Feminist activism influenced the lives of Black women in the areas of sexuality, relationships with men, expectations of fathers, and cultivation of female friendships. Lower-middle-class women discussed these feminist issues consciously as they observed changes in themselves and others. Middle-class Black women also were affected but were more reticent in accepting feminist rhetoric or giving credit for change to feminist activities. Working-class women were even less conscious of the impact of feminism on their lives because of the insular effect of a day-to-day struggle for economic survival. However, their conversations in some ways reflected the influence of the Feminist Period.

Traditionally, Afro-American women married before the age of twenty-five and stayed married for life. They cultivated one or two life-long friends for support and assistance through their rites of passage. Their communication revolved around the events of courtship, marriage, childbirth, and spouse's death. While the extended family provided effective support for unmarried women, both married and unmarried women established secondary relationships through the church, local chapter of Eastern Star, sororities, National

Council of Colored Women, and other formal associations.

Before the 1970s, Black women had not developed the necessary social networks for meeting other women and for having their need for affective communication met through them. Such interpersonal relationships and consequent communication patterns outside of the family and formal associations were unknown to most urban Black women. Moreover, many had not previously considered that these needs might be met outside of these institutions. Since then, Black women have found that through new relationships with both men and women they can meet their basic human needs for affection and acceptance. They are creating new formal associations to bring Black women together. The names of these groups indicate that communication is basic to their purpose: Black Women's Forum, Black Women's Network, Black Women's Caucus, and Women Together. Black women are expanding their circles of friends and increasing the number of significant, informal relationships they maintain with women.

The 1960s and 1970s were accompanied by extensive media coverage through which women were apprised of national social movements. Consequently, a large percentage of Black women were influenced profoundly and rapidly by these social change agents. This influence was manifested by change in communication patterns—old topics were discussed in new ways and new topics reflecting changed values and beliefs were introduced. This change was most apparent in the conversation of lower-middle-class Black women.

Working-class women struggled daily for economic survival. Middle-class women have the wealth and social status which preclude survival level struggle. The lower-middle-class Black woman knows the bitter taste of poverty, yet has sampled the sweetness of academic and economic achievement. She is more aware of the obstacles to full middle-class status and is therefore committed to removing them for herself and her children. She is actively dedicated to social change. Her conversation reflects changed values and beliefs resulting from the influence of sociopolitical movements. It is our hope that this study adds to the literature on Afro-American women by describing a small portion of their world as they perceive it and talk about it.

Notes

1. The open-ended interview format used individually with respondents consisted of establishing rapport and trust, and then posing rather general questions. For example: "What was going on in the United States in the 1950s (or 1960s or 1970s)?" "Who were your friends, male and female?" "What were you talking about with your friends at that time?" Respondents were encouraged to elaborate and explain their answers and comments to these general questions.

2. Guided recall is a technique which prompts the interviewee to recall a past event or a hypothetical event and then describe it in detail. It reflects the assumption that the way people talk about their lives is of significance, and that the language they use and the connections they make reveal the world that they see and in which they act.

References

Bell, Roseann, Bettye Parker and Beverly Guy-Sheftall, eds. 1979. *Sturdy Black Bridges: Visions of Black Women in Literature*. New York: Anchor Press, Doubleday.

Ladner, Joyce A. 1971. *Tomorrow's Tomorrow. The Black Woman*. New York: Anchor Press, Doubleday.

Lerner, Gerda, ed. 1972. *Black Women in White America: A Documentary History*. New York: Vintage Books, Random House.

Moraga, Cherrie, & Gloria Anzaldus, eds. 1981. *This Bridge Called My Back, Writings by Radical Women of Color*. Watertown, Mass.: Persephone Press.

Salaam, Kalamu Ya. 1980. "Our Women Keep Our Skies from Falling," *Six Essays in Support of the Struggle to Smash Sexism/Develop Women*. New Orleans: Nkombo.

Staples, Robert. 1973. *The Black Woman in America: Sex, Marriage, and the Family*. Chicago: Nelson-Hall Publishers.

Sterling, Dorothy. 1979. *Black Foremothers, Three Lives*. New York: The Feminist Press.

Wallace, Michele. 1978. *Black Macho and the Myth of the Superwoman*. New York: The Dial Press.

Washington, Mary Helen, ed. 1975. *Black Eyed Susans, Classic Stories by and about Black Women*. New York: Anchor Press.

Postscript—A Perspective

Women and Language in Transition has focused on language as one of the dimensions in the ongoing process of social change which was actively sought by feminists in the 1970s. It has been argued here that language merits attention because it plays a critical role in the lives of white women and women of color. But the struggle of women to achieve gender equity *in* and *through* language has been merely one part of the overall struggle for self-determination and self-definition. Thus, we must recognize that language change is but one of the many visible signs of transition in which women find themselves. After more than a decade of feminist activism and research, it might be helpful to examine briefly the further dynamics of this transition. In what way have and will women continue the process of self-determination and self-definition in the 1980s and 1990s? From a feminist perspective, what does the second decade of transition hold in store for women? Are there new directions to suggest as well?[1]

While the 1970s brought awareness that women's history had been hidden from them, the 1980s have given birth to research which not only uncovers women's role in history but also suggests a feminist view of *all* aspects of history.[2] Thus, feminist researchers in history, political science, economics, philosophy and other disciplines are challenging the male-dominated assumptions and perspective of the human past and present as they construct a feminist interpretation of events. Many of these researchers have rejected the analytical categories of their disciplines, which were established by and for males, as too narrow to encompass the experiences of women. For example, in economics the definition of labor as wage-based excludes the bulk of women's work, i.e. the child-care and household responsibilities. Feminist economists have argued that this work must be included in GNP (Gross National Product) counts. To name two relevant works, Waring's (1985) *Women, Politics and Power* addresses this issue in the present and Matthaei's (1983) *An Economic History of Women in America: Women's Work, The Sexual Division of Labor and the Development of Capitalism* considers the topic of labor in the past. Drawing on the motto of the feminist movement in the 1970s that "the personal is political," feminist researchers in political science have rejected the male notion of voting as insufficient to encompass women's experiences; instead they have focused on women's attempts to gain control over their lives and have an impact on the society in which they live (Ryan 1981; Hewitt 1984). In summary, the different questions which feminist researchers in various disciplines have raised now challenge the most basic assumptions of these very fields. Feminist scholars have thus contributed significantly to an intellectual dimension of self-definition and to a greater understanding of women's identity and cultural history. There is no doubt also that further demystification of women's language usage (discourse) and language usage in general will continue as new research unfolds.

Many current studies accept the notion that women constitute a culture possessing its own values, system, and psyche, even though the members are at the same time integrated into male networks and frameworks. As more light is shed on the nature of this community or culture, that is, that which is distinctly female, feminist researchers have become more aware of the patriarchal and male-oriented assumptions on which their own research paradigms are based. For example, some feminist philosophers have not found the Kantean notions often assumed in Western philosophy useful in addressing significant issues which directly affect the lives of women, such as, abortion, home labor, or comparable worth applied to child-rearing. *Caring: A Feminine Approach to Ethics and Moral Education* (Noddings 1984) proposes a feminine approach to ethics—a morality of care. Gilligan in her book, *In a Different Voice* (1982), argues for building a theory based on women's experiences. Feminist theory has now placed these experiences at the center of inquiry by accepting the view that the representation of reality begins with the witness of those experiencing that reality.[3] From the above, it is clear that new research questions must be formulated and new theories of language usage must emerge.

Women have continued to re-shape and re-search many dimensions in society, not just those which impinge on their own lives. Now that a considerable knowledge-base has been built up through feminist research, feminists in the 1980s have become aware of the dangers of sharing this knowledge *only* in the domains of women's studies. While women recognize the existence of a feminist community and solidarity, they understand equally that withdrawing into it will lead to continued gender exclusiveness in a male-dominated society. Women cannot afford to isolate themselves or their knowledge from the wider community. The segregation of women's studies from mainstream curriculum is no longer viewed as desirable since issues in women's studies are no longer centered primarily on women but rather address the gender exclusiveness of theories and methodologies in general. Smith-Rosenberg's book *Disorderly Conduct: Visions of Gender in Victorian America* (1985) which considers definitions of masculinity as well as feminity marks a trend that has moved scholarship on women closer to the mainstream of American history.

Feminist researchers in the 1980s have come to understand that a conceptual division by sex leads to dualistic thinking. Thus feminist theory has shifted from placing men and women in separate social spheres defined by sex to assuming a unified social sphere in which the different sexes participate.[4] The current focus in many disciplines is on the concept of "gender" as the socially constructed category of sexual behavior that affects both sexes. There is now greater interest in what Stimpson refers to as "*her*terogeneity" or the study of women as an entry into the multiplicity of heterogeneity.[5]

But as feminists struggle to break the shackles of patriarchal views and actions so that equality across gender might exist, these predominantly white middle- and upper-class females must be careful to avoid suggesting that their perspective is relevant for all women of the world. Women of color, Third World women, and white working-class women have experiences which are uniquely different from those of most academic feminists. Just as men assumed a perspective which was male for all of humankind, feminists must not make the same mistake of assuming for all women a perspective that is white, middle-class, and Western. The voices of women of color and white working-class women must be included in the ongoing process of women in transition. These women must be involved in the dialogue of feminism. This is particularly true in looking at language and women of color. Language holds unique importance to women of color since these women must play the role of "cultural broker" between two or more language communities. Monolingual assumptions and approaches do not capture the complexities inherent in multilingual or bilingual communities, nor do they address the issue of triple oppression under which these women live: as citizens of Third World societies or as members of ethnic minorities in the United States dominated by an industrialized, mostly white world; as poor and unprivileged members within their Third World communities; and as women in a male-dominated world.

The gravest danger, of course, is that women of color will remain anonymous and invisible in the feminist collective, just as women in general were and often still are invisible in the realm of knowledge and theory. A major test of feminism will be how well it can include and incorporate the voices of these female sisters of color.

Notes

1. The discussion in this Postscript owes much to the insight and information obtained at a faculty Seminar on Feminist Theory directed by Susan Gal and sponsored by the Council for Integrative and Cross-disciplinary Studies at Rutgers, the State University of New Jersey. I am grateful to the following speakers who participated: Lourdes Beneria (Rutgers, Economics); Judith Gerson (Rutgers, Sociology); Mary Hartman (Rutgers, History); Alison Jaggar (University of Cincinnati,

Philosophy); Catherine Stimpson (Rutgers, English); Judith Walkowitz (Rutgers, History); and Marilyn Waring (former member of New Zealand Parliament).

2. One of the most successful works by women's historians which applies feminist standards of judgment is Laurel Thatcher Ulrich's book *Good Wives: Image and Reality in the Lives of Women in Northern New England 1650-1750*. (1982).

3. For the application of this notion to feminist criticism, see Catherine Stimpson's article, "Wolfe's *Room*, Our Project: Feminist Criticism Today," in the forthcoming book, *The Future of Literary Theory* by Ralph Cohen.

4. For a discussion of the old model of separate spheres, and the new one see Petchesky (1979).

5. The term *"herterogeneity"* was coined by Catherine Stimpson (personal communication).

References

Gilligan, Carol. 1982. *In a Different Voice*. Cambridge, Mass.: Harvard University Press.

Hewitt, Nancy, 1984. *Women's Activism and Social Change: Rochester, New York 1822-1872*. Ithaca, N.Y.: Cornell University Press.

Matthaei, Julie, 1983. *An Economic History of Women in America: Women's Work, The Sexual Division of Labor and the Development of Capitalism*. New York: Schocken Books.

Noddings, Nell. 1984. *Caring: A Feminine Approach to Ethics and Moral Education*. Berkeley: University of California Press.

Petchesky, Rosalind, 1979. "Dissolving the Hyphen: A Report on Marxist-Feminist Groups, 1-5." In *Capitalist Patriarchy and the Case for Socialist Feminism* edited by Zillah Eisenstein. New York: Monthly Review Press.

Ryan, Mary. 1981. *Cradle of the Middle Class*. New York: Cambridge University Press.

Smith-Rosenberg, Carroll. 1985. *Disorderly Conduct: Visions of Gender in Victorian America*. New York: Knopf.

Stimpson, Catherine. Forthcoming. "Wolfe's *Room*, Our Project: Feminist Criticism Today." In *Future of Literary Theory* edited by Ralph Cohen. New York: Methuen.

Ulrich, Laurel Thatcher. 1982. *Good Wives: Image and Reality in Lives of Women*. New York: Knopf.

Waring, Marilyn. 1985. *Women, Politics and Power*. Wellington, New Zealand: Allen and Unwin.

Notes on the Contributors

T. JEAN ADENIKA is Professor of Education at the University of California, Irvine, with research and teaching interest in multicultural education and other related areas. She is a founder of Adolescent Helpmate, a community agency which works for Black Female Teenagers' development in education and health areas.

ISABEL CROUCH (deceased Dec. 1986) was Professor of Speech Communication at New Mexico State University. She copublished several different articles on language and women. Her interest in performance studies and theatre led her to write and perform many different scripts on language and women, such as "The Inferior Man" and "The Revolutionary Woman." The article in this anthology which she coauthored was originally a theatre script which Crouch enacted for audience participation and entertainment.

BETTY LOU DUBOIS is Professor of Speech at New Mexico State University, Las Cruces. She was coorganizer of a Conference on the Sociology of the Languages of American Women held at New Mexico State in 1976 which resulted in *The Sociology of the Languages of American Women* (1978). Dubois also coedited with Crouch a special issue of the *International Journal of the Sociology of Language* entitled "American Minority Women in Sociolinguistic Perspective."

NANCY M. HENLEY is Professor of Psychology. She is former Director of Women's Studies at UCLA, and former Editor of the journal *Psychology of Women Quarterly*. A cognitive and social psychologist, she is the author of *Body Politics: Power, Sex, and Nonverbal Communication* (1977), and of many journal articles and book chapters on communication and gender. She is coeditor with Barrie Thorne of *Language and Sex: Difference and Dominance* (1975); with Clara Mayo of *Gender as Nonverbal Communication* (1981); and with Barrie Thorne and Cheris Kramarae of *Language, Gender and Society* (1983).

MERCILEE M. JENKINS is an Associate Professor in the Department of Speech and Communication Studies at San Francisco State University. She has previously published articles in Germany and the United States on women's humor and storytelling, as well as a monograph, *Removing Bias: Guidelines for Student-Faculty Communication* (Speech Communication Association, 1984). She is also an experimental theatre artist and oral historian who is currently developing a solo performance piece entitled "The Nuclear Family Experiment."

CHERIS KRAMARAE, Professor of Speech Communication at the University of Illinois at Urbana-Champaign, has published many articles on women and language, as well as several books, including: *Women and Men Speaking: Frameworks for Analysis; Voices and Words of Women and Men, Language, Gender, and Society* (coedited with Barrie Thorne and Nancy Henley); and most recently, *A Feminist Dictionary* (1986) (coauthored with Paula Treichler with the assistance of Ann Russo). She is currently coeditor of *Women and Language News*.

ALLEEN PACE NILSEN is Assistant Dean of the Graduate College and Professor of Education at Arizona State University. She has written several articles on sexism and language and coauthored the books: *Sexism and Language, Language Play, Semantic Theory: A Linguistic Perspective,* and *Pronunciation Contrasts in English*. In her essay in this anthology, Nilsen draws heavily on her experience as coeditor of *The English Journal*.

BEA MEDICINE, a Sioux from the Standing Rock Reservation in South Dakota, has conducted anthropological work for more than twenty years among the Lakota Indians as well as with other tribes in North America. She has published on mental health issues, women's studies, and Native education programs. She is a professor in the Department of Anthropology, California State University, Northridge. Her many publications include "Native American Communication Patterns: The Case of the Lakota Speakers" and "Bilingual Education and Public Policy: the Cases of the American Indians."

JOYCE PENFIELD is an Assistant Professor at Rutgers University, interested in applied sociolinguistic research in bilingualism, intercultural communication, and language planning. She is the author of *Communicating with Quotes: The Igbo Case* (1983) and coauthor of *Chicano English: An Ethnic Contact Dialect* (1985).

KIKANZA NURI ROBINS is an educator in southern California with an interest in sociolinguistics, particularly Black language. Her background is in linguistics and the anthropology of education. Currently she is teaching a course on Afro-American women at Loyola Marymount University. She is the owner of Nuri Webber Associates, a consulting firm which provides training in communication and management for educators and business people.

NAN VAN DEN BERGH is an Associate Professor in the Department of Social Work, California State University at Fresno, where she teaches and carries on research related to women's issues, self-help groups, and alcohol/ drug abuse. She has published several studies on women and social work, particularly related to defining the components of a feminist practice model. She recently coedited a volume published by the National Association of Social Workers entitled *Feminist Visions for Social Work*.

BARBARA WITHERS, church educator and editor employed by the Presbyterian Church, has extensive experience in working in the area of inclusive language and images in printed resources. She teaches study groups and leads workshops on inclusive language, especially God and liturgical language. Withers contributed to and edited *Language About God in Liturgy and Scripture: A Study Guide* (Philadelphia: The Geneva Press, 1980) and *Language and the Church: Articles and Designs for Workshops* (NY: Div. of Education & Ministry, NCCC, 1984).

ANA CELIA ZENTELLA, of Puerto Rican and Mexican parentage, was born and raised in the South Bronx. She is Associate Professor in the Department of Black and Puerto Rican Studies, Hunter College, City University of New York. Her research interest in Spanish-English code-switching has led to studies of this phenomenon in East Harlem, Philadelphia, bilingual classrooms in the Bronx, and high schools in Puerto Rico. Currently she has a Rockefeller Foundation Minority Scholars Grant to study the language behavior and attitudes of the four largest Spanish-speaking groups in New York City.

Index of Names

Index of Topics

Acculturation, xvii
Actions, 65-66
Address, titles of, 8
Affirmative action, 69
Afro-Americans. *See* Blacks
Agents of change, 21, 65-66, 68, 163
American, 169
American Indians, 133, 135, 140, 159-165; Cherokee, 145-146; Lakota Sioux, 159-164
Androgyny, 9
Attitudes: changing of, 131, 133; towards language, 16, 148, 164, 174-175; towards women, 126, 133

Bible, 69-70, 133
Bilingual, xvi-xviii, 162, 164-165, 167, 171, 173-175, 176, 177, 199
Bilingualism, xii, 164-165, 167, 171, 176-177
Birthname. *See* Surname
Black (term), 9, 62, 133
Black muslims, 128
Blacks, 133, 143, 169, 171, 180; women, xvii, 144, 149, 180-181; lower middle class, 181-194; middle class, 181, 184, 186, 188-191; working class, 181, 183, 185-186, 189, 190, 192-194

Center for a Woman's Own Name, 122, 128
Change, 74, 131, 159, 176
Chicanos, 133, 144
Church. *See* Education, church; God; Guidelines, churches; Liturgy
Civil liberty, 118, 120-123
Classroom climate: creating a positive one, 82-83; evaluation of, 74-83
Classroom inequities, 66-67, 70, 74-88, 99-101

Code-switching, 176-177
Consciousness-raising, xiv-xv, 16, 131-132, 134, 145, 147
Conversation, 13, 137-138, 181, 183-195
Culture, xiii-xviii, 132, 168-169, 174, 190-194, 198
Cultural broker, 159, 162-164, 199

Dictionary: feminist, 142, 149, 150
Dual pronoun. *See* Pronouns, dual

Education: church, 69-71; classroom interaction, 66-67, 70, 74-88, 169; curriculum, 65-71, 81, 90-97, 106-114. *See also* Classroom climate; English teachers; Sex Role, stereotyping
Empowerment, xv, 130-132, 134, 140
English Journal, 37, 40-43, 51
English teachers, 38, 41-42, 45-46, 54; *Miss Fidditch*, 45
English language, 55-63, 138, 160, 164, 171, 173-174, 177, 178; Black, 170, 172; Non-standard, 144, 171-172; Puerto Rican, 170, 172-173; Standard, 160, 189

Feminist: activism, 128, 130-131, 133, 137, 180, 193, 197; community, xiii-xv, 191, 197, 198; experience, xi-xvii, 191, 138, 197; movement, xiii-xv, 190, 197; nationalism, xiii-xviii. *See also* Feminists
Feminists, 121, 124, 125, 133, 139, 143, 147
First name. *See* Given name

Gender: equity, xi-xii, 28, 90-98, 118, 197; exclusiveness, 65-69, 198; inclusiveness, xvi, xviii, 5-8, 65-66; in-